The Perennial Philosophy
Series

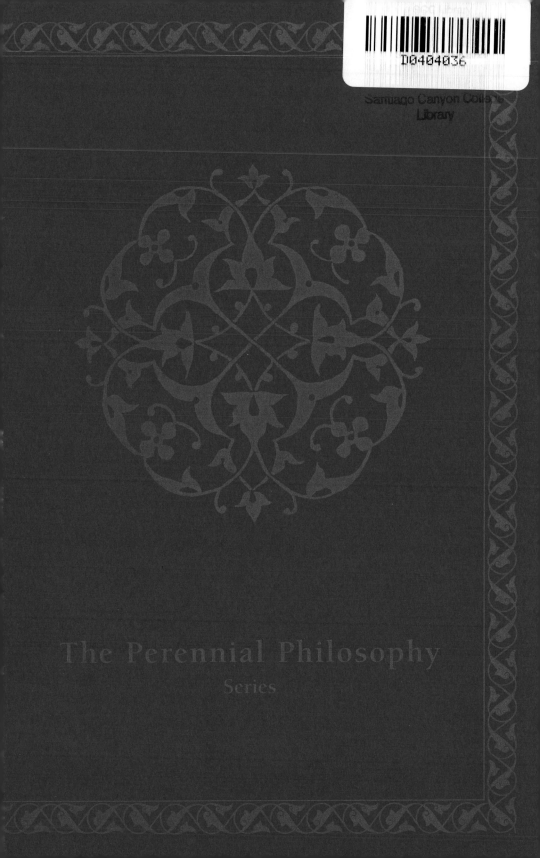

About This Book and its Author

"In a time when religions suffer greatly from a lack of articulate and reasonable spokespersons, believers from any tradition who know Dr. Nasr's work are able to raise their heads high when his name is mentioned and say: 'He makes us all proud to be people of faith.' I have been reading Dr. Nasr for over twenty years and his intelligence, prescience, and relevance astound me still.

"Dr. Nasr was perhaps the first person to identify the *causa profundis* of the current environmental crisis, and in the mid-sixties he was a lone voice in the wilderness calling people's attention to the grave danger that we now all recognize we are in. We ignore him to our own peril. He has much to teach us, and in an age that lacks wisdom, he is surely one of our great sages."

—**Hamza Yusuf**, Director of the Zaytuna Institute

"A masterful introduction to one of the most eminent scholars of our time, and a veritable feast for the educated reader. Remarkably, in twenty-one essays this anthology manages to offer a representative and balanced selection culled from an opus comprising over fifty books and five hundred articles."

—**Wolfgang Smith**, author of *Cosmos and Transcendence: Breaking Through the Barrier of Scientistic Belief* and *The Wisdom of Ancient Cosmology*

"Nasr is one of the major intellects of our day. . . . I know of no one else who is as solidly grounded in both authentic Islam and the complexities of the contemporary Western mind."

—**Huston Smith**, author of *The World's Religions*

"Who speaks for traditional Islam: the Islam lived for centuries by theologians and jurists, by philosophers and scientists, by artists and poets, by Sufis and simple people of faith throughout the Islamic world during fourteen centuries of Islamic history—the Islam which is in fact still followed by the vast majority of Muslims from the Atlantic to the Pacific? There may be still many who speak privately for this tradition but there are only a few writers and, among these few, Seyyed Hossein Nasr is pre-eminent."

—**Charles Le Gai Eaton**, author of *Islam and the Destiny of Man* and *Remembering God: Reflections on Islam*

"This judicious selection of writings from Seyyed Hossein Nasr's prodigious oeuvre confirms that he is one of the era's most profound thinkers and the pre-eminent contemporary exponent of the *philosophia perennis*. He reaffirms the message of Tradition, particularly in its Islamic forms, in a manner attuned to the most urgent imperatives of the age, and thereby kindles the hope that we may yet find a way out of the spiritual and material crises which imperil our very existence."

—**Harry Oldmeadow**, La Trobe University Bendigo, author of *Journeys East: 20th Century Western Encounters with Eastern Religious Traditions*

"A careful and intelligent selection of essays, unique for their range of coverage, by indisputably the most prominent Islamic thinker of today. I highly recommend this collection to anyone interested in comparative religion, science, and the present predicament of human thought."

—**Ashk Dahlén**, Uppsala University and The Swedish Royal Academy of Letters, History, and Antiquities

"Seyyed Hossein Nasr is one of the few scholars who combine modern Western knowledge with a study of Traditional Islam."

—**Inamul Haq**, Benedictine University

"This book is a first-rate anthology which offers to us some of the best pages of Seyyed Hossein Nasr, the most important living thinker in the field of Tradition and Islamic studies. In the darkness and the spiritual fog of the 'modern world,' harrowed by opposite fundamentalisms, where we see a grotesque form of Islam, a ghost and false expression of it, the words of professor Seyyed Hossein Nasr, enlightened interpreter of the deep meaning of Islamic doctrines, convey a message of *peace* and *truth*.

"He plays a pivotal role in the dialogue between the Islamic world and Western civilization because he knows very well both languages, the 'traditional' and the academic. His function as cultural bridge between Islam and the West is highlighted in this book as Nasr opens the mind of modern man, helping him to recover his true nature, forgotten because of a *spiritual amnesia*."

—**Giovanni Monastra**, Director General, National Research Institute for Food and Nutrition, Rome, and author of *Le origini della vita* (*The Origin of Life*)

"Professor Nasr's wisdom covers an immensely wide range of philosophical and religious knowledge, enabling him not only to elucidate the causes of our present dilemmas, but also to guide us in the task of rediscovering a world-view in which Man, Nature, and God are seen in their proper harmony."

—**Carmen Blacker**, University of Cambridge

"The wide corpus of Seyyed Hossein Nasr's writings, which he has so eloquently presented in the last half of the century, pose a challenge for those who want to gain an insight into the complex web of his ideas for the first time. William C. Chittick's lifelong association with Nasr and his writings has provided him with a unique insight into bringing together the essential writings of Nasr for those who would like to gain an understanding of the salient features of his ideas and that of the perennial perspective."

—**Mehdi Aminrazavi**, Professor of Philosophy and Religion, University of Mary Washington

"The profound writings of S.H. Nasr belong to those kinds of fascinating and inspired texts which are universal in their metaphysical essence and, at the same time, reflect the particular historical situation of our contemporary world, which has lost its inner spiritual light and needs to be guided intellectually through the innumerable delusions and perils of modern life. *The Essential Seyyed Hossein Nasr* provides the necessary guidance for any serious spiritual student, whose discrimination increases and spiritual sight is strengthened by those philosophical insights, which reveal the timeless principles and eternal truths hidden in the depths of all the authentic religious traditions of humanity."

—**Algis Uždavinys**, Lithuanian State Institute of Culture, Philosophy, and Arts and editor of *The Golden Chain: An Anthology of Platonic and Pythagorean Philosophy*

"*The Essential Seyyed Hossein Nasr* is a multifaceted work. It contains a portrait of a person who embodies the perennial wisdom of the Eastern tradition as well as the finest scholarly precision of modern Western knowledge. The selected pieces from Nasr's enormous contribution, which he modestly terms 'voicing the rich heritage of Islam,' provides a glimpse into the complexity of the human dilemma of living in the secular age while longing for the certainty of the divine. It also presents a wonderful introduction to Nasr's works that are insightful, revelatory, and comprehensive. The editor of the work, William Chittick, an eminent, fascinating, and insightful scholar in his own right, should be congratulated for being able to make such precise choices from among the ocean of Nasr's contribution to our contemporary knowledge about religion, tradition, Islam, science, the environment, and literally all human scholarly endeavors."

—**Farhang Rajaee**, Carleton University

"At a time when the public opinion too often is dominated by the stereotypes concerning Islam and its culture . . . the significance of the publication of *The Essential Seyyed Hossein Nasr* goes far beyond academic boundaries. One might not share or disagree with some views of S.H. Nasr, yet undoubtedly nobody represents so strongly to the non-Islamic public the image of enlightened Islam.

"Nobody else could present *The Essential Seyyed Hossein Nasr* as brilliantly as Prof. Chittick, not only because he was Nasr's student, but due to the fact that he himself is an outstanding scholar in the field of Islamic thought."

—**Marietta Stepanyants**, Director, Institute of Oriental Philosophy, Russian Academy of Sciences

"*The Essential Seyyed Hossein Nasr*, expertly edited by William Chittick, one of Dr. Nasr's foremost students, is a true gift to humanity. Besides being a leading authority in Islam and Sufism, Seyyed Hossein Nasr is equally at ease with Eastern and Western philosophy and religious thought. His wisdom is more crucially needed today than ever before. It is almost as if the eminent philosopher and mystical poet was meant to be exiled to the West, so that his learning could be understood in a global basis . . . as a bridge between East and West. I wholeheartedly celebrate this book, which is a quintessence of his traditional teachings."

—**Luce López-Baralt**, Professor of Religion and Comparative Literature at Universidad de Puerto Rico

"Among contemporary Muslim scholars few can be considered *living philosophers* and even fewer are known to cover as broad a range of fields as Seyyed Hossein Nasr: metaphysics, cosmology, ethics, philosophy of religion, aesthetics, sciences and technology. The exquisite expert of Sufism, William C. Chittick, has put together a splendid selection of Nasr's writings. Veritable windows of wisdom into the work of a man who has helped revive the idea of perennial philosophy."

—**Tamara Albertini**, University of Hawai'i at Manoa

World Wisdom
The Library of Perennial Philosophy

The Library of Perennial Philosophy is dedicated to the exposition of the timeless Truth underlying the diverse religions. This Truth, often referred to as the *Sophia Perennis*—or Perennial Wisdom—finds its expression in the revealed Scriptures as well as the writings of the great sages and the artistic creations of the traditional worlds.

The Essential Seyyed Hossein Nasr appears as one of our selections in the Perennial Philosophy series.

The Perennial Philosophy Series

In the beginning of the twentieth century, a school of thought arose which has focused on the enunciation and explanation of the Perennial Philosophy. Deeply rooted in the sense of the sacred, the writings of its leading exponents establish an indispensable foundation for understanding the timeless Truth and spiritual practices which live in the heart of all religions. Some of these titles are companion volumes to the Treasures of the World's Religions series, which allows a comparison of the writings of the great sages of the past with the perennialist authors of our time.

Cover: Seyyed Hossein Nasr
Photograph by Harun Tan

The Essential Seyyed Hossein Nasr

Edited by

William C. Chittick

Foreword by

Huston Smith

World Wisdom

Partial underwriting for this book was provided by The Radius Foundation, Inc.

Library of Congress Cataloging-in-Publication Data

Nasr, Seyyed Hossein.
The essential Seyyed Hossein Nasr / edited by William C. Chittick ; foreword by Huston Smith.
p. cm. -- (Perennial philosophy series)
Includes bibliographical references and index.
ISBN-13: 978-1-933316-38-3 (pbk. : alk. paper)
ISBN-10: 1-933316-38-1 (pbk. : alk. paper) 1. Philosophy, Islamic. 2. Sufism. I. Chittick, William C. II. Title.
B741.N3839 2007
181'.5--dc22

2007002527

Printed on acid-free paper in Canada.

For information address World Wisdom, Inc.
P.O. Box 2682, Bloomington, Indiana 47402-2682

www.worldwisdom.com

Table of Contents

Foreword

This valuable book distills the essence of the thought of one of the most important thinkers of our times.

For me, personally, that understates the case. No other thinker that is still alive—the qualification is important, for Seyyed Hossein Nasr would reprimand me if I ranked him with Socrates, Plato, and other historical benchmark thinkers—has influenced my thought as much as he has. And it is easy to say why. It was he who led me to the perennialists—René Guénon, A.K. Coomaraswamy, Frithjof Schuon and others—who with a single stroke settled the dilemma that could have plagued me (by mudding my thinking) for the rest of my life. That single stroke sliced the esoteric from the exoteric—the kernels of walnuts from their shells, so to speak. Esoterically, or in their kernels, the great philosophies and religions of history are one: mystics all speak the same language. Exoterically, they differ importantly. As I am an esoteric by nature this "slice" enabled me to believe wholeheartedly in authentic religions while honoring their differences. I was at peace with the world.

That was my personal tribute to Seyyed Hossein Nasr, but twentieth century history offers a clear, objective tribute as well. The highest honor a *philosopher* can receive is to be nominated by his peers for inclusion in the series of The Library of Living Philosophers, which began with *The Philosophy of John Dewey*, includes *The Philosophy of Alfred North Whitehead*, and whose latest entry is *The Philosophy of Seyyed Hossein Nasr.* And the highest honor a *theologian* can receive is to be invited to deliver the Gifford Lectures in Glasgow, Scotland. Seyyed Hossein Nasr is the only person ever to have received both of these honors. The Gifford Lectures always eventuates in a book, and the one that contains Nasr's lectures is *Knowledge and the Sacred*, one of the most important books of the twentieth century.

I think the above indicates, both objectively and subjectively, the importance of Seyyed Hossein Nasr's thought and the importance of this book, which gathers it together and distills it. It remains only for me to commend William C. Chittick for bringing it out and editing it so skillfully. Specifically, I am grateful that he targeted "Religion and the Environmental Crisis" for inclusion in the first section, for we are standing on a trap door which, if we are not very careful, could open beneath our feet and eliminate humanity, and possibly all life, from the face of our planet.

—Huston Smith

امانت نتوانست کشید

Introduction

Seyyed Hossein Nasr is now the foremost living member of the traditionalist school and is also recognized as a leading spokesman for Islam not only in North America but also world-wide.[1] He was born in 1933 in Tehran, eight years into the reign of the founder of the Pahlavi dynasty, Reza Shah, whose policies were designed largely to bring Iran into the modern world. Nasr's father, Seyyed Valiallah, had been born in 1871, but he only married at the age of sixty, and Seyyed Hossein was the first of his two sons. Both sides of the family had produced scholars and Sufis going back for generations (the title "Seyyed" indicates a paternal line to the Prophet). Seyyed Valiallah was trained as a physician and became the chief administrator of the ministry of education from the end of the Qajar period well into Pahlavi times. He was deeply involved in the transformation of the educational system along modern lines.[2]

Nasr's parents, though part of the modernizing classes, were traditional in their outlook and took great care to instill into him Persian and Islamic culture. At an early age he began memorizing the poetry of Ḥāfiẓ, Rūmī, Saʿdī, and others, though he remarks that during his first period of occidental exile in America, he lost a good deal of what he had learned as a child. His father—a man immersed in traditional Persian culture, a professor at Tehran University, and one of the leading figures in the educational establishment—had numerous friends and acquaintances among the learned classes, many of whom are numbered among the greatest literary figures of the twentieth century. By the age of ten Nasr had met the most important scholars of the day and listened to the debates that often took place in his home. His readings in intellectual matters, including Western philosophy, began at around this age. But, he says, "Most importantly, it was the long hours of discussion with my father, mostly on philosophical and theological issues, complemented by both reading and reaction to the

[1] Nasr has written a detailed "Intellectual Autobiography" for the volume dedicated to him in the Library of Living Philosophers, *The Philosophy of Seyyed Hossein Nasr* (Chicago: Open Court, 2001), and most of what I say about his life derives from that source. The autobiography has been summarized by Zailan Moris in *Knowledge is Light: Essays in Honor of Seyyed Hossein Nasr* (Chicago: ABC International, 1999), pp. 9-32.

[2] See Muhammad Faghfoory, "The Forgotten Educator: The Life and Career of Seyyed Valiallah Khan Nasr," in Moris, *Knowledge is Light*, pp. 209-31.

discourses . . . that constituted an essential aspect of my philosophical education at an early age."[3]

When Nasr was thirteen, his father was injured in an accident and knew that he would not recover. The decision was made to send the boy to America, this in 1945, when the war was scarcely over. After two months alone on the journey, Nasr joined relatives in New York City and was soon enrolled in the Peddie School in New Jersey. He had exhibited his academic talents already in Iran by placing first in national examinations. At Peddie he quickly learned English and graduated four years later as valedictorian, showing exceptional gifts in mathematics and science. Expected by the Peddie establishment to move on to neighboring Princeton, he elected instead to go to MIT to study physics, naively supposing that the field provided the key to the understanding of reality. "It was the possibility of gaining knowledge about the 'nature of things' . . . that was foremost in my mind . . . but [I had] little prescience of the shock that I was soon to receive concerning the real nature of the subject which I had chosen to study."[4]

In 1950 he moved to Boston. His father had died four years earlier, and his mother came from Iran with his younger brother and set up a Persian household in Arlington, thus allowing him to renew his ties to his native cultural ambience. The years at MIT were eventful in many ways, not least because he soon underwent an intellectual and spiritual crisis. He finally decided to leave his chosen field after listening to a lecture by Bertrand Russell, who argued convincingly that there was no possibility of "ontological realism" in the realm of physics. From then on Nasr supplemented his scientific studies with as many humanities courses as he could manage. The most important influence on him during this period was the Italian philosopher Giorgio di Santillana, who among other things taught a one-year course on Dante for Nasr and his friends. When he was asked to teach a course on Hinduism, he took the students straight to "the horse's mouth," meaning the writings of René Guénon. It did not take long for Nasr to discover the writings of Ananda Coomaraswamy and Frithjof Schuon. When he found out that Coomaraswamy's library was right there in Boston, he was able to get permission from Coomaraswamy's widow to make use of its resources. In short, by the time he graduated from MIT in 1954, Nasr was firmly set on the path of traditional wisdom.

[3] "Intellectual Autobiography," p. 9.

[4] Ibid., p. 15.

Given his science degree, however, he went to Harvard in the field of geology and geophysics, in which he received an MA in 1956. He then transferred to the history of science and worked with some of the world's greatest scholars in both this field and in Islamic Studies, including George Sarton, Harry Wolfson, Bernard Cohen, and H.A.R. Gibb. By the time he finished his PhD dissertation in 1958 (published in 1964 as *An Introduction to Islamic Cosmological Doctrines*), Nasr had traveled to Europe, met among others Schuon and Titus Burckhardt, and been initiated into the ʿAlawī branch of the Shādhilī Sufi order.

In the autumn of 1958 Nasr returned to Iran with every intention of studying with the few remaining masters of traditional Islamic wisdom. He quickly married and established a family. He was appointed professor at Tehran University (becoming in 1963 the youngest full professor in the university's history). He read texts in Islamic philosophy in the time-honored, line-by-line way with three of the greatest masters of the twentieth century, Sayyid Muḥammad Kāẓim ʿAṣṣār, ʿAllāmah Ṭabāṭabāʾī, and Sayyid Abu'l-Ḥasan Qazwīnī. He also had many contacts with other masters of both philosophy and Sufism.

The twenty-one years that he remained in Iran made up an enormously productive period in his life. Not only did he publish a series of groundbreaking books in both English and Persian, but he also undertook heavy teaching and administrative loads that helped sow the seeds for a revival of traditional education in the context of the modern university system. When I went to Tehran in 1966 to study with him at Tehran University's Faculty of Letters, he was director of both the Faculty's library and the foreign students program in which I was enrolled, and he was a very popular teacher in the philosophy department. Every year he also taught a well-attended course on Islam or Persian culture in English for the expatriate community, and he was constantly writing books and articles. At the same time, he was busy with the comings and goings that are standard fare in the extended families of which his own was a good example. Despite his almost frenetic schedule, during the day he could usually be counted on to be sitting at his desk in the midst of the library stacks, and I had frequent reason to visit him there in the process of becoming oriented to a totally new environment. In 1968 he was appointed dean of the Faculty of Letters, and from there he moved on to become academic vice-chancellor of the university and, in 1972, chancellor of Aryamehr University (Iran's answer to MIT). In the dozen years I spent in Iran up to the revolution, I was constantly astounded by his energy and his ability to wear several hats at once.

I was able to observe Nasr most closely after he almost single-handedly arranged for the founding, in 1974, of the Imperial Iranian Academy of Philosophy. This was a fruitful period in the recovery of traditional Iranian intellectuality. The Academy hosted courses taught by many important Iranian philosophers, held frequent conferences, and published a bilingual journal, *Sophia Perennis*. The primary foreign faculty were the prolific and highly influential experts in Islamic thought, Henry Corbin and Toshihiko Izutsu. Especially interesting to watch was the manner in which Nasr was able to twist the arms of the foremost scholars of the country to produce important books, an extraordinary number of which were published—mainly in Persian and Arabic—while he was director. At the same time he remained chancellor of Aryamehr University, professor of philosophy at Tehran University, and, from 1978, the director of the private bureau of the empress, the Shahbanou of Iran.

Nasr left Iran in January of 1979 with the intention of returning in two weeks, but things happened quickly and he found himself and his family stranded in London with no place to go. A quickly-arranged visiting professorship at the University of Utah brought him to America, followed by an appointment at Temple University, and then, from 1984, by his current position as University Professor at George Washington University.

Shortly before leaving Iran, Nasr had been invited to deliver the well-known Gifford Lectures on "Natural Theology" in Scotland. The series had begun in 1888, and the list of lecturers includes many well-known philosophers and scientists, such as Werner Heisenberg, William James, Albert Schweitzer, Paul Tillich, Arnold Toynbee, and Alfred North Whitehead. Despite the turmoil in Nasr's life at this time, the loss of his library, and his lack of a permanent location, he sat down and produced what he calls "a gift from Heaven." He was able to write ten long lectures with an ease that he had never before experienced. The result, published as *Knowledge and the Sacred*, is his most comprehensive statement of his philosophical position. He acknowledges, with modest hesitation, that the book is "in a sense my most important philosophical work and has had perhaps greater impact outside the circle of scholars of Islamic thought than any of my other writings."[5]

Nasr's years in America have been especially productive in terms of books written, lectures delivered, and students trained. One wishes

[5] Ibid., pp. 77-78.

him many more years of flourishing and the opportunity to return to his beloved Iran.

* * *

Most of Nasr's earlier writings apply the traditionalist perspective to Islamic intellectuality, specifically the teachings of Muslim philosophers and Sufis. His major studies of Islamic cosmology, science, psychology, and spirituality offer a fresh interpretative stance not found earlier in the academic mainstream. Three out of four of his first books in English (*An Introduction to Islamic Cosmological Doctrines*, *Three Muslim Sages*, and *Science and Civilization in Islam*) were published by Harvard University Press, and they immediately established him as a major and original voice in Islamic Studies. His strong endorsement of the writings of Schuon and Burckhardt in these books were in turn instrumental in bringing the traditionalist school to the notice of official academia.

The newness of his approach to the field of Islamic Studies can perhaps be illustrated by an anecdote from my undergraduate years. I spent the academic year of 1964-65 at the American University of Beirut, having gone mainly with the intention of getting out of Ohio. For various reasons, I became interested in Sufism, and I proceeded to read much of the English secondary literature on the subject, with the aim of writing a paper to fulfill the requirements for a one-semester independent project. After several months studying the standard Orientalist accounts, I was fairly confident that I had mastered the topic. Then I attended a public lecture by Nasr on "The spiritual path in Islam." I did not know what he was talking about. It dawned on me that something important was missing from all those academic accounts that I had been reading. This led me to his *Three Muslim Sages*, in particular the chapter on Ibn ʿArabī, and from there on it was easy to see that whole dimensions of Islamic intellectuality are lost when it is read without an understanding of the world view that underlies it and the yawning gulf that separates that world view from our own received wisdom.

In short, Nasr brought a new perspective to mainstream Islamic Studies, but it was already familiar to those involved in careful readings of pre-modern Muslim texts, because it was simply an articulate re-expression, in a more universal and contemporary language, of the underlying presuppositions of the writings. At the same time, Nasr has always been concerned to clarify the nature of the traditionalist perspective itself, first to the university community in his native Iran (which was then dominated by the methodologies taught on the French academic scene) and second to the West. His *Knowledge and the Sacred* is his comprehensive statement of what tradition entails, and the fact that it was conceived in Iran but written in America highlights a turning point in Nasr's life and career, his shift from primary emphasis on the Islamic tradition to a more intense focus on tradition per se.

This slight shift in emphasis in Nasr's writings can be observed by studying the course of his writings. The closest thing to a complete bibliography of his publications, covering the period from 1961 to 1999, is provided in *The Philosophy of Seyyed Hossein Nasr.* The fifty-odd books and monographs and 500 articles pertain generally to the two broad fields of Islamic Studies and the *philosophia perennis.* The majority of works before *Knowledge and the Sacred* offer traditionalist readings of Islamic thought and culture. Nasr did not neglect the traditionalist approach per se, however, as is shown for example by his Rockefeller lectures at the University of Chicago in 1966, published two years later as *The Encounter of Man and Nature.* This work demonstrates that he had already assimilated the approach at an early stage in his career, since he applies it there to the history of Western thought, the birth of the modern world, the study of religion generally, and the crisis of the environment, the last of which was just beginning to attract some attention in academic circles.

Since coming to America, Nasr has continued his prolific output in both Islamic and traditionalist studies, with much of his effort focused on bringing to light the riches of Islamic philosophy, as in his recent *Islamic Philosophy from Its Origin to the Present: Philosophy in the Land of Prophecy.* Nonetheless, there is a general trend in his writings and activities to bring the traditionalist approach to a broader audience. This is reflected not only in two major books, *The Need for a Sacred Science* (1993) and *Religion and the Order of Nature* (1996), but also in numerous public lectures all over the globe.

Choosing Nasr's "essential" writings from his vast corpus has been no easy task. I have been guided by the assumption that readers will either not be familiar with his writings and/or would like to have an overview of his main points. The first of the book's three parts introduces Nasr's evaluation of the significance of the traditionalist perspective for the understanding of religion in the contemporary situation. The second part illustrates his application of the traditionalist perspective to Islam and the manner in which this approach fits seamlessly into the Islamic approach to the spiritual and intellectual life. The third part deals with main themes of the traditionalist school: metaphysics, cosmology, spiritual psychology, art, pre-modern science, and the shortcomings of modern thought.

—William C. Chittick

Religion

1. Living in a Multi-Religious World

As a young student enrolled at a Christian preparatory school in New Jersey for several years, I was required to go to church nearly every Sunday while being a Muslim fully rooted in the Islamic tradition. That direct experience of another religion contributed to my own awareness of living in a world with many religions. It brought home realities which were to confront me later in life both theologically and philosophically. I began to ponder over the meaning of living in a world in which, while being aware of one's own religious roots, one has contact on both a personal and an intellectual plane with others who belong to a religious universe different from one's own. My own experience as a Muslim studying in the West had confronted me with the problem of living in a multi-religious world.

Much has been said about the new adventures of the man of the twentieth century, the age known for the use of atomic power and flight into space. However, I personally believe that there is in truth only one new experience of real significance which confronts twentieth century man, one which his ancestors did not face. That experience is not one of discovering new continents and even planets, but one of journeying from one religious universe to another. For a very long time human beings lived in a world in which their religion was *the* religion, in which the knowledge and experience of God as the Absolute were directly reflected in man's seeing his religion as absolute. Here I use the word *absolute* metaphysically and theologically despite all the positivistic criticisms against such terms. Even in worlds where God was not mentioned, such as the non-theistic religions of Buddhism and Taoism, in whose perspective one speaks only of the Void or the Supreme Principle, the knowledge and experience of Ultimate Reality or the Absolute was also reflected in the sense of the absolute experienced by adherents of these religions in their own religious teachings, forms, and rites. To have lived a religion was to have lived in a world whose values and perspectives reigned supreme and in an absolute manner over human life.

That is what the normal situation of man always was and in fact should be. But today, in contrast to normal times, the situation has altered wherever modernism has spread its influence. The normal human situation can be understood by citing how man views himself in the cosmos. Astronomically and also "theoretically," we accept the presence of other suns in a vast expanding universe; yet we live on the surface of the earth as if our sun were *the* sun revolving, as it appears to the eye, around the earth. Otherwise, we would lose our sanity and sense of peace and stability. Our sanity requires that we look at the sun as *the* sun, which it is in fact for *our* world. In the same way, the consciousness of humanity in normal circumstances demanded that the sun, whether it was s-u-n or s-o-n, of a particular universe, be *the* sun or son and, therefore, be absolute for that universe.

For better or for worse, however, that homogeneous religious universe has now been broken for a large segment of humanity, although not where traditional societies survive to any appreciable degree. There are Moroccan fishermen or Burmese farmers who live "exclusively" in the world of Islam or Buddhism without awareness of other religions, as there are also Italian peasants, or perhaps even farmers in this part of the country, that is, the American South, for whom the presence of other religions is not an existential reality, Judaism being an exception because it is seen as preceding and being the immediate background of the Christian revelation and therefore holding a special position with respect to Christianity. It is, therefore, seen as a part of the same tradition by the Christians whom we have in mind here. However, for much of the Western and modernized world, and this includes in particular the Western intelligentsia, a new situation has arisen which is due in large part to the erosion of the boundaries of the closed religious universe that constituted the traditional world of Christianity within which Western man lived until modern times.

It is interesting to note that contiguity or the physical presence of two religions in one place is not in itself sufficient to warrant this new awareness of other religions. For many centuries, for example, Christians lived across the river from the Muslims of Isfahan in Iran. Many of them were friends and traded and bargained in the bazaars of Isfahan. They rarely, however, wrote treatises comparing Christianity and Islam, although there are one or two exceptions. Or, again, most people think of India as a place where there is a general awareness of diverse religious traditions. Yet there are many people in India who have never heard of Tibetan Buddhism or for that matter have never even heard of Tibet. There are also those who have not even heard of the great religion of Buddhism itself, which arose in India but which gradually disappeared from that land from the fifth century A.D. onward, surviving nevertheless in the peripheral areas of the Indian subcontinent such as Nepal and Sri Lanka. Still, in that very land of India, during a particular period of history, Islam and Hinduism met on the highest level, with far-reaching results for the religious life of the subcontinent as a whole.

It is, therefore, not simply the proximity of two religious communities which creates an awareness of the need to take cognizance of a religious world other than one's own. Many other factors are involved. As far as the modern West is concerned, it is the destruction of the absoluteness of the Christian vision of the world in the minds of Western man that has confronted him today with a new situation whose main features and characteristics cannot be neglected by any intelligent person interested in the phenomenon of religion or belonging to the world of faith.

* * *

Contemporary man is confronted with several realities of religious character belonging to diverse religious traditions, whose religious and spiritual nature is very difficult to negate unless we negate the reality of religion itself. The first of these is art, that most tangible and visible manifestation of an alien religious world. We see and also hear various forms of sacred art belonging to many different worlds. Today no well-educated Westerner who is sensitive to the architecture of the Chartres Cathedral and who is well informed can pass over with indifference the beauty of a Cairene mosque, a southern Hindu temple, or the temples of Kyoto. Nor can anyone who is interested in serious Western sacred music from the Gregorian chant to Palestrina and who is musically educated fail to appreciate the sacred character—I do not use the word *religious* but *sacred*—of this music without also being at least aware of what the music of the Sufis, or Hindu music, or Buddhist chanting can imply as bearers of a spiritual message. One could go down the list of all of the other arts. Let us take poetry, for example. Can anyone with a solid literary education read St. John of the Cross and be moved religiously by it, and yet not be touched by the religious significance of the poetry of Jalāl al-Dīn Rūmī? That is hardly an aesthetic or artistic possibility for the person who has experienced the modern world and who at the same time is sensitive to religious and mystical poetry.

Therefore, it can be safely asserted that the very presence of the sacred art of other religions has already brought these religions into the life of Western man through what one might call the back door. Many an individual has bought a Taoist landscape painting and put it in his or her home without realizing that it is really an icon; that is, it is a presentation of nature with profound metaphysical and religious significance in the form of a landscape painting, belonging to the artistic tradition of another civilization. Today those in the West who are really educated have to acknowledge and be aware of the presence of sacred art as a gateway to the inner courtyard of various religious traditions of East and West.

A second reality involves doctrine. The term doctrine as used in Christianity, *docta* in Latin, does not have its exact equivalent in certain traditional languages such as Sanskrit, Chinese, or Japanese, although Hinduism, Buddhism, Taoism, Confucianism, and Shintoism certainly possess metaphysical teachings which correspond to doctrine in Western languages. In any case the word does have an equivalent in Arabic, the term *ʿaqīdah.* Now, anyone who takes religious doctrine seriously, who has read St. Bonaventure or St. Thomas Aquinas, cannot remain totally impervious to the religious character of doctrines which are purported to be of a religious nature and are written by followers of other religions. Even in the Middle Ages, at the height of religious fervor in the Christian West, when Albertus Magnus and St. Thomas were reading Avicenna and al-Ghazzālī in the newly translated Latin versions that appeared by way of Toledo in the 1170s and 1180s, they were fully aware that these texts were of a religious significance. That is why the apologetic literature of the period said something to the effect that, "Well, Islam is not a true religion, but these texts are of religious significance and should be studied from the point of view of religious philosophy." The debates of the Latin Averroists and the Thomists as well as other theological and philosophical discussions in the thirteenth and fourteenth centuries point to this fact.

Today this awareness of non-Christian religious doctrine has become much more universalized and it has also become necessary to go beyond the polemical position of the medieval theologians who lived in a homogeneous Christian universe and who could afford to ignore the universality of revelation and the reality of religion in diverse forms. One cannot read the Bhagavad-Gita seriously in this day and age without becoming aware of the religious character of this text. Nor could any one in good conscience call it pagan ramblings. Therefore, the doctrines of the other religions which are now available in the form of sacred scripture, open metaphysical exposition, theological formulation, or inspired literature of one kind or another, convey a metaphysical, theological, and religious significance which must be taken seriously by men and women of good faith.

Finally and perhaps more important than these two realities, there is the presence of human beings of spiritual nature belonging to other religions. It is perhaps simple for some to brush aside sacred art or to refuse to read metaphysical and doctrinal treatises belonging to another tradition. It is difficult, however, to confront a religious and spiritual presence in the person of a saintly individual from another religious tradition and refuse to acknowledge that presence for what it is. This, incidentally, had already been recognized as a reality before modern times in certain periods and cultures where it was appreciated in a positive sense, a prime example of it being India. When the great saints of Sufism first went to India, the Hindu sages immediately recognized their extraordinary nature and there were many encounters between the two groups in Kashmir, Sind, and the Punjab. More meetings between the sages and the holy men of the two traditions occurred later when the various Sufi orders, especially the Chishtī, spread to the heartland of India. It is impossible for a person of spiritual awareness to meet his counterpart and not to realize the spiritual nature of the other side, as impossible as a mathematician encountering another gifted mathematician and not taking cognizance of the fact that he knows mathematics.

In the twentieth century the presence of human beings from another religious tradition poses on a larger scale than ever before the question of the authenticity of the religion which has nurtured them. The encounter with authentic representatives of other religions raises this question because of the ethical behavior and self-discipline of such human beings and the fact that they live in a world in which they obviously draw from inner spiritual sources which one cannot deny without denying the reality of religion as such. The fact that many such figures correspond so precisely to what Christ said a human being should be makes it very difficult for a Christian not to take them seriously. This was the problem which confronted many of the English who went to India in the nineteenth century and there met a man like Ramakrishna. And it has continued to our own day. We have accounts of men such as Charles Foucauld, the famous Catholic missionary in Algeria and Morocco, who, in his first encounter with Sufi saints, recognized in them the sanctity he had found in figures belonging to the Christian tradition. It was very difficult for him to act as if these people were merely pagans needing to be saved.

In the modern world one observes for the first time on the general cultural and social scene the presence of these three major religious realities namely, art, doctrine, and spiritual and saintly human beings of other religions. On a wider circle than ever before the sincere person is forced to take these religious realities outside his or her own religion seriously into consideration under pain of losing attachment to his or her own religion itself.

The situation obviously poses a difficult problem for the individual who does take religion seriously, particularly in the West. There are many reasons for this dilemma, one of the most important of which is the fact that a metaphysics of comparative religion, although already formulated in a magisterial fashion by F. Schuon and others, is very difficult to come by in general religious and academic circles. This in turn is the result of the philosophical background of the study of other religions, a background that is limited almost exclusively to positivism, relativism, or some form or other of one-dimensional existentialism. The metaphysical dimension disappeared for the most part from Western philosophy and world view a long time ago. Therefore, a modern Westerner in search of the metaphysical doctrines that alone can make an understanding in depth of other religions and the "transcendent unity of religions" possible is not in the same metaphysical universe as a Hindu or a Muslim, who would have easy access to modes of thought which accept the metaphysical dimension of reality as part and parcel of the world view of their traditions. It is important to realize the fact that Western man has come to this crucial problem of the multiplicity of religions at a time when the philosophical scene is essentially the legacy of nineteenth century rationalism plus the logical positivism of the twentieth century in the Anglo-Saxon world and existentialist philosophy on the Continent. The situation would have been very different if Meister Eckhart, St. Bonaventure, or Nicholas of Cusa were living philosophical influences in the West rather than being taught exclusively in a few seminaries or courses on the history of philosophy.

Now, this absence of a veritable metaphysics in the West makes it much more difficult to confront the philosophical problems that have been encountered by Western historians and philosophers of religion. As a result, few among the academic scholars of religion are able to provide an answer that would really be satisfying from a scholarly and philosophical as well as a religious point of view.

* * *

The problem so difficult for modern scholars and philosophers of religion to solve can be analyzed as follows: If God is absolute in the metaphysical and theological sense, and if He speaks as the Absolute within a religion which then claims to be *the* religion, how is it possible to have a multiplicity of religions, which seems to imply a multiplicity of absolutes? Does this not already relativize the Absolute? That is the first and fundamental question. Let us turn to a concrete example. Christ said, "I am the way, the truth, and the life." The Prophet of Islam said, "No one sees God unless he has seen me." One could go down the list of statements of this kind mentioned by founders of other religions. What does this imply? If we take the sayings of the New Testament seriously as Christians, or those of the Quran and *Ḥadīth* seriously as Muslims, or those of the Bhagavad-Gita seriously as

Hindus, and so forth, how then does one come to terms with the absoluteness implied by such statements in religions other than one's own? That is, what shall we do with the very idea of the sense of absoluteness in religion and the concept of the absolute in metaphysics?

This is a fundamental question that has led many to the relativization of religion itself, and therefore to the destruction of religion, which ceases to be religion if it does not come from and lead to the Absolute. The attack which was carried out in the nineteenth century by such agnostic and atheistic philosophers as Karl Marx and Ludwig Feuerbach and positivists like Auguste Comte against religion was actually based not only upon the negation of the metaphysical and supernatural elements of religion, but also in part upon the multiplicity of religions. Moreover, on the popular level, knowing the Christian teaching that "celibacy is good," or that "one can marry only one wife," and then seeing Muslims or Hindus, or for that matter prophets of the Old Testament who had, or in the case of the former still have, more than one wife has caused doubt as to the "absoluteness" of religious edicts. As a result, both the skeptical and atheistic philosophers and many common believers have concluded that everything is relative and therefore religion has no ultimate meaning. It is hardly necessary to repeat that no religion can survive without a sense of the absolute. Absoluteness of religion is in fact a necessary consequence of the absoluteness of its Origin. The sense that a good Christian or a good Muslim, as people of faith, have that they are walking upon the right path and that when they die they are in the Hands of God, is based on religious certitude, which itself issues from the sense of the absolute in religion and ultimately the absoluteness of God.

What happens when this absoluteness is destroyed? We are left with only three possibilities. One possibility is to reject the claim of every religion regarding the absoluteness of its message and to say that the teachings of all religions are relative. To do this is ultimately to destroy all religions and religion as such. One ends up with one form or another of one of two positions: The first is a historicism, which reduces all religions to merely historical and social phenomena. One attempts to study who has influenced whom in such a manner that if one were to carry it to its ultimate conclusion, one would end up reducing the most sublime teachings to the cosmic soup of molecules which, according to evolutionists, has produced everything. That is of course metaphysically absurd, but nevertheless certain people continue to practice this reductionist, historicistic method. The second position is to acknowledge that the matter of personal faith and personal commitment are the heart of religion, but that religion has no permanent and immutable intellectual or for that matter ethical content. Consequently, one should not speak of religion in an absolute sense but should remain aware of the subjective nature of religious assertions and claims. In either case, this possibility means the destruction of religion or at best its impoverishment in one way or another.

A second possibility is to accept only one's own religion as being absolute and reject all other religions, an attitude which many people hold. This attitude has, moreover, been normal to traditional humanity and one cannot but have respect for the majority of ordinary believers who hold such a position. From the point of view of a pious Muslim or Hindu, surely it would be preferable to be considered a "heathen" by a believing Christian than to be accepted as an equal by a secularist and agnostic on the condition of accepting to live in a world without transcendence or religious meaning. I do not of course mean to imply that bigotry and intolerance are preferable to tolerance, but that religious faith, even if exclusivist, is better than no faith at all, as the history of the twentieth century has borne out so amply. Therefore, this position should not be belittled in a world given to denial of the transcendent and relativization. It is better to cling to a particular form of the Truth while negating or neglecting other forms of the Truth than to deny Truth altogether.

To cling with all possible strength to the bonds which relate man to God at a time when he feels threatened by both agnosticism and alien religious worlds is not to be criticized out of hand so easily, at least in the case of those who still live within a homogeneous religious universe. It must be remembered that the first duty of man, according to every religion, is to save his soul. We are really only responsible to God for our soul at the moment of death. We are not responsible to Him for solving the problems arising from the multiplicity of religions. No religion has said that if one does not solve the problems of comparative religion, one will not go to Heaven. Therefore, remaining bound within one's own religion for those not touched by the reality of other religions cannot be simply criticized and brushed away. I have heard Christian fundamentalists say that all Muslims are heathens. I have also, needless to say, encountered individuals all over the globe who think that all people should be brothers and sisters but who do not believe in God or the world of the Spirit. Provided he is free to practice his religion, a Muslim, one for whom the Absolute is the center of life, would certainly prefer the first category to the second, despite the limitations of that perspective.

The problem with this position, however, is that, as mentioned above, there are already cracks in the wall of the homogeneous religious world, and for certain human beings it is not enough to assert simply the truth of only one's own religion. For such men and women, it would mean the loss of their faith if a satisfactory answer were not given to the question as to why there are many religions and not only one religion. There is many a person who has lost his simple faith in religion precisely as a result of his awareness of other traditions. Such a person becomes aware, for example, that there are Buddhist monks who do not believe in God in the Christian sense of the term, yet they fast constantly, while he believes in God but cannot fast even three days. This is the sort of problem that has obviously bothered a great many people everywhere, but especially in this country and Europe. Yet, this second possibility of considering only one's religion to be true and its values absolute certainly exists even in today's diversified world, but obviously it does not lead to the possibility of the serious study and understanding of other religions.

Before proceeding any further, it must be mentioned that one of the consequences of the failure of scholars in the West to provide a genuine solution concerning the encounter of religions, which would be at once intellectually and religiously satisfying, is precisely strife among religions on the one hand and the strengthening of opposition to all religions on the other. This is a fact of great importance which must be understood and which it is not possible to discuss here except in passing. Many in the modern world assume that modernism automatically brings with it open-mindedness in religious matters, that the more modern one becomes, the more open-minded he will be towards the faith of other men. This is fallacious, as is borne out by recent historical experience. There is a story which I heard from a great and venerable teacher in Iran who died over ten years ago at an advanced age. I studied Islamic philosophy and Sufism for nearly twenty years with him and he was like an uncle to me. One day he said, "It is fine to be open-minded. To be open-minded is like having the windows of the mind open. It is like opening up the windows of a house. Now it is wonderful to open the windows of your house provided your house has walls. But if there are no walls, say just two windows in the middle of the desert, it does not matter whether you close them or open them."

The idea that as one becomes more modern one becomes open-minded in a religiously meaningful sense is totally absurd. Even if there is open-mindedness on a certain level, it is irrelevant because for the modernists there are no religious principles which must be defended at all cost against error. For them immutable principles are identified with dogmatism and narrow-mindedness. Anyone over sixty years old who is familiar with the Middle East, and even anyone younger with some experience of the less modernized areas of the region, knows that a Muslim, Jew, or Christian in the Middle East was much more religiously tolerant a generation ago than today, and also today much more tolerant in the less modernized areas of that world than in the big cities. This is a tragic fact with profound reasons underlying it.

Putting aside the political issues that have caused this particular problem in that region of the world, there are also religious reasons. One of these reasons is that the very attack of modernism against religious identity has caused many people to emphasize that identity on the basis of exclusiveness. Exclusivity has created a new phenomenon which was not predicted by earlier Western sociologists of religion. Nor did they predict the revival of religion throughout much of the world. Religion was supposed to become outmoded and disappear in the so-called underdeveloped world after a few five-year economic programs; and, of course, that simply did not happen, as the case of many countries such as Iran and Egypt bear out. Modernism brought in its wake in the non-Western world not only the erosion of religion but also its revival in a more exclusivist form.

But putting this fact aside and returning to the second possibility, that is, the view that one's religion is alone true and everything else is false, it needs to be repeated that this is certainly one of the prevalent positions in the modern world. However, that is not sufficient unto itself, because of factors mentioned in the first part of this lecture, in which I spoke of the reality of the universal character of religious presence, which must be taken into account by anyone who is both sincere with himself and has had a genuine encounter with religion and spirituality beyond the borders of his own religious world. Also, obviously this view is not sufficient because of the evident human and social need to create peace and better understanding among followers of different religions.

The third possibility is to assert that all religions which come from Heaven are true. This does not mean to imply that all religious claims are true. There is always need for the principle of discernment. But if one asserts that all the revealed religions, all the historical traditions, all the millennial religions of mankind which have produced civilizations, sacred art, theology, and saints who have manifested the phenomenon of sanctity—which is an extremely important criterion for the judgment of the authenticity of a religion—are true, then one is faced with two important questions. First, is there, then, no falsehood? For if religiously speaking everything is true, then there is no falsehood and in fact no truth. Two and two is four; if for the sake of generosity we say that it might be five or that charity requires that six also be true, then mathematically speaking nothing is true. The first question is thus one of truth.

The second is the question of authority, that is, who can make assertions about the truth of various religions and by what authority? These are two fundamental questions, the second being especially important when one moves outside a particular religion. As long as one remains within a single religion, there is always, within that religion, an inerrant authority which is guaranteed by Heaven for those who accept that religion. Otherwise in the long run there would be no religion at all. Whether it be the Holy Spirit, the Magisterium, the Imams, the *Ummah* (Muslim community), the Wheel of *Dharma* or other similar realities, in every religion there must be an authority and a guarantee of the truth of that religion. Otherwise one would not follow that religion with the assurance of the authenticity of its teachings. The believers of a particular religious tradition live with the certitude that there is an authority which guarantees its authenticity and a voice which can speak the truth.

Now once one moves out of the framework of a single religion and asserts that all revealed religions are true, the first question which comes up is, "According to whose authority are you speaking?" This is a basic question to be answered in addition to the question which arises with regard to religious truth and the criterion for truth. If one claims that all religions are true, then why is Hinduism true and the Jonestown phenomenon not true? According to what criterion can one distinguish between true and false religions? Should it be said that all people have the right to be prophets, just as everyone has the right to vote? Even in this age of egalitarianism few would answer this question in the affirmative. This leaves then the questions of authority and truthfulness. Now these questions have been definitively answered; they are not unanswerable questions. However, the fact remains that the definitive answers that have been given have not been heard very widely in current religious and academic circles.

* * *

First, however, it is necessary to recapitulate the major schools in the West which have tried to study the phenomena of religious diversity. It is necessary because these schools are responsible for the eclipse of the profounder studies of religious diversity and are the reason why the satisfactory answers to the questions of truth and authority in a multi-religious universe have not been as widely heard as they should. The definitive answers to these fundamental questions come from the perspective of the oft-neglected traditional school, which asserts that it is both possible and necessary to accept the truth of all revealed religions without destroying the truth and innate orthodoxy of each of them. I shall deal with this school shortly.

First, however, I would like to focus upon scholarship in the West, both Christian and secular, which has tried to deal with the multiplicity of religious forms. This is obviously important for the understanding of the study of religion today. Before modern times, the Western world, and here I refer primarily to the Christian, was already in a peculiar situation with regard to its relationship with other religions. Western Christianity, which had little intellectual exchange with the eastern churches after the early centuries of the Christian era, remained in a sense isolated in one corner of the Eurasian land mass. This is a rather peculiar way of speaking, perhaps, if one is sitting in London. However, if one lives in Delhi or Tehran, the situation appears this way. One observes a large land mass in the Western corner of which is located a place called Europe. Western Christianity remained isolated in that corner during its period of growth and crystallization throughout the early and even High Middle Ages. It knew nothing at all about Hinduism or Buddhism and very little about Zoroastrianism. (Zoroaster, for example, appeared as a mathematician in Europe during early Christian centuries, and the early texts in Greek and Latin often considered him to be a scientist or alchemist, whereas he never wrote a treatise on mathematics or any of the other sciences). As for Manichaeism, it became known mostly through the writings of St. Augustine simply as the arch-heresy of Christianity. There remained one particular exception, however, and that was Islam, which, in a sense, surrounded all of Western Europe and acted as both an obstacle against the penetration by the West of Africa and Asia and an obstacle to contact with other religions.

For a long time for Western Christianity, the world was divided into two parts, the Christian world and the pagan or heathen one, the latter being identified mostly with the Islamic world. The situation remained more or less this way until the sixteenth and seventeenth centuries, when Europeans traveled to many faraway lands, and such groups as the Jesuits went to China and wrote to Catholic authorities in Rome informing them of the religions and culture of China. It is true that in the hope of having a kind of Christian pincer movement to destroy Islam, the Pope had sent an ambassador to the Mongols when they invaded Persia in the thirteenth century. Also earlier in the twelfth century, word had spread in Italy and France that there were Christians on the other side of the Muslim territories and that if some kind of an alliance could be made with them, then it would be possible to defeat the Muslims. Despite the sending of such an embassy, however, its result was not sufficient to change the consciousness of Western Europe concerning the presence of other religions. When Christianity came to America, it brought this vision of a world divided among Christians and pagans with it. And despite the later contact of Christianity with other religions, something of this earlier attitude survived in Christian circles, especially as far as Islam was concerned.

Now, this historical experience of Christianity was very different from the experience of either Islam, Hinduism, Buddhism, or the Chinese religions. In the case of Islam it is particularly interesting to note that it is the only religion before the modern era which had confronted every major religious tradition of mankind, with the exception of Shintoism and the American Indian religions. It had encountered Christianity and Judaism in its birthplace, Zoroastrianism, Manichaeism, and Mithraism in Persia, Shamanism—which in its Asian form is a sister religion of Shintoism and the North American Indian religions—in Central Asia and Mongolia, the native African religions south of the Sahara, and, of course, Hinduism and Buddhism in India and eastern Persia.

Thus an intelligent, educated person, sitting in Isfahan four hundred years ago, could read books in Persian and Arabic on Hinduism and Buddhism and familiarize himself to some extent with these traditions. There existed many books on comparative religion in Arabic and Persian in which various religions were discussed. It is true that they were not completely consistent with what the followers of those religions themselves accepted, but neither are most of the books of comparative religion today. I do not wish to imply, therefore, that those books were perfect, but nevertheless they were there and available to the intelligent reader. In contrast an intelligent person in Paris during that same period had hardly any access to traditions outside the Abrahamic world, while his view of Islam was restricted to the conception of the heathen and the pagan inherited from the earlier period of European history. Like his contemporary in Isfahan, a Hindu intellectual in India would know Buddhism and Jainism, and would certainly have heard of the Chinese religions because of the trade routes going back and forth. He would also of course have had direct experience of Islam, which existed in India at that time. Among major Asian civilizations, perhaps Japan was the only exception, being an island culture isolated from the rest of the world except for Korea and China. It can be said in general that the other important Asian civilizations had already developed an awareness of other religions during that period which the West calls the Middle Ages and in which Western civilization was formed.

As a result of this unique historical experience, when in the nineteenth century serious encounter with other religions became a reality for Western Christianity, Western Europe began from a very special position. To this experience must be added the theological structure of Christianity, which saw itself for the most part as the only religion and interpreted the saying of Christ, "I am the way, the truth, and the life" as meaning "I am the only way, the only truth, and the only life." Despite exceptions found in the works of such a theologian as Nicholas of Cusa, the exclusivism of Christian theology complemented the historical experience of Western Christianity and made the serious approach to other religions particularly difficult.

Moreover, as a result of the Renaissance and the Age of Enlightenment, Europe came to consider itself as superior in every way to other civilizations. There is also this fact to consider that at a time when Europeans were debunking Christianity inside their homeland, European missionaries were being sent abroad to propagate it. The difference in the attitude of the French government toward the Catholic Church in Paris and the Catholic Church in Algeria and Morocco is very interesting and telling. The same could be said of the British government, although there did not exist the same anti-clericalism in England as in France, since the British king or queen served as the head of the Anglican Church. Nevertheless, the British attitudes to Christianity at home and abroad were quite different. Despite missionary activity in Asia, Africa, and elsewhere, within European intellectual circles there existed an opposition to Christianity combined with a sense of superiority to everyone else and to other religions, all of which were considered as "childish" and their followers simpletons who had not as yet benefited from the fruits of the Age of Enlightenment. Once they read Montesquieu, Voltaire, Rousseau, and the like, they would stop believing in the religions to which they still clinged. Nineteenth-century European scholars thus began to write from a perspective of superiority with results which seem amusing when read today.

Many works came to be written in the field of comparative religion by famous scholars. It needs to be remembered, furthermore, that even the most famous of them, Max Müller, the founder of the "science of religion" who contributed so much to drawing attention to the importance of the study of other religions and supervised the translation of the sacred scripture of eastern religions, wrote that he did not consider the Upanishads to be false, but to be like the work of little children compared to the New Testament, which is like that of grown-up men. At least he had some respect for the New Testament, but what he said about Hinduism appears unbelievable today.

From this background emerged the sort of historical, evolutionary, and positivist interpretation of religion that attempted to deal with the entire religious phenomenon from the point of view of a gradual evolutionary growth. This evolutionary perspective can be seen in the well-known Comptian distinction between the metaphysical, theological, and rational stages of the growth of mankind, or in the work of others who spoke of the evolution of man from mythology to theology to philosophy. There were many different ways in which man's religious life was considered in an evolutionary and progressive sense. At that time many Christian theologians adopted this prevalent evolutionary perspective because they thought it would serve their purpose. They saw religion as evolving gradually from simple early forms to its perfection, which was Christianity, forgetting for the most part the embarrassing postscript which is Islam. That is why, as the discipline of comparative religion developed, less attention was paid to Islam than to any other major religion and also why to this day there are so many departments of religion in America where there is no professor of Islamic studies. This is the result of the fact that departments were built and continue to be built, often unconsciously, with this philosophy in the background. Hinduism and Buddhism and, of course, Judaism were studied and made to fit into this evolutionary pattern since they preceded Christianity. But the case of Islam remained an enigma that many decided to ignore, rather than relinquish the evolutionary and historicistic ideology inherited from the nineteenth century.

This evolutionary approach to the study of religion with its dogmatic historicism began, however, to confront challenges in the early part of the twentieth century from new philosophical currents such as phenomenology. Many realized that one could not subjugate one religion in grandeur, beauty, or truth to another simply because it appeared earlier or later in the history of mankind. And so gradually the evolutionary and historicistic approach was complemented by the school of phenomenology, which has had several branches, the late Mircea Eliade at the University of Chicago being its most famous representative in America. An entire generation of scholars developed who instead of trying to be purely historical, attempted to base their studies on the religious phenomenon itself irrespective of historical influences but also divorced for the most part from theological considerations and the question of metaphysical truth.

The question of the innate meaning of religion and religious truth is not the concern of this school. Its interest resides in the description of the phenomena of religion in themselves. Something like the "rites of initiation" might be chosen and then studied in Egypt, Mesopotamia, etc., without much interest in the way in which such a rite forms an integral part of the Egyptian or the Mesopotamian traditions. This approach, moreover, has ignored the theological significance of religion entirely. Hence, many Christians have been quite unhappy with the fruit of research by those who have followed the methods of this school.

Moreover, interestingly enough, this school has had to leave the treatment of Islam for the most part out of its treatment of religion. This kind of phenomenological approach has been more suitable for the mythological form of religion but has had greater difficulty in dealing with a religious tradition such as Islam which is essentially metaphysical and abstract. It is significant to note that this school has not produced any Islamicist of note, while it has produced many well-known scholars of the Indian and Far Eastern religions.

Several decades ago there came to the fore a number of American and European Christian scholars who felt that things should be set straight by emphasizing the pole of faith rather than the pole of the phenomena of religion as phenomena. Foremost among them is perhaps Wilfred Cantwell Smith, a Christian minister of Canadian origin and one of the most famous scholars in the field of the theology and philosophy of comparative religion today and also a noted Islamicist. In a series of books Professor Smith has attempted to distinguish between belief and faith and to place the whole of religion upon the basis of faith, essentially leaving the pole of knowledge to the philosophers and to those who want to deal with religion only rationally rather than "existentially." I must add on a personal note that I have been debating with Cantwell Smith for several decades concerning the matter of religion in a pluralistic setting and feel sympathetic to many of his concerns. We were both Islamicists before turning to the field of comparative religion, and we have been friends since he came back from India and Pakistan in the 1950s and I was studying at Harvard. I have followed his intellectual development and have respect for much that he has done. However, what he does not accentuate is precisely the question of the primacy of objective truth, that is, "What is the criterion for objective truth in religion?" That is a question which cannot really be answered unless one has recourse to traditional metaphysics.

Along with schools of thought which have made a contribution to the Christian theological study of other religions, of which W.C. Smith is an outstanding example, we have what for want of a better term one could call the "Neo-Hindu" school, although the approach we have in mind embraces a whole array of varying groups not all of which are related to Hinduism and the Vedanta. I am, of course, aware that the "Neo-Hindus" would never accept the appellation of "sentimental," but this is what characterizes the attitude to other religions of many of their members. Their view is based on the idea that all religions are the same and equal and that what differs among them is unimportant, this sense of equality being based more on sentimentality and less on metaphysical discernment. This position, which came to the fore early in this century, actually developed out of the theosophical movement associated with Madame Blavatsky and Annie Besant and the late nineteenth and early twentieth-century groups in England and Germany associated with them, and it was perpetuated later by the Ramakrishna Mission, the World Council of Faiths, and several other groups, some of which did not have any Hindu connections. A figure such as Baron von Hügel, who played a major role in this movement, was an influential person seeking to establish friendly relation among religions. Perhaps the most colorful and influential figure of this type of approach which saw unity in religions without paying attention to the diverse metaphysical, theological, and social teachings which they obviously entail was, however, the Indian Swami Vivekananda, who was a student of the great saint Ramakrishna. Now, Swami Vivekananda, unlike his master Ramakrishna, who attested to the inner unity of religions through spiritual experience and vision, was not an orthodox or traditional Hindu. Rather, he was a modernist who thought that, by putting aside the distinct metaphysical, theological, and social teachings of various religions, he could create religious unity and bring the religions together in a healthy, friendly, and brotherly fashion.

Now, brotherhood and sisterhood are positive human attitudes; it is good to be brothers. I would be the last person to negate the virtue of such an attitude and in fact in Islam, the devout call each other brothers and sisters. Yet that "feeling" of brotherhood is certainly not going to solve the problem of the plurality of religions, because it leaves aside the basic question of religious truth, which is related to knowledge rather than sentiment. Nevertheless, this school did play a considerable role upon the religion scene for a long time, to the extent that most scholars of comparative religion finally reacted against it by saying, "Please do not talk about religions being the same; in fact they are not at all the same and in most cases they have nothing to do with each other." Their reaction went to the opposite extreme, and the type of treatment of comparative religion popular in the thirties and forties, which had even penetrated into scholarly circles and the academic world, was brushed aside. The last fifty years have seen great opposition to this approach among academicians and scholars of comparative religion, without this opposition being able in its turn to address successfully the questions posed at the beginning of this essay concerning the truth of religion in a universe with multiple religious forms.

2. The Traditionalist Approach to Religion

To understand the approach of the traditional school, or the *philosophia perennis* as here understood, to the study of religions as well as religion as such, it is necessary to point out certain fundamental features of the vision of reality or the metaphysics which underlies all the teachings of this school. According to the *philosophia perennis*, reality is not exhausted by the psychophysical world in which human beings usually function, nor is consciousness limited to the everyday level of awareness of the men and women of present-day humanity. Ultimate Reality is beyond all determination and limitation. It is the Absolute and Infinite from which issues goodness, like the rays of the sun that of necessity emanate from it. Whether the Principle is envisaged as Fullness or Emptiness depends upon the point of departure of the particular metaphysical interpretation in question. If a critic asserts, as in fact has been done, that according to this or that Oriental sage *māyā* is *Ātman* or *samsāra* is *nirvāṇa*, one can answer that such an assertion is only possible if one first realizes that *māyā* is *māyā* and *samsāra* is *samsāra*. The Principle can be envisaged as the Pure Object but also as the Pure Subject or the Supreme "I," in which case ordinary consciousness is then seen as an outward envelope of the Supreme Self rather than the descent of the Supreme Reality into lower realms of the universal hierarchy. But in either case, whether seen as the Transcendent or the Immanent, the Principle gives rise to a universe which is hierarchical, possessing many levels of existence and states of consciousness from the Supreme Principle to earthly man and his terrestrial ambience.

It is in this hierarchic universe that man's life takes place and possesses meaning. Religion is not only the key to the understanding of this universe, but also the central means whereby man is able to journey through the lower stages of existence to the Divine Presence, this journey being nothing other than human life itself as it is understood traditionally. The doctrines, symbols, and rites of a religion possess therefore a meaning which is not confined to the spatiotemporal realm. In contrast to most modern theologians, philosophers, and scholars of religion, who have either consciously or unconsciously adopted the scientistic view that reduces Reality as such to physical or historical reality, the traditionalists refuse to reduce the existence of religion to only the terrestrial and temporal realm. Religion for them is not *only* the faith and practices of a particular human collectivity which happens to be the recipient of a particular religious message. Religion is not *only* the faith of the men and women who possess religious faith. It is a reality of Divine Origin. It has its archetype in the Divine Intellect and possesses levels of meaning and reality like the cosmos itself. If a religion were to cease to exist on earth, that does not mean that it would cease to possess any reality whatsoever. In this case its life cycle on earth would have simply come to an end, while the religion itself as an "Idea" in the Platonic sense would subsist in the Divine Intellect in its trans-historical reality. The efficacy of its rites here on earth would cease, but the archetypal reality which the religion represents would persist.

The traditional school does not neglect the social or psychological aspects of religion, but it refuses to reduce religion to its social or psychological manifestations. Religion in its earthly manifestation comes from the wedding between a Divine Norm and a human collectivity destined providentially to receive the imprint of that Norm. From this wedding is born religion as seen in this world among different peoples and cultures. The differences in the recipient are certainly important and constitute one of the causes for the multiplicity of religious forms and phenomena, but religion itself cannot be reduced to its terrestrial embodiment. If a day would come when not a single Muslim or Christian were to be left on the surface of the earth, Islam or Christianity would not cease to exist nor lose their reality in the ultimate sense.

The radical difference between the traditionalists and most other schools of thought concerned with the study of religions comes precisely from this vast difference in the views they hold concerning the nature of reality. The traditionalists refuse to accept as valid that truncated vision of reality currently held in the Western world and arising originally from the post-medieval rationalism and empiricism that became prevalent in Europe and came to constitute the background for most of religious studies, especially in academic circles. It must be remembered, however, that the perspective held by the traditionalists is the same as the world view within which the religions themselves were born and cultivated over the millennia until the advent of the modern world. That is why the traditional studies of religion are able to penetrate into the heart of the subject in such a fashion and also why these studies, in contrast to those of most modern scholars of religion, are so deeply appreciated by the traditional authorities of different religions outside the modern Western world and its cultural extensions into other parts of the globe.

The school of the *philosophia perennis* speaks of tradition and traditions. It believes that there is a Primordial Tradition which constituted original or archetypal man's primal spiritual and intellectual heritage received through direct revelation when Heaven and earth were still "united." This Primordial Tradition is reflected in all later traditions, but the later traditions are not simply its historical and horizontal continuation. Each tradition is marked by a fresh vertical descent from the Origin, a revelation which bestows upon each religion lying at the center of the tradition in question its spiritual genius, fresh vitality, uniqueness, and the "grace" that makes its rites and practices operative, not to speak of the paradisal vision which constitutes the origin of its sacred art, or of the sapience which lies at the heart of its message. But because the Origin is One and also because of the profound unity of the human recipient, despite important existing racial, ethnic, and cultural differences, the fact that there is both the Primordial Tradition and traditions does not destroy the perennity and universality of the *philosophia perennis.* The anonymous tradition reflects a remarkable unanimity of views concerning the meaning of human life and the fundamental dimensions of human thought in worlds as far apart as those of the Eskimos and the Australian Aborigines, the Taoists and the Muslims.

The conception of religion in the school of the *philosophia perennis* is vast enough to embrace the primal and the historical, the Semitic and the Indian, the mythic and the "abstract" types of religions. Tradition, as understood by such masters of this school as Schuon, embraces within its fold all the different modes and types of Divine Manifestation. The doctrine of tradition thus conceived makes it possible to develop a veritable theology of comparative religion—which in reality should be called a metaphysics of comparative religion—able to do theological justice to the tenets of each religion while enabling the student of religion, who is at once interested objectively in the existence of religions other than his own and is at the same time of a religious nature himself, to cross frontiers as difficult to traverse as that which separates the world of Abraham from that of Krishna and Rama, or the universe of the American Indians from that of traditional Christianity.

In the same way that the rejection of the reality of hierarchy in its metaphysical sense by so many modern scholars has affected their world view and methodology in every field and domain, the acceptance of this reality constitutes an essential feature of the traditionalist school in its study of religion in its different aspects. Religion itself is hierarchically constituted and is not exhausted by its external and formal reality. Just as the phenomenal world necessitates the noumenal—the very word *phenomenon* implying a reality of which the phenomenon is the phenomenon—the formal aspect of religion necessitates the essential and the supraformal. Religion possesses at once an external, outward, or exoteric dimension concerned with the external and formal aspect of human life, but, because it is religion, it is in itself sufficient to enable man who follows its tenets and has faith in its truths to lead a fully human life and to gain salvation. Religion also possesses an inner or esoteric dimension concerned with the formless and essential with means to enable man to reach the Supernal Essence here and now. Moreover, within the context of this most general division, there are further levels within both the exoteric and the esoteric, so that altogether there exists within every integral religion a hierarchy of levels from the most outward to the most inward, which is the Supreme Center.

There is also in religion a hierarchy of approaches to the Ultimate Reality which can again be summarized in a schematic fashion as the ways of work, love, and knowledge, the famous *karma mārga*, *bhakti mārga*, and *jñāna mārga* of Hinduism or *al-makhāfah*, *al-maḥabbah*, and *al-maʿrifah* of Islam. Likewise, there is a hierarchy among followers of religion or human types seen from the religious perspective corresponding to these modes of approach to the Ultimate Reality. It is to these types that the sapiential tradition of the ancient Greeks referred as the *hylikoi*, *psychoi*, and *pneumatikoi*. Islam also distinguishes between the *muslim*, the *muʾmin*, and the possessor of spiritual virtue or *iḥsān*, who is referred to in the Quran as *muḥsin*, although this latter term is not as common in later religious literature as the first two.

The hierarchy of ways to God or of human types in their religious quest is innate to the paths or ways in question, the higher comprehending the lower in the sense of both understanding and encompassing it, but the lower not able to comprehend what stands beyond and above it. Hence the inner tension between various religious schools and paths even in traditional settings. These traditional oppositions, however, are very different in nature from the modern attack against the whole hierarchic perspective of the traditionalist school on the charges that it is "elitist" or something of the sort. If by this charge is meant that the traditional school accepts the saying of Christ that "Many are called but few are chosen," then yes, it is elitist. This school asserts that not everyone is able to know everything, but it also affirms strongly that all levels of religion are precious and from Heaven, that all human beings can be saved if only they follow religion according to their own nature and vocation. It also asserts that with respect to the possibility of being able to call upon God and ultimately to reach the Divine, all human beings are equal by virtue of being human, without this equality destroying the hierarchy mentioned or obliterating the obvious distinctions between human types, their aptitudes and capabilities. Being based on the primacy of knowledge, the *philosophia perennis* is elitist in the sense that it distinguishes between those who know and those who do not, according to the famous Quranic verse, "Are they equal, those who know and those who know not?" (39:9), which the Quran answers with a strong nay. What is difficult to understand is why this charge of elitism is even made by certain scholars, unless it be to keep up with current fads, but in that case one wonders why modern physics is not called elitist, since some people are able to understand it and others are not able to master its tenets.

The *philosophia perennis* sees a unity which underlies the diversity of religious forms and practices, a unity which resides within that quintessential truth at the heart of religions that is none other than the *philosophia perennis* itself. But this unity is not to be found at the level of external forms. All religions do not simply say the same thing, despite the remarkable unanimity of principles and doctrines and the profound similarity of applications of these principles. The traditionalist school is opposed to the sentimental ecumenism which sees all religions as being the same at the expense of reducing them to a common denominator or of putting aside some of their basic teachings. On the contrary, the traditionalists respect the minutiae of each sacred tradition as coming ultimately from Heaven and to be treated with reverence, as every manifestation of the sacred should be. They are fully aware of the particular spiritual genius of each religion and its uniqueness and insist that these features are precise proof of the transcendent origin of each religion and the reality of its archetype in the Divine Intellect. These characteristics also demonstrate the falsehood of the view which would reduce a religion to simply historical borrowing from an earlier religion.

The unity to which the traditionalists refer is, properly speaking, a transcendental unity above and beyond forms and external manifestations. The followers of this school would accept the current criticism of academic scholars against that leveling "unity of religions" movement that emanated mostly out of India during the last decades of the nineteenth and early decades of the twentieth century. Wherein they differ from most academic scholars of religion is that the traditionalists breathe within the traditional universe in which the reality of a thing—most of all religious forms, rites, and symbols—is not exhausted by its spatiotemporal aspect. Each form possesses an essence, each phenomenon is related to a noumenon, each accident issues from a substance. Using the language of traditional Western philosophy, hallowed by its employment by the representatives of the *philosophia perennis* in the Latin Middle Ages, the traditionalists distinguish between the external form and the essence which that form manifests, or form and substance, so the external forms of a religion are seen as "accidents" which issue forth from and return to a substance that remains independent of all its accidents. It is only on the level of the Supreme Essence even beyond the Logos, or on the level of the Supreme Substance, standing above all the cosmic sectors from the angelic to the physical within which a particular religion is operative, that the ultimate unity of religions is to be sought. If as the Sufis say "The doctrine of Unity is unique" (*al-tawḥīd wāḥid*), one can also say that the transcendent unity underlying the diversity of religions cannot be but the Unique or the One Itself. Below that level, each religion possesses distinct qualities and characteristics not to be either neglected or explained away.

Within the particular genius and structure of each religion, however, one can discern certain features which are again universal. There is at the heart of every religion what Schuon calls the *religio perennis*, consisting ultimately of a doctrine concerning the nature of reality and a method for being able to attain what is Real. The doctrinal language varies from one religion to another and can embrace concepts as different as those of *śūnyatā* and Yahweh. The method can also vary in numerous ways ranging from Vedic sacrifices to Muslim daily prayers. But the essence and goal of the doctrine and method remain universal within every religion.

The traditionalist school does not, moreover, simply place all religions alongside each other in the manner of a certain type of phenomenological approach which would collect religious phenomena without any normative judgment, as if one were collecting mollusks. Basing itself on the knowledge provided by the *philosophia perennis*, the traditional school judges between grades of Divine manifestation, various degrees and levels of prophecy, major and minor dispensations from Heaven, and lesser and greater paths, even within a single religion. It possesses a normative dimension and studies religions in the light of a truth that for it is truth and not something else, but it does so without falling into subjectivism. On the contrary, this truth alone permits the individual scholar to escape from the prison of subjectivism and the passing fads of a particular period within which the scholar in question happens to live, for this truth is supra-individual in nature, being a *sophia* that is at once perennial and universal.

It is in the light of this truth embodied in the *philosophia perennis* that the traditionalist school can also speak about truth and falsehood in this or that religious school as well as greater and lesser truth. The presence of this truth is also the reason why this school is able to be judgmental about a particular religious phenomenon and speak about authentic and pseudo-religion without falling into a narrow dogmatism on the one hand or simply indifference to truth on the other, two alternatives which dominate much of the religious scene in the modern world. . . .

The traditional school studies the ethics, theology, mysticism, or art of each religion in the light of the absoluteness of its Divine Origin, without either negating the other manifestations of the Absolute or the possibilities of change and transformation which all things that exist in time must of necessity undergo. This school does not, however, identify the reality of religion only with its historical unfolding. Each religion possesses certain principial possibilities contained in its celestial archetype. These possibilities are realized or become unfolded in the historical period and within the humanity providentially determined to be the temporal and human containers of the religion in question. Each religious phenomenon is both a phenomenon of religious character in itself, not to be reduced to any other category, and a phenomenon which reveals its full meaning only in the light of the archetypal reality of the tradition in question along with its historical unfolding. Not all religions, therefore, have at their disposal all of their possibilities in a state of actuality at a given moment of human history. Religions decay and even die in the sense that their earthly careers terminate. They can also become revived as long as the nexus between their earthly manifestation and their celestial origin remains intact. For the traditionalist school it is not a question of which religion is "better," since all authentic religions come from the same Origin, but there does exist the question from the operative and practical point of view of what possibilities are available at a particular juncture of history, of what one can in practice follow, and of what is no longer in fact available at a given historic moment within a particular religion.

3. Religion and the Environmental Crisis

For the title of my lecture, "The Spiritual and Religious Dimensions of the Environmental Crisis," I have chosen both the words *spiritual* and *religious.* That was done on purpose, because the present usage of the word *religion* in many quarters often leaves out precisely the spiritual element. Those people who are looking for the inner dimension of religious experience and of religious truth are seeking for another word to supplement the word *religion.* It is tragic that this is so, but it is nevertheless a fact. The word *spirituality* in its current sense, and not the Latin term from which it derives, is a modern term. As far as my own research has shown, the term *spirituality* as it is used today began to be employed by French Catholic theologians in the mid-nineteenth century and then crept into English. We do not find the use of this term as we now understand it earlier than the nineteenth century. Today it denotes for many people precisely those elements of religion which have been forgotten in the West and which therefore have come to be identified wrongly with spirituality as distinct from religion. From my point of view, which is always of course a traditional one, there is no spirituality without religion. There is no way of reaching the spirit without choosing a path which God has chosen for us, and that means religion (*religio*). Therefore, the reason I am using both words is not for the sake of expediency, but to emphasize that I mean to include a reality which encompasses both spirituality and religion, in the current understanding of these terms, although traditionally the term *religion* would suffice, since in its full sense it includes all that is understood by spirituality today.

It is important we remember that all of us on the globe share in destroying our natural environment, although the reasons for this are different in different parts of the globe. In the modern world the environment is destroyed by following the dominating philosophy, while in what remains of the traditional world it is done in spite of the prevailing world view and most often as a result of external coercion as well as temptation, whether it be direct or indirect. I have repeated this truth in many places and have caused some people to become angry, but the fact is that the only action in which nearly everybody participates at the present moment of human history, from communist and socialist to capitalist, from Hindu and Muslim to atheist, from Christian to Shinto, is in living and acting in such a way as to cause the destruction of the natural environment. This fact must seep fully into our consciousness while at the same time we remember the differences in motive and perspective among religious and secularized sectors of humanity. Obviously, for those for whom religion is still a reality, it is much easier to appeal to religion and the religious view of nature to discover the means through which a solution would be found for the crisis from which we all suffer.

* * *

We often forget that the vast majority of people in the world still live by religion. And yet most Western intellectuals think about environmental issues as if everyone were an agnostic following a secular philosophy cultivated at Oxford, Cambridge, or Harvard, and so they seek to develop a rationalist, environmental ethics based on agnosticism, as if this would have any major effect whatsoever upon the environmental crisis. It is important to consider in a real way the world in which we live. If we do so then we must realize why in fact religion is so significant both in the understanding and in the solution of the environmental crisis. Let us not forget, I repeat, that the vast majority of people in the world live according to religion. The statistic that is often given, saying that only half of humanity does so, is totally false because it is claimed that in addition to the West one billion two hundred million Chinese are atheists or non-religious. This is not at all the case. Confucianism is not a philosophy, but a religion based upon ritual—I shall come back to that in a few moments. There are at most a few hundred million agnostics and atheists spread mostly in the Western world, with extensions into a few big cities in Asia and Africa. But this group forms a small minority of the people of the world. Those who live on the other continents, as well as many people in Europe and America, still live essentially in a religious world. Although in the West the religious view of nature has been lost, even here it is still religion to which most ordinary people listen, while the number is much greater in other parts of the globe. That is why any secularist ideology that tries to replace religion always tries also to play the role of religion itself. This has happened with the ideology of modern science in the West, which for many people is now accepted as a "religion." That is why the people who try to sell you many kinds of goods on television do so as "scientists"—as agents of "authority"—and always wear a white robe, not a black robe of traditional priests. They are trying to look like members of the new "priesthood." They function as the priesthood of a pseudo-religion. Their whole enterprise is made to appear not as simply ordinary science but as something that replaces religion. For people who accept this thesis it would be feasible to accept a rationalistic ethics related to science, but the vast majority of people in the world still heed authentic religion. Consequently, for them, no ethics would have efficacy unless it was religious ethics.

In the West, for four hundred years, philosophers influenced by scientism have been trying to develop secular ethics and, sure enough, there are many atheists who are very ethical in their life. But by what norm are they to be considered as ethical? By no other than the very norms which religion instilled in the minds of people in the West. If somebody murders his neighbor we think it is unethical. But why is it unethical? What is wrong with that? The television programs you watch on nature in Africa show that animals are eating each other all the time. If we are just animals, then what is wrong if we kill one another? The fact that everybody says "no" to such an act is precisely because there are certain religious values instilled even into the secular atmosphere of the modern West which speaks of so-called secular ethics. The values of this ethics really have their roots in religion. In any case no secular ethics could speak with authority except to those who would accept the philosophical premises of such ethics.

The fact remains that the vast majority of people in the world do not accept any ethics which does not have a religious foundation. This means in practical terms that if a religious figure, let us say, a mulla or a brahmin in India or Pakistan, goes to a village and tells the villagers that from the point of view of the *Sharīʿah* (Islamic law) or the Law of Manu (Hindu law) they are forbidden to cut this tree, many people would accept. But if some graduate from the University of Delhi or Karachi, who is a government official, comes and says, for rational reasons, philosophical and scientific reasons, that it is better not to cut this tree, few would heed his advice. So from a practical point of view the only ethics which can be acceptable to the vast majority, at the present moment in the history of the world, is still a religious ethics. The very strong prejudice against religious ethics in certain circles in the West which have now become concerned with the environmental crisis is itself one of the greatest impediments to the solution of the environmental crisis itself.

* * *

There is a second reason why religion is so important in the solution of the environmental crisis. There are many elements involved here but I will summarize. We all know and, even if we are not personally concerned with the metaphysical, spiritual, and cosmological roots of the environmental crisis, we are nonetheless aware of the fact, that outwardly (I do not say inwardly) this crisis is driven by the modern economic system appealing to human passions, especially the passion of greed intensified by the creation of false needs, which are not really needs but wants. This is in opposition to the view which religions have espoused over the millennia, that is, the practice of the virtue of contentment, of being content with what one has. The modern outlook is based on fanning the fire of greed and covetousness, on trying to do everything possible to attach the soul more and more to the world and on making a vice out of what for religion has always been a virtue, that is, to keep a certain distance and detachment from the world; in other words, a certain amount of asceticism. There is a famous German proverb, "There is no culture without asceticism"; and this is true of every civilization.

We are living in the first period in human history in the West in which, except for a few small islands here and there of Orthodox or Catholic or Anglican monasticism and a few people who try to practice austerity, asceticism is considered to be a vice, not a virtue. It is not taught in our schools as a virtue; it is taught as a vice, preventing us from realizing ourselves, as if our "selves" were simply the extension of our physicality. This idea of self-realization is, of course, central to Oriental and certain Occidental traditions. But it has become debased in the worst way possible and transformed into the basis for modern consumerism, which can be seen in its most virulent form in America—now fast conquering Europe, and doing a good job of reaching India, China, Indonesia, etc. (within the next decade we will have several billion new consumers in such countries thirsting for artificial things which they have lived without for the last few thousand years). And what this will do to the earth God alone knows. It is beyond belief and conjecture what will happen if present trends continue. So what is it that can rein in the passions, either gradually or suddenly? Nothing but religion for the vast majority of people who, believing in God and the afterlife, still fear the consequences of their evil actions in their lives in this world. If it were to be told to them that pollution and destruction of the environment is a sin in the theological sense of the term they would think twice before indulging in it. For the ordinary believer the wrath of God and fear of punishment in the afterlife is the most powerful force against the negative tendencies of the passionate soul. For nearly all people on the earth who continue to pollute the air and the water, and whose lifestyle entails the destruction of the natural environment, what is it that is going to act as a break against the ever-growing power of the passions except religion? The religions have had thousands of years to deal with the slaying of the passionate ego, this inner dragon, to use the symbol mentioned in so many traditions. St. Michael's slaying of the dragon with his lance has many meanings, one of which is, of course, that the lance of the Spirit alone is able to kill that dragon; or what in Sufism is called *nafs*, that is the passionate soul, the lower soul within us. We rarely think of that issue today. But where is St. Michael with his lance? How are we going to stop people from wanting more and more if not through the power of the Spirit made accessible through religion? And once you have opened up the Pandora's box of the appetites, how are you going to put the genie back into the box? How are you going to be able, with no more than rational arguments, to tell people to use less, to be less covetous, not to be greedy, and so forth? No force in the world today, except religion, has the power to do that unless it be sheer physical coercion.

For the vast majority of people there is no other way to control the great passions within us which have now been fanned by, first of all, the weakening of religion and, secondly, the substitution of another set of values derived from a kind of pseudo-religion whose new gods are such idols as "development" and "progress." But such notions do not have the power to help us control our passions. On the contrary they only fan the fire of those passions. We have been witness during the last generation alone to the ever greater debunking of the traditional religious attitudes towards the world, especially what we call in Arabic *riḍā*, that is contentment with our state of being, a virtue which is the very opposite of the sin of covetousness. Of course, the Muslims have been criticized by the West for a long time for simply being fatalistic in the face of events, of being too content with their lot. This same debunking has also been directed towards similar Christian values. But that is because of a deep misunderstanding. Where, in the current educational system in the West, is attention being paid to these traditional virtues? Even from a purely empirical, scientific point of view, these virtues must be seen as being of great value, seeing that they have made it possible for human beings to live for thousands of years in the world without destroying the natural environment as we are currently doing. These traditional virtues that allowed countless generations to live in equilibrium with the world around them were at the same time conceived as ways of perfecting the soul, as steps in the perfection of human existence. These virtues provided the means for living at peace with the environment. They also allowed man to experience what it means to be human and to fulfill his destiny here on earth, which is always bound to try to inculcate such virtues within oneself.

* * *

Another cardinal and central role of religion in the solution of the environmental crisis, one that goes to its very root, is much more difficult to understand within the context of the modern mind-set. This role is related to the significance of religious rituals as a means of establishing cosmic harmony. Now, this idea is meaningless in the context of modern thought, where ritual seems to have no relation or correspondence with the nature of physical reality. In the modern world view, rituals are at best personal, individual, subjective elements that create happiness in the individual or establish a relationship between him or her and God. That much at least some modern people accept. But how could rites establish cosmic harmony? From the modern scientific point of view such an assertion seems to make no sense at all. But it is not nonsense; it is a very subtle truth that has to be brought out and emphasized. From both the spiritual and the religious perspective, the physical world is related to God by levels of reality which transcend the physical world itself and which constitute the various stages of the cosmic hierarchy. It is impossible to have harmony in nature, or harmony of man with nature, without this vertical harmony with the higher states of being. Once nature is conceived as being purely material, even if we accept that it was created by God conceived as a clockmaker, this cosmic relationship can no longer even be conceived much less realized. Once we cut nature off from the immediate principles of nature—which are the psychic and spiritual or angelic levels of reality—then nature has already lost its balance as far as our relation to it is concerned.

Now rituals, from the point of view of religion, are God-made. I am not using the term ritual as seen from the secular point of view, as if one were putting on one's gown and going to some commencement exercise or some other humanly created action, often called a "ritual" in everyday discourse today. I am using it in the religious sense. According to all traditional religions, rituals descend from Heaven. A ritual is an enactment, or rather re-enactment, here on earth of a divine prototype. In the Abrahamic world, that means that rituals have been revealed to the prophets by God and taught by them to man. The "repetition" of the Last Supper of Christ in the Eucharist, or the daily prayers of Muslims—where do they come from? According to the followers of those religions, they all come from Heaven. In Hinduism and Buddhism one observes the same reality. The differences are of context and world view, but the fundamentals are the same. There is no Hindu rite which was invented by someone walking along the Ganges who suddenly thought it up. For the Hindus they are of divine origin. The Muslim daily prayers, which we have all seen in pictures, were given by the Prophet to Muslims on the basis of instructions received from God.

Even the Prophet did not invent them. The Eucharist "re-enacts" the Last Supper which, as the central rite of Christianity, was first celebrated by Christ himself.

Now, these rites, by virtue of their re-enactment on earth, link the earth with the higher levels of reality. A rite always links us with the vertical axis of existence, and by virtue of that, links us also with the principles of nature. This truth holds not only for the primal religions, where certain acts are carried out in nature itself—let us say the African religions or the Aboriginal religion of Australia, or the religions of the Native American Indians—but also in the Abrahamic world, in the Hindu world, and in the Iranian religions. Whether one is using particular natural forms such as a tree or a rock or a cave or something like that, or man-made objects of sacred and liturgical art related to rites carried out inside a church, synagogue, mosque, or Hindu temple, it does not make any difference. The same truth is to be found in all these cases. From a metaphysical point of view a ritual always re-establishes balance with the cosmic order.

In the deepest mystical sense, nature is hungry for our prayers, in the sense that we are like a window of the house of nature through which the light and air of the spiritual world penetrate into the natural world. Once that window becomes opaque, the house of nature becomes dark. That is exactly what we are experiencing today. Once we have shut our hearts to God, darkness spreads over the whole of the world. This, of course, is something very difficult to explain to an agnostic mentality. But from a practical, expedient point of view at least, it should be taken into consideration even by those who do not take rites seriously, seeing what has happened to nature at the hands of those sectors of humanity who no longer perform traditional rites.

All religious people who believe in the efficacy of rites and perform them have a way of looking at the natural world and their place in it which is very different from the secularist way that has itself led us to the environmental crisis. You have all read or heard about examples of various religious rituals and their relation to nature, even in lesser known religions. Perhaps the best known, as far as displaying the direct relation between rituals and the natural world is concerned, is the rain-dance of the Native Americans, about which skeptics make jokes. But some people take it very seriously and go to Native American medicine men, the shamans, to try to get help from them to bring rain. Of course, such a thing is laughed at by official science, but that does not matter, for such a science neglects the *sympathaeia* which exists between man and cosmic realities.

We have similar rituals all over the Islamic world, the Hindu world, the Buddhist world, and in the traditional Christian world. But in the modern Western world this has now become more or less eclipsed, although it has not disappeared completely. In Greece, once you go out of big cities, you still see it, and in Italy, in the villages, when there is news of an earthquake, people recite the beginning of the Gospel of John in Latin, which many still know by heart. The faithful recite it in a ritual sense to help recreate balance and harmony with the natural world by calling upon Divine Mercy. I can hardly overemphasize the significance of this aspect of religion, because it is impossible for a human collectivity to live in harmony with nature without this ritualized relationship with the natural world and harmony with God and the higher levels of cosmic hierarchy. If we do not have this relationship, nature is reduced to an "it," to a pure fact, to a material lump, not in itself, of course, but for us, and we must bear all the consequences which such a view entails.

* * *

Along with providing a sound basis for ethics, perhaps the most important role of religion in the understanding of the roots of the environmental crisis (and here I would include especially the spiritual element of religion, because it is the spiritual, metaphysical, and esoteric dimension of religion which emphasizes this element), is that religion possesses an extensive doctrine about the nature of the world in which we live. That is, religion, when it was integral and not truncated as it has become today in the West, provided not only a doctrine about God, not only a doctrine about the human state, but also a doctrine about the world of nature. And here, by doctrine, I mean knowledge (*docta*), not only opinion, but authentic knowledge which is not in any way negated by the scientific knowledge of the world. Every religion provides not only teachings pertaining to the emotional and sentimental realm, not only principles for ethical action, but also knowledge, knowledge in the deepest sense of the term, of God, of the human state, and also of nature. There is no major religion whose integral tradition does not provide such a knowledge. Some religions emphasize one element, some religions another. Certain religions, such as Confucianism, do not speak about cosmogony and eschatology, but they have a vast cosmology. Of other religions, the reverse is true. But these three types of knowledge, that is, knowledge of God or the Ultimate Principle, of the human state, and of nature, have to exist in all integral religions.

Now, one does not need to look very far to see what has happened in the modern world. Gradually, from the seventeenth century onwards, first in the West, then spreading in recent decades to other parts of the world, the legitimacy of the religious knowledge of nature has been rejected. Most people who study the views of an Erigena or a St. Thomas Aquinas on nature do so as historians. But their views are not accepted by the mainstream of modern Western society as legitimate knowledge of the world. What has been lost is a way of studying nature religiously, not simply as "poetry," as this term is used today in a trivializing sense and not of course in a positive one. True poetry possesses a great message as far as nature is concerned, a message which itself is usually religious. In any case modern society has disassociated knowledge of nature from religion as well as sapiential poetry itself, and relegates the religious attitude and knowledge of nature to sentiment or "simply" to poetic sensibility.

We have wonderful examples of nature poetry in the great poetry produced in the nineteenth century in England. The Romantic poets produced beautiful poetry about nature. But what effect did it have on the physics departments of the universities? Absolutely none, precisely because the science that developed in the seventeenth century, through very complicated processes which I cannot go into now, began to exclude from its world view the possibility of a religious or metaphysical form of knowledge of nature. This science even excluded the poetic view of nature in so far as it claimed any intellectual legitimacy and sought to be more than what some would call "mere poetry." Modern science has clung to that monopoly very hard, even in this pluralistic age of ours, in which everything other than science is relativized. Post-modernists usually deconstruct everything except modern science because, if this were to be done, the whole world view of modernism along with post-modernism would collapse. So you have a kind of scientific exclusivity and monopoly which has been created and accepted by most although not all people in the modern world. Goethe, the supreme German poet as well as a scientist, rebelled very strongly against this monopolistic claim of modern science. There were also certain scientists, such as Oswald, who was a reputable chemist, who rejected scientific mechanism; and one can name others. But these are exceptions to the rule. The rule became that there is no other knowledge of nature except what is called scientific knowledge. And if someone claims that there is a religious knowledge of nature, then it is usually claimed that it is based on sentiment, on emotions, or, in other words, on subjective factors. If, for example, you see a dove flying and you think of the Holy Spirit, that is simply a subjective correlation between your perception of the dove and your own sentiments. There is no objectivity accorded to the reality of nature as perceived through religious knowledge. That is why even symbolism has become subjectivized—it is claimed to be "merely" psychological, à la Jung. The symbols which traditional man saw in the world of nature as being objective and as being part of the ontological reality of nature have been all cast aside by this type of mentality which no longer takes the religious knowledge of nature seriously.

During the last thirty years, when the thirst for a more holistic approach to nature made itself felt, something even worse occurred because neither mainstream religion nor modern science showed any interest whatsoever in the religious and symbolic knowledge of nature and the holistic approach to it. The water sought for in this thirst seeped under the structures of Western culture and came out in the form of New Age movements, nearly all of which are very much interested in the science of the cosmos. But what they claim as science is really a New Age pseudo-science of the cosmos. It is not an authentic traditional science, because a traditional science of the cosmos always has to be related to a traditional religious structure. In this New Age climate the word "cosmic" has gained a great deal of currency precisely because of the dearth of an authentic religious knowledge of the cosmos in the present-day world. Somehow the thirst had to be satisfied. So we have had both excavation of the earlier Western esoteric teachings about nature—usually presented in distorted fashion—or borrowings from Oriental religions and their teachings about nature, often distorted. Even the famous and influential book of Fritjof Capra, *The Tao of Physics*, does not really speak of Hindu cosmology or Chinese physics, but only mentions certain comparisons between modern physics and Hindu and Taoist metaphysical ideas.

To be sure there are many profound correlations and concordances to be found between certain aspects of biology, astronomy, and quantum mechanics on the one hand and Oriental doctrines of nature, of the cosmos, on the other. I would be the last person to doubt that truth. But what has occurred for the most part is not the kind of profound comparison we have in mind, but its parody, a kind of popularized version of a religious knowledge of nature, usually involving some kind of occultism or even some kind of an existing cult. The great interest shown today in Shamanism in America, in the whole phenomenon of the Native American tradition (which is one of the great and beautiful primal traditions that still survives to some extent), with weekend Shamanic sessions, is precisely because such teachings appeal to a kind of mentality that seeks some sort of knowledge of nature of a spiritual and holistic character other than what modern science provides. This phenomenon is one of the paradoxes of our day and has not helped the environmental crisis in any appreciable way. Indeed, it has created a certain confusion in the domain of religion and created a breach between the mainstream religious organizations which still survive in the West—whether they be Catholic, Protestant, or Orthodox—and these pseudo-movements and the New Age phenomenon, which they rightly oppose. The fact that these pseudo-religious movements are very pro-environment, yet in an ineffectual manner, has caused many people in the mainstream to take a stand against the very positions which they should be defending. So we have the paradoxical situation in America today where the most conservative Christian groups are those which are least interested in the environment. This phenomenon was not originally caused by the rise of the New Age religions but is certainly related to it and strengthened by it.

Islam

4. One God

At the heart of Islam stands the reality of God, the One, the Absolute and the Infinite, the Infinitely Good and All-Merciful, the One Who is at once transcendent and immanent, greater than all we can conceive or imagine, yet, as the Quran, the sacred scripture of Islam, attests, closer to us than our jugular vein. The One God, known by His Arabic Name, Allah, is the central reality of Islam in all of its facets, and attestation to this oneness, which is called *tawḥīd*, is the axis around which all that is Islamic revolves. Allah is beyond all duality and relationality, beyond the differences of gender and of all qualities that distinguish beings from each other in this world. Yet He is the source of all existence and all cosmic and human qualities as well as the End to Whom all things return.

To testify to this oneness lies at the heart of the credo of Islam, and the formula that expresses the truth of this oneness, *Lā ilāha illa'Llāh*, "There is no god but God," is the first of two testifications (*shahādah*) by which a person bears witness to being a Muslim; the second is *Muḥammadun rasūl Allāh*, "Muhammad is the messenger of God." The oneness of God is for Muslims not only the heart of their religion, but that of every authentic religion. It is a reassertion of the revelation of God to the Hebrew prophets and to Christ, whom Muslims also consider to be their prophets, the revelation of the truth that "The Lord is one," the reconfirmation of that timeless truth that is also stated in the Catholic creed, *Credo in unum Deum*, "I believe in one God." As the Quran states, "We have never sent a messenger before thee except that We revealed to him, saying, 'There is no god but I, so worship Me'" (21:25). Like countless Muslims, when I read the names of the prophets of old in the Quran or in the traditional prayers, I experience them as living realities in the Islamic universe, while being fully conscious of the fact that they are revered figures in Judaism and Christianity. I also remain fully aware that they are all speaking of the same God Who is One and not of some other deity.

The One God, or Allah, is neither male nor female. However, in the inner teachings of Islam His Essence is often referred to in feminine form and the Divinity is often mentioned as the Beloved, while the Face He has turned to the world as Creator and Sustainer is addressed in the masculine form. Both the male and the female are created by Him and the root of both femininity and masculinity are to be found in the Divine Nature, which transcends the duality between them. Furthermore, the Qualities of

God, which are reflected throughout creation, are of a feminine as well as a masculine nature, and the traditional Islamic understanding of the Divinity is not at all confined, as some think, to a purely patriarchal image.

The Quran, which is the verbatim Word of God for Muslims, to be compared to Christ himself in Christianity, reveals not only the Supreme Name of God as Allah, but also mentions other "beautiful Names" of God, considered by traditional sources to be ninety-nine in number, Names revealing different aspects of the Divinity. The Quran states, "To God belong the most beautiful Names (*al-asmāʾ al-ḥusnā*). Call on Him thereby" (7:180). These Names are divided into those of Perfection (*kamāl*), Majesty (*jalāl*), and Beauty (*jamāl*), the first relating to the essential oneness of God Himself beyond all polarization and the last two to the masculine and feminine dimensions of reality *in divinis* (in the Divine Order). The Names of Majesty include the Just, the Majestic, the Reckoner, the Giver of Death, the Victorious, and the All-Powerful, and those of Beauty, the All-Merciful, the Forgiver, the Gentle, the Generous, the Beautiful, and Love. For Muslims the whole universe consists of the reflection in various combinations of the Divine Names, and human life is lived amid the polarizations and tensions as well as harmony of the cosmic and human qualities derived from these Names. God at once judges us according to His Justice and forgives us according to His Mercy. He is far beyond our reach, yet resides at the center of the heart of the faithful. He punishes the wicked, but also loves His creatures and forgives them.

The doctrine of God the One, as stated in the Quran, does not only emphasize utter transcendence, although there are powerful expressions of this truth such as *Allāhu akbar*, usually translated as "God is great," but meaning that God is greater than anything we can conceive of Him, which is also attested by the apophatic theology of both the Catholic and Orthodox churches as well as by traditional Judaism. The Quran also accentuates God's nearness to us, stating that He is closer to us than ourselves and that He is present everywhere, as when it states: "Whithersoever ye turn, there is the Face of God" (2:115). The traditional religious life of a Muslim is based on a rhythmic movement between the poles of transcendence and immanence, of rigor and compassion, of justice and forgiveness, of the fear of punishment and hope for mercy based on God's love for us. But the galaxy of Divine Names and the multiplicity of Divine Qualities reflected in the cosmos and within the being of men and women do not distract the Muslim for one moment from the oneness of God, from that Sun before whose light all multiplicity perishes. Striving after the realization of that oneness, or *tawḥīd*, is the heart of Islamic life; and the measure of a successful religious life is the degree to which one is able to realize *tawḥīd*, which means not only oneness, but also the integration of multiplicity into Unity.

Moreover, since there is no official sacerdotal authority in Islam like the magisterium in Roman Catholic Christianity, the authenticity of one's faith in Islam has by and large been determined by the testification of *tawḥīd*, while the degree of inward realization of this truth has remained a matter to be decided by God and not by external authorities. This has been the general norm in Islamic history, but there have also been exceptions, and there are historical instances when a particular group or political authority has taken it upon itself to determine the authenticity or lack thereof of the belief in *tawḥīd* of a particular person or school. But there has never been an Inquisition in Islam, and there has been greater latitude in the acceptance of ideas, especially mystical and esoteric ones, than in most periods of the history of Western Christianity before the penetration of modernism into Christian theology itself.

Now, although Islam is based on the reality of God, the One, in His Absoluteness and Suchness, it also addresses humanity in its essential reality, in its suchness. Man, in the traditional sense of the term corresponding to *insān* in Arabic or *homo* in Greek and not solely the male, is seen in Islam not as a sinful being to whom the message of Heaven is sent to heal the wound of the original sin, but as a being who still carries his primordial nature (*al-fiṭrah*) within himself, although he has forgotten that nature now buried deep under layers of negligence. As the Quran states: "[God] created man in the best of stature (*aḥsan al-taqwīm*)" (95:4) with an intelligence capable of knowing the One. The message of Islam is addressed to that primordial nature. It is a call for recollection, for the remembrance of a knowledge kneaded into the very substance of our being even before our coming into this world. In a famous verse that defines the relationship between human beings and God, the Quran, in referring to the pre-cosmic existence of man, states, "'Am I not your Lord?' They said: 'Yes, we bear witness'" (7:172). The "they" refers to all the children of Adam, male and female, and the "yes" confirms the affirmation of God's Oneness by us in our pre-eternal ontological reality.

Men and women still bear the echo of this "yes" deep down within their souls, and the call of Islam is precisely to this primordial nature, which uttered the "yes" even before the creation of the heavens and the earth. The call of Islam therefore concerns, above all, the remembrance of a knowledge deeply embedded in our being, the confirmation of a knowledge that saves, hence the soteriological function of knowledge in Islam.

Islam addresses the human being not primarily as will, but as intelligence. If the great sin in Christianity is disobedience, which has warped the will, the great sin in Islam is forgetfulness and the resulting inability of the intelligence to function in the way that God created it, as the means to know the One. That is why the greatest sin in Islam and the only one God does not forgive is *shirk*, or taking a partner unto God, which means denying the Oneness of God, or *tawḥīd*.

This direct address from God, the One, to each human being in his or her primordial state requires total surrender to the Majesty of the Absolute, before whom ultimately nothing can in fact exist. In an ordinary sense it means the surrender of ourselves to God, and in the highest sense it means the awareness of our nothingness before Him, for, as the Quran says, "All that dwells [in the heavens and the earth] perishes, yet there abideth the Face of thy Lord, Majestic, Splendid" (55:26-27). The very name of the religion, Islam, comes from this reality, for the Arabic word *al-islām* means "surrender" as well as the peace that issues from our surrender to God. In fact, Islam is the only major religion, along with Buddhism (if we consider the name of the religion to come from *Buddhi*, the Divine Intellect, and not the Buddha), whose name is not related to a person or ethnic group, but to the central idea of the religion. Moreover, Islam considers all authentic religions to be based on this surrender, so that *al-islām* means not only the religion revealed through the Quran to the Prophet Muhammad, but all authentic religions as such. That is why in the Quran the prophet Abraham is also called *muslim*, that is, one who is in the state of *al-islām*.

True surrender is not, however, only concerned with our will. It must involve our whole being. A shallow understanding of surrender can lead to either a passive attitude, in which one does not strive in life as one should according to the promulgations of the religion, or to mistaking one's own imperfect understanding of Islam for the truth and performing acts that are against God's teachings while claiming that one is acting in surrender to God. Islam states that a person must be the perfect servant (*ʿabd*) of God in the sense of following His commands. But since God has given us many faculties, including free will and intelligence, our surrender must be complete and total, not limited to only certain faculties. It must involve the whole of our being. Otherwise, hidden thoughts and emotions as well as false ideas can combine with a fallacious sense of external surrender of one's will to God to produce acts in the name of religion that can have calamitous consequences.

Such acts have appeared from time to time historically and can be seen especially in this day and age, but they are deviations rather than the norm.

The norm by which the vast majority of Muslims have lived over the ages has meant surrender to God with one's whole being, following the Divine Law and the ethical teachings of Islam to the extent possible, striving in life according to religious teachings to the extent of one's ability, and then being resigned to consequences that ensue and accepting what destiny has put before us. It is in this sense that the common Arabic saying *maktūb*, "It is written," marking the sign of resignation to a particular event or results of one's actions, must be understood. This surrender has certainly not meant either fatalism or an individualistic interpretation of Divine norms in the name of surrender. It has, on the contrary, led to an inward and outward striving combined with serenity that characterizes traditional patterns of Islamic life, in contrast to both modernistic and many of the so-called fundamentalist currents found in the Islamic world today.

* * *

Since the One God is Infinite and Absolute as well as the Infinitely Good, He could not but create. His infinitude implies that He contains within Himself all possibilities, including that of negating Himself, and this possibility had to be realized in the form of creation. Moreover, as St. Augustine also stated, it is in the nature of the good to give of itself, and the Infinitely Good could not but radiate the reality that constitutes the world and, in fact, all the worlds.

But creation or radiation implies separation, and it is this ontological separation from the Source of all goodness that constitutes evil. One might say that evil is nothing but separation from the Good and privation, although it is real on its own level, in a sense as real as our own existential level on which we find it. And yet the good belongs to the pole of being and evil to that of nonbeing.

Throughout the history of Islam there have been numerous profound metaphysical and theological discussions concerning the question of evil, as there have been in other religions, especially Christianity. But in contrast to the modern West, in which many people have turned away from God and religion because they could not understand how a God who is good could create a world in which there is evil, in the Islamic world this question of theodicy has hardly ever bothered the religious conscience of even the most intelligent people or turned them away from God. The emphasis of the Quran upon the reality of evil on the moral plane combined with the sapiential and theological explanations of this question have kept men and women confronted with this problem in the domain of faith. The strong emphasis in Islam on the Will of God has also played a role in resigning Muslims to the presence of evil in the world (which they must nevertheless combat to the extent possible), even when they cannot understand the causes involved.

In any case, God has created the world, in which there is imperfection and evil, but the world itself is considered by the Quran to be good, a view corresponding to that found in the book of Genesis. And creation has a purpose, for, as the Quran says, "O Lord, Thou didst not create this [the world] in vain" (8:190). The deepest purpose of creation is explained by a famous *ḥadīth qudsī* (a sacred saying of the Prophet not part of the Quran in which God speaks in the first person through the mouth of the Prophet): "I was a hidden treasure. I loved to be known. Therefore, I created the creation so that I would be known." The purpose of creation therefore is God's love for the knowledge of Himself realized through His central agent on earth, humanity. For a human being to know God is to fulfill the purpose of creation. Moreover, God loved to be known. Hence, the love of God and by God permeates the whole universe, and many Islamic mystics or Sufis over the ages have spoken of that love to which Dante refers at the end of the *Divine Comedy* when he speaks of "the love that moves the sun and the stars."

This sacred *ḥadīth* (*ḥadīth qudsī*) also speaks of God's being "a hidden treasure," which is a symbol of the truth that everything in the universe has its origin in the Divine Reality and is a manifestation of that Reality. Everything in the total cosmos both visible and invisible is a theophany, or manifestation, of the Divine Names and Qualities and is drawn from the "treasury" of God. The Wisdom of God thus permeates the universe, and Muslims in fact see the cosmos as God's primordial revelation. Everything in the universe, in reflecting God's Wisdom, also glorifies Him, for, as the Quran says, "There is nothing but that it hymns His praise" (17:44). In fact, the very existence of beings is nothing but their invocation of God's Names, and the universe itself is nothing but the consequence of the breathing upon the archetypal realities of all beings in the Divine Intellect, or the Breath of the Merciful (*nafas al-Raḥmān*). It is through His Name *al-Raḥmān*, which means the Infinitely Good and also Merciful, that the universe has come into being. It is significant to note that much of the Quran is devoted to the cosmos and the world of nature, which play an integral role in the traditional life of Muslims. All Islamic rites are harmonized with natural phenomena, and in general Muslims view the world of creation as God's first revelation, before the Torah, the Gospels, the Quran, and other sacred scriptures were revealed. That is why in Islam, as in medieval

Judaism and Christianity, the cosmos is seen as a book in which the "signs of God," the *vestigia Dei* of Christian authors, are to be read.

The Islamic understanding of anthropogenesis, the creation of human beings, resembles those of Judaism and Christianity in many ways, but also differs on certain significant issues. In fact, there are also important differences between Judaism and Christianity when it comes to the question of original sin. As for Adam's original creation, the Quran speaks of God creating Adam from clay and breathing His Spirit into him, "And I breathed into him My Spirit" (15:29). The Quran also says,

> And when thy Lord said unto the angels: "Verily! I am about to place a vicegerent (*khalīfah*) on earth," they said, "Wilt Thou place therein one who will bring corruption therein and will shed blood, while we, we hymn Thy praise and sanctify Thee?" He said: "Surely, I know that which ye know not."
>
> And He taught Adam all the names, then showed them to the angels, saying: "Inform Me of the names of these, if ye are truthful."
>
> They said: "Be glorified! We have no knowledge save that which Thou hast taught us" (2:30-32).

The angels were then asked by God to prostrate before Adam, and all did so except Iblīs, that is, the Devil or Satan, who refused because of pride. God placed Adam and his wife in paradise and permitted them to eat of the fruits there, except the fruit of the forbidden tree. But Satan "caused them to deflect therefrom," and the Fall ensued. But a revelation was sent to Adam. He repented and became the first prophet as well as the father of humanity.

The Quranic account contains all the main features of the sacred anthropology of Islam and its view of the nature of men and women. First of all, God chose the human being as His vicegerent (*khalīfah*) on earth, which means that He has given human beings power to dominate the earth, but on the condition that they remain obedient to God, that is, being God's servant, or *ʿabd Allāh*. There are numerous Quranic references to this truth. The two primary features of being human are servanthood and vicegerency: being passive toward Heaven in submission to God's Will, on the one hand, and being active as God's agent and doing His Will in the world, on the other. Moreover, Adam was taught all the names, which means that God has placed within human nature an intelligence that is central and the means by which he can know all things. It also means that human beings themselves are the theophany, or visible manifestation, of all of God's Names. There is in principle no limit to human intelligence in knowing the nature of things (the question of knowing the Divine Essence is a different matter) unless there is an obstacle that prevents it from functioning correctly. That is why Muslims believe that any normal and wholesome intelligence will be naturally led to the confirmation of Divine Oneness and are at a loss when rationalist skeptics from the West refuse to accept the One (most Muslims are unaware of the obstacles in the soul of such a skeptic that reduce the intelligence to analytical reason and prevent it from functioning in its fullness). Adam, the prototype of humanity, is superior to the angels by virtue of his knowledge of the names of all things as well as by being the reflection of all the Divine Names and Qualities.

As for Iblīs, his rebellion comes from pride in considering his nature, which was made of fire, superior to that of Adam, who was made of clay. He refused to prostrate himself before Adam, because fire is a more noble element than earth or clay. He could not see the effect of the Spirit that God had breathed into Adam. Satan was therefore the first to misuse analogy, to try to replace intelligence with ordinary logical reasoning. His fall was thus also connected to the domain of knowledge. The lack of total knowledge on his part created the sense of pride, which in Islam, as in Christianity, is the source of all other vices.

The Quran mentions Adam's wife, but not her name. *Ḥadīth* sources however confirm that her name was Ḥawwā', or Eve. In fact, the Islamic names for the first parents of humanity, Ādam and Ḥawwā', are the same as in Judaism and Christianity. The Quran, however, does not mention how she was created. Some traditional commentators have repeated the biblical account of her creation from Adam's rib, while other authorities have mentioned that she was created from the same clay from which God created Adam. It is important to note for the Islamic understanding of womanhood and women's roles in both religious and social life that, in contrast to the biblical story, Eve did not tempt Adam to eat the forbidden fruit. Rather, they were tempted together by Iblīs and therefore Eve was not the cause of Adam's expulsion from paradise. He was also responsible; they shared in performing the act that led to their fall, and therefore both men and women are faced equally with its consequences. As far as the forbidden fruit is concerned, again, the Quran does not mention it explicitly, but according to traditional commentaries it was not an apple, as believed by Christians and Jews, but wheat.

The creation of human beings complements the creation of the cosmos and adds to the created order a central being who is God's vicegerent, capable of knowing all things, of dominating the earth, given the power to do good, but also to wreak havoc and, in fact, corrupt the earth. According to a famous *ḥadīth*, "God created man upon His form," although here form does not mean physical image, but rather the reflection of God's Names and Qualities. But human beings are also given the freedom to rebel against God, and Iblīs can exercise power over them. The human being contains, in fact, all possibilities within himself or herself. The soul itself is a vast field in which the signs of God are manifested. As a Quranic verse states, "We shall show them Our signs (*āyāt*) upon the horizons and within their souls until it becomes manifest unto them that it is the truth" (41:53). Therefore, in a sense, the human being is itself a revelation like the macrocosm.

It might be said that from the Islamic point of view creation and revelation are inseparable, and that there are in fact three grand revelations: the cosmos, the human state, and religions—all three of which Islam sees as "books." There is, first of all, the cosmic book to be read and deciphered. Then there is the inner book of the soul, which we carry within ourselves. And finally there are sacred scriptures, which have been sent by God through His Mercy to guide humanity throughout the ages and which are the foundations of various religions and keys for reading the other two books, that of the cosmos and that of the soul.

5. Many Prophets

In the Islamic perspective, the oneness of God has as its consequence not the uniqueness of prophecy, but its multiplicity, since God as the Infinite created a world in which there is multiplicity and this includes, of course, the human order. For Islam, revelation and prophecy are both necessary and universal. Humanity, according to the Quran, was created from a single soul, but then diversified into races and tribes, for, as the Quran states, "He created you [humanity] from a single soul" (39:6). The single origin of humanity implies the profound unity within diversity of human nature, and therefore religion based on the message of Divine Oneness could not have been only meant for or available to a segment of humanity. The multiplicity of races, nations, and tribes necessitates the diversity of revelations. Therefore, the Quran asserts on the one hand that "To every people [We have sent] a messenger" (10:48), and, on the other hand, "For each [people] We have appointed a Divine Law and a way. Had God willed, He could have made you one community. But that He may try you by that which He hath given you. So vie with one another in good works. Unto God ye will all return, and He will then inform you concerning that wherein ye differed" (5:48). According to these and other verses, not only is the multiplicity of religions necessary, but it is also a reflection of the richness of the Divine Nature and is willed by God.

Religion (*dīn*), revelation (*waḥy*), and prophecy (*nubuwwah*) have a clear meaning in the context of the Islamic world view and therefore need to be carefully defined in the modern context, where all of these terms have become ambiguous in ordinary discourse. The closest word to the English term "religion" in Arabic is *dīn*, which is said by many to have been derived from the root meaning "to obey, submit, and humble oneself before God." *Al-dīn* means religion in the vastest sense as the sacred norm into which the whole of life is to be molded. It is the total way of life grounded in teachings that have issued from God. These teachings reach humanity through revelation, which means the direct conveying of a message from Heaven (revelation being understood apart from all the psychological entanglements it has acquired in much of modern Western religious thought). Revelation, moreover, must not be confused with inspiration (*ilhām*), which is possible for all human beings.

Islam sees revelation not as incarnation in the Hindu or Christian sense, but as the descent of the Word of God in the form of sacred scripture to a prophet. In fact, the Quran uses the term "Book" (*kitāb*) not only for the Quran, but also for all other sacred books and the totality of revelations. The Quran considers all revelations to be contained in that "archetypal book," or *Umm al-kitāb* (literally, "the Mother Book"), and the sacred scriptures to be related in conveying the same basic message of the primordial religion of unity in different languages and contexts. As the Quran states, "We never sent a messenger save with the language of his people" (14:4). Even when the Quran states that "The religion with God is *al-islām*" (3:19) or similar statements, *al-islām* refers to that universal surrender to the One and that primordial religion contained in the heart of all heavenly inspired religions, not just to Islam in its more particular sense. There is, moreover, a criterion of truth and falsehood as far as religions are concerned, and the Quran's confirmation of the universality of revelation does not mean that everything that has passed as religion yesterday or does so today is authentic. Throughout history there have been false prophets and religions, to which Christ also referred, as well as religions that have decayed or deviated from their original form.

Islam sees itself as heir to this long chain of prophets going back to Adam and believes all of them, considered to be 124,000 according to tradition, to be also its own. It does not believe, however, that it has inherited their teachings through temporal and historical transmission, for a prophet owes nothing to anyone and receives everything from Heaven, but it does believe that its message bears the finality of a seal. Islam sees itself as at once the primordial religion, a return to the original religion of oneness, and the final religion; the Quran itself calls the Prophet of Islam the "Seal of Prophets." And, in fact, fourteen hundred years of history have confirmed Islam's claim, for during all that time there has not been another plenary manifestation of the Truth like the ones that brought about the births of Buddhism and Christianity, not to speak of the earlier major religions. The two characteristics of primordiality and finality have bestowed upon Islam its trait of universality and the capability to absorb intellectually and culturally so much that came before it. It has also made spiritually alive the prophetic presences that preceded it, so that, for example, such figures as Abraham, Moses, and Christ play a much greater role in the spiritual universe of Islam than Abraham and Moses do in the Christian universe.

While speaking of the finality of the Islamic revelation for this cycle of human history, which will last until the eschatological events at the end of historic time, something must be said, from the Islamic point of view, about the "order" and "economy" of revelation. Muslims believe that each revelation takes place through the Divine Will, but also on the basis of a spiritual economy and is not by any means ad hoc. Each revelation fulfills a major function in human history seen from the religious point of view. For example, around the sixth to fifth century B.C., which also marks the transition from mythological time to historic time, a qualitative change took place in the march of time, which for Islam, as for Hinduism, is not simply linear. This is the period when the myths of Homer and Hesiod recede as Greek history flowers and the stories of mythical Persian dynasties are left behind as the Persian Empire takes shape. From the human point of view, this qualitative change in the terrestrial life of humanity required new dispensations from Heaven, and from the metaphysical perspective, these new dispensations themselves marked the new chapter that was to begin in human history.

This period, which philosophers such as Karl Jaspers have called the Axial Age, was witness to the appearance of Confucius and Lao Tzu in China and the new crystallization of the primal Chinese tradition into Confucianism and Taoism, and the appearance of Shintoism in Japan and the beginning of the terrestrial life of the solar emperors, who marked the beginning of historical Japanese civilization. This age was also witness to the life of the Buddha, whose teaching spread throughout India and Tibet and soon transformed the religious life of East and Southeast Asia. At nearly the same time, we see the rise of Zoroaster, who established Zoroastrianism in Persia and whose teachings greatly influenced later religious life in western Asia. Finally, around the same time we have the rise of Pythagoras and Pythagoreanism, which was central to the spiritual life of ancient Greece and from which Platonism was born. This remarkable cluster of figures, which also includes some of the Hebrew prophets, figures whom Muslims would call prophets, transformed the religious life of humanity, although the still living and viable religions of the earlier period such as Judaism and Hinduism survived. Moreover, this list of figures does not exhaust all the notable sages and prophets of the Axial Age.

One would think that the cycle of revelation would have been terminated in the Axial Age. But the decadence of the Greek and Roman religions around the Mediterranean Basin and the weakening of the northern European religions created a vacuum that only a new revelation could fill. Therefore Christianity was revealed by God. Although originally a Semitic religion, providentially it soon became, to some extent, Hellenized, and Christ was transformed almost into an "Aryan" solar hero for the Europeans, who were destined to find the path of salvation through this new dispensation from Heaven. It certainly was no accident that in Europe Christianity remained strong and unified, while in the eastern Mediterranean and North Africa, destined to become part of the future "Abode of Islam," it splintered into numerous small denominations fighting among themselves as well as against Byzantium.

This latter situation, added to the inner weakness of Zoroastrianism in the Persian Empire and certain other religions elsewhere, created another vacuum to be filled, this time by a new Semitic religion—Islam. Islam, like Judaism, remained faithful to its Semitic origin, but, like Christianity, was not confined to a particular ethnic group. Islam thus came to reassert the full doctrine of Divine Oneness on a universal scale after the Axial Age and the appearance of Christianity, placing in a sense the last golden brick in that golden wall that is revelation. With it, the structure of the wall became complete, and, as far as Muslims are concerned, although small religious movements may take place here and there, there is to be no plenary revelation after Islam according to the Divine Providence and the spiritual economy of God's plans for present-day humanity. When asked how they know such a truth, Muslims point to the Quran itself and the fact that no previous revelation had ever made such an explicit claim. Being the final religion of this cycle, Islam is not only closely related to its sister monotheisms, Judaism and Christianity, but also possesses an inward link to the religions of the Axial Age as well as to Hinduism. It is this link that made it easier for Islam than for Christianity to incorporate so much of the wisdom of Hinduism and of the religions of the Axial Age, from Buddhism and Pythagoreanism to Zoroastrianism and even later to Confucianism, within its sapiential perspective.

Paradoxically, the insistence of Islam upon God as the One and the Absolute has had as its concomitant the acceptance of the multiplicity of prophets and revelations, and no sacred scripture is more universalist in its understanding of religion than the Quran, whose perspective concerning the universality of revelation may be called "vertical triumphalism." In contrast, in Christianity, because of the emphasis on the Triune God, God the One is seen more in terms of the relationality of the three Hypostases, what one might call "Divine Relativity"; the vision of the manifestation of the Divine then became confined to the unique Son and Incarnation, in whom the light of all previous prophets was absorbed. In Christianity the vision is that of the Triune God and a unique message of salvation and savior, hence *extra ecclesiam nulla salus* (no salvation outside the church), whereas in Islam there is the One God and many prophets. Here is to be found the major difference between how Muslims have viewed Jews and Christians over the centuries and how Christians have regarded Jews and Muslims as well as followers of other religions. For Muslims, the Quran completes the message of previous sacred texts without in any way denigrating their significance. In fact, the Torah and the Gospels are mentioned by name as sacred scriptures along with the Quran in the text of the Quran. Likewise, although the Prophet terminates the long chain of prophecy, the earlier prophets lose none of their spiritual significance. Rather, they appear in the Islamic firmament as stars, while the Prophet is like the moon in that Islamic sky.

* * *

The sacred scripture of Islam, known in Arabic by many names, of which the most famous is *al-Qurʾān*, "the Recitation," is considered by all Muslims, no matter to which school they belong, as the verbatim revelation of God's Word made to descend into the heart, soul, and mind of the Prophet of Islam through the agency of the archangel of revelation, Gabriel, or Jibraʾīl in Arabic. Both the words and meaning of the text are considered to be sacred, as is everything else connected with it, such as the chanting of its verses or the calligraphy of its phrases. Muslims are born with verses of the Book, which Muslims call the Noble Quran, read into their ears, live throughout their lives hearing its verses and also repeating certain of its chapters during daily prayers, are married with the accompaniment of Quranic recitations, and die hearing it chanted beside them.

The Quran (also known as the Koran in English) is the central theophany of Islam, the fundamental source of its metaphysics, cosmology, theology, law, ethics, sacred history, and general world view. In a way the soul of the traditional Muslim is like a mosaic made up of phrases of the Quran, which are repeated throughout life, such as the *basmalah*, "In the Name of God, the Infinitely Good, the All-Merciful," with which all legitimate acts begin and are consecrated; *al-ḥamdu li'Llāh*, "Praise be to God," with which one terminates an act or event in the attitude of gratefulness; *inshāʾ Allāh*, "If God wills," which accompanies every utterance concerning the future, for the future is in God's Hands and nothing takes place save through His Will. Even the daily greeting of Muslims, *al-salāmu ʿalaykum*, "Peace be upon you," which the Prophet taught to his companions as the greeting of the people of paradise, comes from the Quran. As some Western scholars of Islam have noted, there is perhaps no single book that is as influential in any religion as the Quran is in Islam.

To fully understand the significance of the Quran, a Westerner with a Christian background should realize that, although the Quran can in a sense be compared to the Old and New Testaments, a more profound comparison would be with Christ himself. In Christianity both the spirit and body of Christ are sacred, and he is considered the Word of God. The Quran is likewise for Muslims the Word of God (*kalimat Allāh*), and both its inner meaning, or spirit, and its body, or outer form, the text in the Arabic language in which it was revealed, are sacred to Muslims. Arabic is the sacred language of Islam and Quranic Arabic plays a role in Islam analogous to the role of the body of Christ in Christianity. Moreover, as Christians consume bread and wine as symbols of the flesh and blood of Christ, Muslims pronounce, using the same organ of the body, that is, the mouth, the Word of God in the daily prayers. The rationalist and agnostic methods of higher criticism applied by certain Western scholars to the text of the Quran, which was not compiled over a long period of time like the Old and the New Testaments, is as painful and as much a blasphemy to Muslims as it would be to believing Christians if some Muslim archeologists claimed to have discovered some physical remains of Christ and were using DNA analysis to determine whether he was born miraculously or was the son of Joseph.

In any case, for Muslims themselves, Sunni and Shi'ite alike, there is but a single text of the Quran consisting of 114 chapters of over 6,000 verses revealed to the Prophet of Islam in Mecca and Medina over the twenty-three years of his prophetic mission. As verses were received and then uttered by him, they would be memorized by companions, who were Arabs with prodigious memories. The verses were also written down by scribes. The order of the chapters of the Quran was also given by the Prophet through Divine command. During the caliphate of the third caliph, 'Uthmān, some twenty years after the death of the Prophet, as many of those who had memorized the Quran were dying in various battles, the complete text of the Quran was copied in several manuscripts and sent to the four corners of the Islamic world. Later copies are based on this early definitive collection.

It is said in Islam that God gives to each prophet a miracle corresponding to what was important in his time. Since magic was so significant in Egypt, God gave Moses the power to turn his staff into a serpent. Since medicine was such an important art at the time of Christ, God gave him the miracle of raising the dead to life. And since poetic eloquence was the most prized of all virtues for pre-Islamic Arabs, God revealed through the Prophet by far the most eloquent of all Arabic works. In fact, the greatest miracle of Islam is said to be the eloquence of the Quran. Its eloquence not only moved the heart and soul of those Arabs of the seventh century who first heard it, but also moves to tears Muslim believers throughout the world today, even those whose mother tongue is not Arabic, although Arabic is the language of daily prayers for all Muslims, Arab and non-Arab alike. The grace, or *barakah* (corresponding both etymologically and in meaning to the Hebrew *berakha* [or *brakah*]), of the text transcends its mental message and moves souls toward God in much the same way that hearing Gregorian chant in Latin would for centuries in the West deeply affect even those who did not understand the Latin words. Of course, the same can be said for the Latin Mass itself, whose beautiful liturgy was of the deepest significance for some fifteen hundred years even for those Catholics who did not know Latin.

The Quran has many names, each revealing an aspect of its reality. It is *al-Qurʾān*, or "recitation," which also means "gathering" or "concentration." It is *al-Furqān*, or "discernment," because it provides the criteria for discerning between truth and falsehood, goodness and evil, beauty and ugliness. It is *Umm al-kitāb*, the archetypal book containing the root of all knowledge, and it is *al-Hudā*, the guide for the journey of men and women toward God. For Muslims, the Quran is the source of all knowledge both outward and inward, the foundation of the Law, the final guide for ethical behavior, and a net with which the Divine Fisherman ensnares the human soul and brings it back to Unity.

The Quran contains several grand themes. First of all, it deals with the nature of reality, with the Divine Reality and Its relation to the realm of relativity. Second, the Quran says much about the natural world, and in a sense the Islamic sector of the cosmos participates in the Quranic revelation. Then the Quran contains many pages on sacred history, but the episodes of this history are recounted more for their significance as lessons for the inner life of the soul than as historical accounts of ages past. Sacred history in the Quran contains, above all, moral and spiritual lessons for us here and now.

The Quran also deals with laws for the individual and society and is the most important source of Islamic Law, or the *Sharīʿah*. Furthermore, the Quran comes back again and again to the question of ethics, of good and evil, of the significance of living a virtuous life. Finally, the Quran speaks, especially in its last chapters, in majestic language about eschatological events, about the end of this world, about the Day of Judgment, paradise, purgatory, and hell. The language of the Quran, especially in dealing with eschatological realities, is concrete and symbolic, not abstract, nor descriptive in the ordinary sense, which would in any case be impossible when one is dealing with realities our earthly imaginations cannot grasp. This trait has caused many outsiders to criticize the Quran for its sensuous description of the delights of paradise as if they were simply a sublimation of earthly joys and pleasures. In reality every joy and delight here below, especially sexuality, which is sacred for Islam, is the reflection of a paradisal prototype, not vice versa.

According to the Prophet and many of the earliest authorities such as ʿAlī and Jaʿfar al-Ṣādiq, the Quran has many levels of meaning, of which the highest is known to God alone. In the same way that God is both the Outward (*al-Ẓāhir*) and the Inward (*al-Bāṭin*), His Book also has an outward and an inward dimension or, in fact, several levels of inner meaning. Throughout Islamic history, Quranic commentaries have been written from both points of view, the outward and the inward. The first is called *tafsīr* and the second *taʾwīl*. Works of both categories are crucial for the understanding of the text of the Quran, each word and letter of which is like a living being with many levels of significance, including a numerical symbolism, which is studied in the science called *jafr*, corresponding to Jewish and Christian Kabbala.

The chapters (*sūrahs*) and verses (*āyahs*) of the Quran are both the path and the guidepost in the Muslim's earthly journey. The root of everything Islamic, from metaphysics and theology to law and ethics to the sciences and arts, is to be found in it. Every movement that has begun in Islamic history, whether religious, intellectual, social, or political, has sought legitimization in the Quran, and the permanent flow of the daily life of traditional Muslims unaffected by such movements has also been marked in the deepest sense by the presence of the Quran. Jurists have sought to interpret its legal verses and Sufis its inner meaning. Philosophers have drawn from its philosophical utterances and theologians have debated its assertions about the nature of God's Attributes and His relation to the world. Today, as when it was revealed, the Quran remains the central reality of Islam and the heart of Muslim life in both its individual and social aspects.

* * *

The Prophet of Islam, to whom we shall henceforth refer simply as the Prophet, is for the West the most misunderstood reality within the Islamic universe. For over a millennium he has been maligned in various European sources as an apostate, a pretender, and even the Antichrist, and one has had to wait well over a thousand years until the twentieth century to see fair treatments of him appear in European languages. Until recently, Christians usually compared him, of course very unfavorably, to Christ, assuming that he holds the same position in Islam as Christ does in Christianity. Westerners therefore called Islam Mohammadanism until a few decades ago, a term detested by Muslims, and concentrated their attacks against him in order to vilify Islam. Even those who admitted to his remarkable achievements in this world refused to accept him as a prophet. Christian attacks against him were, in fact, the most painful and divisive element in Islam's relationship with Christianity over the centuries. Even today the general misunderstanding of the Prophet in the West remains a major obstacle to mutual understanding. In modern times certain Western writers opposed to Christianity tried to use the Prophet as an instrument in their attacks on Christianity without any real appreciation or understanding of the Prophet himself. Rarely does one find in earlier Western history a figure such as the German poet Goethe, who harbored deep respect and even love for the Prophet.

To understand the heart of Islam it is, therefore, essential to understand the significance of the Prophet from the point of view of traditional Muslims—not that of either Muslim modernists who neglect his spiritual dimension or the so-called puritan reformers who for other reasons belittle his significance in the total religious economy of Islam. The Quran asserts clearly that the Prophet was a man and not divine, but also adds that God chose him as His final messenger, the "Seal of Prophets," that he was given the most exalted and noble character, and that he was chosen as a model for Muslims to emulate, as mentioned in the verse, "Verily you have in the Messenger of God an excellent exemplar for him who looks to God and the Last Day and remembers God often" (32:21). This verse is the basis for the emulation of the *Sunnah*, or wonts (in the sense of actions and deeds) of the Prophet, that is central to the whole of Islam. For Muslims, the Prophet is a mortal man (*bashar*), but also God's most perfect creature, or what the Sufis, the mystics of Islam, call the Universal Man (*al-insān al-kāmil*). As a Sufi poem recited often throughout the Islamic world asserts,

> Muhammad is a man, but not like other men.
> Rather, he is a ruby and other men like stones. . . .

To comprehend the significance of the Prophet in Islam, it is necessary to remember that the great founders of religions are of two types. The first constitutes the category of those figures who preach detachment from the world and a spiritual life that does not become entangled with ordinary worldly matters with all their ambiguities and complexities. Supreme examples of this type are found in Christ and the Buddha, both of whom founded what were originally small spiritual communities divorced from and not integrated into the political, social, and economic conditions of the larger society. Christ, who said that his kingdom was not of this world, did not marry and was not the leader and ruler of a whole human society, and the Buddha left the married life of a prince to devote himself to the monastic life and the attainment of illumination.

The second type is exemplified by Moses, David, and Solomon in the Abrahamic world and by Rama and Krishna in Hinduism. Such figures, whether seen as prophets or *avatārs*, entered into the complexity of the ordinary human order to transform and sanctify it. The Hebrew prophets as well as some avataric figures from Hinduism were also political leaders and rulers of a human community. They were married and had children and therefore appear to those who have been brought up gazing upon the dazzling spiritual perfection of Christ or the Buddha as being too immersed in the life of the world and therefore less perfect. Such a judgment neglects the truth that once Christianity and Buddhism became religions of a whole society, they too had to deal with the earthly realities of human society, with justice, war and peace, and the question of family and sexual relations.

In any case, the Prophet must be seen as belonging to the second category. His contemplativeness was inward, while outwardly he had to face nearly every possible human situation. He experienced being an orphan, living the life of a merchant, suffering persecution. He grieved deeply the loss of his beloved wife Khadījah and his two-year-old son Ibrāhīm, but he also knew the happiness of family life and of final triumph in the world. He, who loved solitude and contemplation, had to deal with the affairs of men and women, with all their frailties and shortcomings. He had to rule over a whole society and to sit as judge in cases of one party's complaints against another. One might say that his mission was to sanctify all of life and to create an equilibrium in human life that could serve as the basis for surrender and effacement before the Divine Truth.

In every religion all the virtues of its adherents derive from those existing in the founder of the religion. In the same way that no Christian can claim to have any virtue that was not possessed to the utmost extent by Christ, no Muslim can have any virtue that was not possessed in the most eminent degree by the Prophet. More specifically, the Prophet exemplifies the virtues of humility; nobility, magnanimity, and charity; and truthfulness and sincerity. For Muslims, the Prophet is the perfect model of total humility before God and neighbor; nobility and magnanimity of soul, which means to be strict with oneself but generous, charitable, and forgiving to others; and finally, perfect sincerity, which means to be totally truthful to oneself and to God. This crowning Islamic virtue requires the melting of our ego before God, for, as a Sufi saying asserts, "He whose soul melteth not away like snow in the hand of religion [that is, the Truth], in his hand religion like snow away doth melt."[1]

Love for the Prophet is incumbent upon all Muslims and in fact constitutes a basic aspect of Islamic religious life. It might be said that this love is the key for the love of God, for in order to love God, God must first love us, and God does not love a person who does not love His messenger. The Prophet is also held in the greatest esteem and respect. He has many names, such as Aḥmad ("the most praiseworthy of those who praise God"), ʿAbd Allāh ("servant of God"), Abu'l-Qāsim ("Father of Qāsim"), and al-Amīn ("the Trusted One"), as well as Muhammad. Whenever any of these names are mentioned, they are followed with the formulaic phrase, "May peace and blessings be upon him." It is considered a sign of disrespect to mention his name or the name of any of the other prophets without invoking the benediction of peace upon them.

The invocation of benediction upon the Prophet is so central for Muslims that it might be said to be the only act that is performed by both God and human beings, for, as the Quran says, "Verily, God and His angels shower blessings upon the Prophet. O ye who have faith! Ask blessings on him and salute him with a worthy salutation" (33:56).

The love and respect for the Prophet also extends to other prophets who remain spiritually alive in the Islamic universe. In fact, Muslims do not consider the fact that the message of the Prophet was conclusive to mean that it was also exclusive. The Prophet is for them both the person they love and admire as God's most perfect creature and the continuation of the long chain of prophets to whom he is inwardly connected. A pious Muslim would never think of praising the Prophet while denigrating the prophets who came before him, particularly those mentioned in the Quran. In the metaphysical sense, the Prophet is both a manifestation of the Logos and the Logos itself, both the beginning of the prophetic cycle and its end, and, being its end and seal, he contains from an essential and inward point of view the whole prophetic function within himself.

[1] Martin Lings, *A Sufi Saint of the Twentieth Century* (Berkeley: University of California Press, 1973), p. i.

6. The Nature of Man

The Islamic conception of man is summarized in the doctrine of *al-insān al-kāmil*, the universal or perfect man, a doctrine whose essence and full manifestation is to be found in the Prophet of Islam and whose doctrinal exposition and formulation was left to later sages and saints such as Ibn ʿArabī and Jalāl al-Dīn Rūmī. In fact Islamic gnosis (*al-ʿirfān*) revolves nearly always around the two axes of unity (*al-tawḥīd*), dealing with God and His Names and Qualities, and *al-insān al-kāmil*, dealing with man and the cosmos. The first is concerned with the Origin and Source of creation and the second with manifestation and the return of things to the Source. Or one could say that the first corresponds to the first "witness" or *Shahādah* of Islam, *Lā ilāha illa'Llāh*, there is no divinity but God, and the second to the second "witness," *Muḥammadun rasūl Allāh*, Muhammad is the Messenger of God. Muhammad is the Universal Man *par excellence* and also the quintessence of all creation, of all that is positive in cosmic manifestation. The Universal Man contains all degrees of existence within himself and is the archetype of both the cosmos and man. Therefore, metaphysically and of course not physically and quantitatively, there is a profound correspondence between man and the cosmos. Although outwardly a small part of the cosmos, man contains inwardly and within himself a reality that is the source of the cosmos itself—and that is why even fallen man, he who has forgotten his own true nature, has the power to dominate nature.

> From the pure star-bright souls replenishment is ever coming to the stars of heaven.
>
> Outwardly we are ruled by these stars, but our inward nature has become the ruler of the skies.
>
> Therefore, while in form thou art the microcosm, in reality thou art the macrocosm.
>
> Externally, the branch is the origin of the fruit; intrinsically the branch came into existence for the sake of the fruit. (Rūmī)[1]

The spiritual man, although outwardly dominated by nature, inwardly rules over things, most of all because he has conquered his own inner

[1] R. A. Nicholson, *Rūmī, Poet and Mystic* (London: Allen and Unwin, 1950), p. 124.

nature. Might one not add that today, when man boasts most about conquering nature, the reverse process has taken place, namely an apparent and outward conquest of nature combined with complete lack of asceticism, spiritual discipline, and self-negation, which therefore makes man more than ever a prisoner of his own passions and natural inclinations. But the spiritual man who has overcome his passions and who is the reflection of Universal Man and its realization and embodiment is the pole toward which the universe itself is attracted, to the extent that Jalāl al-Dīn Rūmī, that supreme poet of the spirit, could say,

> Wine in ferment is a beggar suing for our ferment;
> Heaven in revolution is a beggar suing for our consciousness;
> Wine was intoxicated with us, not we with it;
> The body came into being from us, not we from it.[2]

The Universal Man, whose full metaphysical doctrine cannot be expounded here, is then the sum of all degrees of existence, a total mirror before the Divine Presence and at the same time the supreme archetype of creation. It is the prototype of man, the reality that man carries potentially within himself and can always realize if there is aspiration, persistence, and of course divine succor. It is enough for man to realize the total possibility of his own existence, to become fully conscious of himself, to gain that treasure of true felicity and peace which he seeks outwardly here and there but never seems to find.

> You who wander in deserts away from your own consciousness,
> Come back to yourself to find all existence summed up in you.
> You are the way and reality of perfection.
> One in whom the great consciousness of God dwells.
> (Abu'l-Mawāhib al-Shādhilī)[3]

One is here reminded of Shakespeare's advice: "This above all; to thine own self be true."

The cosmic dimension of man may bring certain protests from theologians that this would obliterate the distinction between grace and nature and reduce man to simply "natural man." Christianity, having expanded in a world which suffered from too much emphasis upon rationalism and

[2] *Ibid.* p. 141.

[3] M. Smith, *The Sufi Path of Love* (London: Luzac and Co., 1954), p. 72.

naturalism, had to draw a sharp distinction between nature and grace, at least in its official theology. But Islam was not faced with the same situation. For this and for other reasons its doctrines are such that it considers nature itself as a handiwork of God in whose arteries flows the grace issuing from the Creator Himself. Man also is from a certain point of view a "natural being," yet without being deprived of grace. He is natural without being reduced to the natural man of the Renaissance or of Rousseau and the French encyclopaedists. The questions of natural law, original sin, the role of nature in spiritual realization, and the like are approached in a different light in Islam, and these questions have of course their bearing on the understanding of man and his function in the world. By considering man in his primordial nature (*al-fiṭrah*) and bestowing upon each Muslim the priestly and sacerdotal function, Islam removed the sharp distinction between the religious and secular, or sacred and profane, making of man a natural being who is yet the most direct symbol of the spiritual world in nature and in direct contact with that world.

Furthermore, by virtue of being the *khalīfah* of God on earth and occupying the central position he does hold, man is the channel of grace for nature. The spiritual man is the means whereby nature breathes of the spiritual life and is prevented from suffocation and destruction, as also confirmed by Western Hermetical and alchemical writers like Flamel and Jakob Boehme. Were man to cease completely to follow the spiritual life and lose his contact with the spiritual world, he would also cease to be a source of light for nature and in fact would turn toward the destruction and vilification of nature. The relation between modern industrial societies and virgin nature should provide an occasion to pause and meditate on this relationship.

The constitution of man and his relation with God and nature cannot be fully understood without analyzing the meaning and role of intelligence and reason, by means of which man seeks to master the world.

First of all a clear distinction, often forgotten today, must be made between the intellect, the faculty which knows immediately and totally, and reason whose Latin root (*ratio*) reveals its function of analysis and division. Islam appeals to the intellect in man, whose function it is to know the principles of things and which will arrive at the basic Islamic doctrine of Unity (*al-tawḥīd*) if it functions normally and is wholesome (*salīm*). In fact the role of revelation is to remove those obstacles which prevent the intelligence from functioning in a wholesome manner. Otherwise the intellect within man confirms the revealed truths of religion and Islam bases itself on a truth which is evident and in the nature of things.

As for reason, it is like the shadow and reflection of the intellect. If it remains subservient to the intellect and also to revelation, which likewise issues forth from the Supreme Intellect or Logos, then it is a positive instrument which can aid man to journey from multiplicity to Unity. But if it rebels against its own source, against both the intellect and revelation, then it becomes the source of disharmony and dissolution. Other creatures have intelligence in the sense that they reflect certain aspects of the divine and also cosmic intelligences. But only man possesses this subjective polarization of true intelligence which we call reason. And that is why only he can destroy the natural harmony of nature.

If modern man has been able to dominate but at the same time destroy nature and himself more than men of all other civilizations, it is precisely because with him more than ever before reason has been made independent of its principle. In such a condition reason becomes like an acid burning through the tissues of the cosmos and at the same time is powerless before the infra-human and irrational forces that revolt against it from below, in the same way that it has rebelled against the intellect above it. The relation between rationalism and the spiritual and intellectual heritage against which it rebelled on the one hand, and the irrationalism of modern times on the other, is very similar and in fact nearly the same thing as the humanism which rebelled against the theomorphic concept of man only to end in being threatened by the infrahuman forces it has itself liberated. Islam, while considering man as essentially an intelligence that also has willpower and performs actions, and emphasizing knowledge as a means of salvation and deliverance, yet rejects the position of rationalism and its limiting of the intellect to its reflection, which is reason as ordinarily understood. For Islam the world of the mind is much more vast than we usually envisage. It is in fact the locus of the Presence of the Divine Spirit, but man must penetrate beneath the surface of the mind with which he usually identifies himself in order to become aware of this Presence.

Again to quote Rūmī:

What worlds mysterious roll within the vast,
The all-encircling ocean of the Mind!
Cup-like thereon our forms are floating fast,
Only to fill and sink and leave behind
No spray of bubbles from the Sea upcast.
The Spirit thou canst not view, it comes so nigh.
Drink of this Presence! Be not thou a jar
Laden with water, and its lip stone-dry;

Or as a horseman blindly borne afar,
Who never sees the horse beneath his thigh.[4]

It is the very centrality and totality of the human state which makes any "linear" and "horizontal" evolution of man impossible. One cannot reach a more central point in a circle than the center itself. Once at the center one can always move either upward or downward but no further in the horizontal direction. The evolutionary view of man as an animal, which even from the biological point of view is open to question, can tell us little as to the real nature of man; no more than can the theories of many anthropologists who discuss anthropology without even knowing who man, the *anthrōpos*, is and without realizing the complete states of universal existence which man carries with him here and now.

Once it was asked of ʿAlī, the cousin and son-in-law of the Prophet: What existed before Adam? He answered Adam, and to the question what existed before that Adam he again answered Adam, adding that were he to be asked this question to the end of time he would repeat Adam. This saying means that irrespective of when he appeared in the time-space matrix of this world, the metaphysical reality of man, of the Universal Man, has always been. It could not become but is, because it transcends time and becoming. It is, furthermore, this eternal archetype that determines the meaning of the human state and which man always reflects and bears potentially within himself in all time and space. Those who speak of the future evolution of man perhaps do not realize that higher possibilities of existence do not lie in some future time ahead of man but here and now above him, yet within his reach. Frankly, it must be said that the way man is "evolving" today makes it ever more difficult for him to attain these higher states of consciousness and being, whose very existence he has begun to doubt in general, while a certain number of people in this very climate of doubt seek to reach these states through the short-cut of drugs and pills rather than through spiritual discipline. One might say that the total and central nature of the human state, deriving from man's theomorphic nature, makes his relation with other states of being not a temporal one but a spatial one. Man stands at the crossing of the vertical and horizontal dimensions containing the amplitude and breadth of universal existence within himself here and now. It is for him to delve into himself in order to realize who he is, to realize these states which comprise his full nature.

[4] Nicholson, *Rūmī*, p. 106.

No development in time, especially in a process during which man lives increasingly on the surface of his being, fleeing from himself and the needs of his inner nature, will ever automatically bring an evolution to higher planes for the human species.

Rather, the urgent problem today is to prevent man from falling into an infrahuman world, which he faces because he has rejected his own transcendent origin and prototype. Modern man wants to kill the gods without destroying himself. He wants to reject the Divine and yet remain fully human. Islam has considered this question fully and has provided an answer with which we shall conclude this discussion. In several places in the Quran mention is made of the term "Face" or "Countenance of God" (*wajh Allāh*), for example the verses: "There remaineth but the Countenance of thy Lord, Majestic, Splendid" (55:27) and "Everything will perish save His Countenance" (28:88).

Nearly all Muslim sages have agreed that the Countenance of God, which alone endures and persists, is the spiritual aspect of man's nature. Ultimately the body dies and even the inferior psychic elements perish or at least are integrated into a higher degree of being, namely that of the spirit. It is only the spiritual element which is eternal. It is the face that man has turned toward God. But it is also the face that God has turned toward man. The Countenance of God embraces a total reality, one aspect of which is man's spiritual countenance and the other God's countenance toward his creation and especially his vicegerent on earth, man. And it is this same reality which in Shi'ite Islam comprises the inner nature of the Imam. The Imam is the link between God and man, a spiritual being in whom the divine and the human orders meet.

To meditate on the theme of the Face of God is to realize that man cannot destroy the divine image without destroying himself. The poetical cry of Nietzsche in the nineteenth century that "God is dead," a cry which has now been turned into a theological proposition in certain quarters and is advertised far beyond its purport and significance by those who seek after the sensational and who seem to have little reverence for the belief of those living and dead for whom God is eternally present and alive, cannot but have its echo in the assertion that man is dead, man as a spiritual and free being. Man cannot destroy the face that God has turned towards him without destroying the face that man has turned towards God, and therefore also all that is eternal and imperishable in man and is the source of human dignity, the only reality that gives meaning to human life. The inexhaustible richness of the symbol of the Countenance of God should possess much meaning for modern man who seeks desperately for meaning in human life and the preservation of human dignity, but is too rarely concerned with the other half of this reality, namely the Countenance of God, that aspect of the Divine that has turned toward us as human beings.

To know himself, man must come to know the Face of God, the reality that determines him from on high. Neither flights into outer space nor plunges beneath the seas, nor changes of fashions and modes of outward living alter the nature of man and his situation vis-à-vis the Real. Nor can biological or conventional psychological studies, which deal only with the outward aspects of human nature, reveal to man who he is and how he should "orient" himself in that journey whose end is the meeting with the Real. Man can know himself only by realizing his theomorphic nature. It is only in remaining conscious of the divine imprint upon his soul that man can hope to remain human. Only the attraction of the celestial can prevent man from being dragged by gravity to the abysses of subhuman existence. And it is a remarkable feature of the human state that no matter where and in what condition he may be, man always finds above him the sky and the attraction which pulls him toward the Infinite and the Eternal.

7. The Integration of the Soul

What do we mean by integration? Not only do I want to pose this question from the point of view of Sufi metaphysics, but also of other forms of metaphysics as well. Oneness in its absoluteness belongs to the Absolute alone. It is only the One who is ultimately one. This is not a pleonasm, not simply a repeating of terms. It is the reassertion of a truth which we are easily apt to forget while we are seeking the One in Its reflections on lower levels of reality and on the plane of multiplicity. We must always remember this metaphysical truth: that oneness in its highest and absolute sense belongs only to God as the Absolute, to Brahman, Allah, the Godhead, the Highest Reality, the Ultimate Reality. Precisely because of this truth, no benefit could be gained in our search for unity by being immersed only in multiplicity. In fact, without the One, multiplicity itself could not exist. It would be nonexistent, because multiplicity always issues from the One, always issues from the Supreme Principle. If we remember this truth, we shall then be able to understand what is truly meant by integration.

Nearly everybody is in favor of integration these days, without bothering to search fully for its meaning. In the modern world attempts are often made to achieve integration by seeking to bring forces and elements together on a single plane of reality without recourse to the Transcendent Principle or a principle transcending the level in question. But this is metaphysically impossible. It is only a higher principle that can integrate various elements on a lower level of reality. This truth is repeated throughout all of the levels of the hierarchy of the universe. Throughout the universe it is ultimately only the Divine Principle—God—who either by Himself, or possibly through His agents, makes possible the integration of a particular level of reality and the integration of that level itself into the whole of existence. On all levels, from the *deva*s of the Brahmic world or the archangels or whatever corresponding language you wish to use, to the lower angelic world, to the psychological world, and finally to the physical world, it is always by means of a higher principle that the elements and forces involved on lower levels of reality are integrated. Let us give a concrete example.

Take the human state. It is composed of body, soul, and spirit. There is no way one can integrate the body without the presence of the soul. That is why when the soul departs, the body falls apart. Furthermore, the remarkable, integrated functioning of various parts of our body is one of the greatest miracles, to which we usually pay little attention. By accepting

Descartes' reductionist conception of the body as a machine, we have fallen into the crisis concerning the relation between body and soul that we now face. The body is not a machine at all. If we look at the body, we see that it has this remarkable integrative function. But the moment the soul departs, the principle of integration departs and the body begins gradually to decompose. The same truth holds *mutatis mutandis* for the soul. Our souls and minds are scattered, like particles dispersing from a center—we usually live in a scattered world. The common everyday English usage of the term "scatter-brain" reflects the fact that in a sense the mind is scattered. There is absolutely no way to integrate the soul and the mind without the presence of the spirit and intellect, which are ultimately the same reality. It is only the spirit that is able to integrate the psyche, and the intellect the mind. The vital power of integration is not only related to God as the Supreme Reality, but also involves higher principles in relation to every level of reality down to the physical world in which we live; although of course the power of integration on all levels of reality comes ultimately from the Supreme Principle, which is One.

To speak seriously about integration, we must accept the vertical dimension of reality. The reason that we have such difficulty to integrate anything in the present-day world is the eclipse of knowledge of that vertical dimension. We are always trying to integrate and bring together various realities in a united and harmonious manner. We talk about how people should be friends, society should become integrated, races should seek harmony, religions should be in accord and not in conflict. But of course that is only for the most part wishful thinking, as we can observe from what is going on in our world. The most fundamental unit of our society, the family, is going the other way; it is breaking up to an ever greater degree, because there are so few people who possess an integrated inner being. The reason for this state of affairs is that we refuse to accept a principle above the individual order, we have forgotten the vertical dimension of existence and have fallen into a state of dementia.

Now, it is in light of these metaphysical truths that I wish to discuss Sufism and its relationship to the integration of man, first inwardly and then outwardly. Sufism is the esoteric or inward dimension of Islam, as you have heard mentioned many times. Islamic esoterism is, however, not exhausted by Sufism. It has certain manifestations within Twelve-Imam Shi'ism and Isma'ilism in its classical forms, but the main manifestation and the most important and central crystallization of Islamic esoterism is to be found in Sufism. Let us now ask what is meant by esoterism. It is a somewhat dangerous word to use in the modern world if not well defined, because it is confused often with occultism, or with the simply obscure and incomprehensible. It should be noted, however, that it is only in the modern West that the phenomenon that we know as occultism arose. There was no occultism in classical Hindu, Islamic, or Buddhist civilizations or in the Christian West when esoterism was fully present and accessible. So, by esoteric, I do not mean occult and certainly not obscure, although of course for those who do not possess the necessary intellectual and spiritual qualifications, it might appear as obscure and inaccessible, as would higher mathematics for someone who is not mathematically inclined. But in neither case is the subject obscure in itself for those qualified to know it. In any case, by esoterism I mean the inner dimension of both religion and reality itself—of manifested reality.

Everything in this world issues from the hidden to the state of manifestation. We ourselves are born from the wombs of our mothers. We come from darkness into light, to the manifest or external world. As you know, the water of life in all mythologies flows from a dark cave where its source and fountain are to be found. This darkness is not, however, simply emptiness or nothingness; rather, it symbolizes the hidden or non-manifested level of being. Everything in this world that we are able to experience or study (even in the field of quantum mechanics), issues in a sense from the unmanifested to the manifested, or from the hidden to the apparent. Furthermore, metaphysically the hidden or inward refers to a transcending reality which is also immanent as, symbolically speaking, the esoteric also means that which transcends appearances as well as being immanent to them. Of course, as far as religion is concerned, the exoteric dimension does not issue from the esoteric but, like the esoteric, comes from God. But the esoteric represents both the inner reality of the exoteric and that which lies on a higher level of reality, and in this sense transcends it. This is how these dimensions are experienced as one marches on the way to that Truth which is the Transcendent, as well as the Immanent as such. In any case, instead of using the image "from inside, out," we can also use "from up, down," which is more familiar to those who come from an Abrahamic background. (For Hinduism, especially of the school of the Vedanta, of course it would be the other way around.) Let us for the moment just keep to the vertical hierarchy of existence.

In the Islamic context there is first of all God, the One (*al-Aḥad*), one of whose Names is *al-Ḥaqq*, the Truth, to which Christ also referred in the Gospels. As for truth, when one refers to the truth of this or that matter, this is called *al-Ḥaqīqah* in Arabic, which also means reality. The two terms *al-Ḥaqīqah* and *al-Ḥaqq* are related etymologically and on the higher level refer to the same Reality. The term *Ḥaqīqah* means truth as it is grasped and lived at all different levels, while *al-Ḥaqq* is the Name of God, who is Truth in the most exalted meaning of the term. So, *Ḥaqīqah* at its highest level of meaning also refers to the Divine Truth, which lies at the heart and center of the Islamic religion and is, from the Islamic point of view, the ultimate goal of human life. Then there is the level of the path or *Ṭarīqah*, the spiritual path leading to *Ḥaqīqah*, the path which is associated with Sufism. The phrase *al-ṭarīq ila'Llāh*, that is, the path towards God in Arabic, is practically synonymous with Sufism, although in its early history, up to the end of the eleventh Christian century, Sufism had not as yet been ordered and crystallized into what we call *ṭarīqah*s or Sufi orders today. After the period in question, *ṭarīqah*s came into being bearing the names of their founders such as the Rifāʿiyyah, Qādiriyyah, Shādhiliyyah, Niʿmatullāhiyyah, Naqshbandiyyah, and the Chishtiyyah orders, the latter being so widespread in India. Nevertheless, the idea of a *ṭarīqah* or *ṭarīq ila'Llāh* goes back to a *ḥadīth* of the Prophet of Islam himself in which he said, "The number of paths (*ṭuruq*, pl. of *ṭarīqah*) to God is equal to the number of children of Adam." That is, it is the path, the *Ṭarīqah* that connects each of us to God, and before each human being there stands a path to Him as long as he or she follows the Divine Law or *Sharīʿah* by virtue of which that person stands on the circumference of a circle every point of which is connected by a radius (*Ṭarīqah*) to the Center (*Ḥaqīqah*). That does not mean of course that there are 5.5 billion individual *ṭarīqah*s, but that there are many possible paths which have become crystallized over time, as far as Islam is concerned, into the various orders, each of which leads us to God.

The actual named orders came somewhat later, but the reality of Sufism begins with the inner dimension of the Quran and the *Sunnah* and the spiritual power of the Prophet of Islam and originates everywhere from these sources. At the foundation of Islamic religious life there stands the *Sharīʿah*, the Divine Law, which defines Islamicity on the external plane of life. So you have a vertical hierarchy, of the *Sharīʿah*, the *Ṭarīqah*, and the *Ḥaqīqah* on the human plane, corresponding to the macrocosmic hierarchy. Furthermore, in the case of the *Sharīʿah*, *Ṭarīqah*, and *Ḥaqīqah*, it is also the higher principle that integrates that which belongs to a lower-level order on the hierarchy of human existence.

The goal of all levels and domains of Islamic reality is of course *tawḥīd*, which means both unity and integration. This word in Arabic also exists in all other Islamic languages, including many of the languages of India, such as Gujurati, Punjabi, and Bengali. This term possesses several shades and levels of meaning in the original Arabic and is really untranslatable into a single term in European languages. It is a noun implying a state while at the same time implying action. It is both a noun meaning oneness or unity and it implies the act and process of integration, of bringing into unity, the act of making into one. One therefore needs to use more than one term in English to bring out its full meaning. It is important to bear this point in mind when trying to understand what Sufism means by integration.

In the Islamic perspective then integration means to achieve *tawḥīd*, to become embellished with a quality which on the highest level belongs only to God, for God alone is One. One should never forget that supreme *tawḥīd* belongs to God alone. We can never achieve complete unity unless we realize that ultimately we are nothing and God is everything. It is through *fanāʾ*, the awareness of our nothingness before God, that the Sufis believe we can achieve that supreme unity. In the Hindu tradition this corresponds very much to "That art Thou"—that is, "Thou art the Supreme Reality," which cannot but be one. Every aspect of life bears the imprint of that unity whether we are aware of it or not, and everything that we do should direct us more and more towards *tawḥīd*. This begins at the level of the *Sharīʿah*, the Divine Law, with which I will not deal here in detail, but I just want to add the following by way of a parenthesis.

There are too many imponderables in the world of chaotic multiplicity in which we live for our unaided intelligence to impose order and integration upon the chaos of this world; especially this modern world, which is itself the result of man seeking to live as if he no longer had any need of God's laws. The chaotic nature of this age is mentioned not only in traditional Islamic sources, but also in the classical texts of Hinduism concerning the Kali Yuga in which we live. This is an age in which many flaunt the Divine Law, the Hindu *dharma*, something that would have been unimaginable in days of old. The situation is not the same today as when classical Sufi authors invited men to journey beyond the outward teachings of the *Sharīʿah*—which were taken for granted—to the Divine Truth. There are of course some pseudo-Sufis today who make the call to cast aside the *Sharīʿah* in order to reach the Divine, while misusing some of the sayings of certain Sufis of old. These days it is much easier to cast away the *Sharīʿah* than before without, however, reaching the Divine at all, in fact falling below forms rather than transcending them. Contrary to what many pseudo-Sufis claim, by abandoning the *Sharīʿah*, one is in danger of falling easily into the bottom of the well rather than being able to reach the Empyrean. The reason the books of certain so-called Sufi teachers sell well in the West is that they claim that one can disregard and flaunt the

Sharīʿah, and yet reach the *Ḥaqīqah*; that one does not need to do the hard work that serious spiritual effort requires. They claim that it is enough just to read the poetry of Rūmī and so forth in order to achieve integration. But that is not possible, least of all in the chaotic, modern world in which we live, where the need for the order given by God's laws is greater than ever before. Seeking inner integration seriously can only bear fruit if it is based on following God's laws on the outward plane, whichever religious universe one happens to be living in.

As for Islam specifically, to achieve inner integration requires that one must first of all accept and practice the *Sharīʿah* as the norm which integrates our everyday life and provides a cadre that prevents the soul from falling into various pitfalls. By disciplining the soul horizontally, divine laws prepare the soul to journey vertically, and there is no possibility of the vertical journey without certain boundaries and limitations on the horizontal plane. He who seeks to achieve freedom merely horizontally will never achieve true freedom. The history of the modern and post-modern worlds has demonstrated that truth sufficiently.

At the first stage in integration, it is on the basis of accepting and practicing the *Sharīʿah* that the teachings of Sufism become operative. Now, according to the *Sharīʿah* in its ordinary understanding, God judges us by the actions that we perform. If one has the intention of murdering someone, but does not do so, then that person is not punished by the Law. Sufism starts from this basic, external position, but then takes a further step internally. It is interested most of all in our *niyyah*, our intention, in performing an act. According to a *ḥadīth* of the Prophet, "Actions (*al-aʿmāl*) are judged [by God] according to our inner intentions (*niyyāt*)." It is essential to follow the *Sharīʿah*, but more than that, one must seek to integrate the soul and purify intentions through the inner practices and methods of the *Ṭarīqah*.

It is even more difficult to integrate the soul than the body, much of whose organic and integrating functions are beyond our control. How many of us are healthy physically but are psychologically dispersed; often the body is doing a much better job of integration than our psyche. One of the maladies of modern human beings is to live in a state of scatteredness and dispersion, rather than being integrated within the psyche while at least temporarily being physically healthy, even though the health of the body and the psyche are interrelated and the two react often upon each other in many ways. Sufism enters into human life to heal the psyche and make it whole; which means to integrate it. But even this laudable goal is not the ultimate end. The final goal of Sufism is not the health of the psyche of the adept (as with modern psychiatry or psychology, which is really a parody of traditional psychology), and spiritual teachings like Sufism are not there to provide us with only physical health. The end of Sufism is *tawḥīd,* that is, union or unity, and preparation of the soul for proximity to God, who is One.

Sufism turns to the higher levels of the human microcosm without neglecting the outward physical domain. It tries to integrate the psyche both within itself and through its wedding to the spirit, and in a sense also includes the body in this process of integration. But how does it go about achieving this process of integration? First of all, it always emphasizes the effect that the body has upon the psyche and vice versa. Sufism never deals with the psyche as an abstraction, as a dismembered mind floating in the air. Every aspect of the action of the body is of some importance. One's postures, the way one sits and walks, the traditional courtesy or comportment (*adab*, which again is a very difficult word to translate)—all of these elements play a role in the life of the soul as well as the body. Does the body play a role in the final integration of the human state? The answer is yes, for one cannot just be indifferent to the body. Not only actions, which are to be governed by the Divine Law, but also the way people dress, the way they display certain gestures, the way they act with the body, all have an effect on the soul. This cause and effect is to be found in spiritual climes everywhere, as can be seen in the traditional teachings of Hindu and Buddhist spirituality, as in other religions.

The body, however, has a dual purpose in the spiritual life. Sometimes it has a negative role to play and becomes an impediment to the integration of the soul, and sometimes it has a positive role. There are all kinds of possibilities in Sufism's training of the soul, which aims at integrating the soul into its center, whilst not divorcing it from the body. As Rūmī says, the body is the horse, the steed on which we ride in this life. And there is a profound relationship between the nature of the steed and the ultimate goal toward which body and soul together transport us. The body also has a positive role in this journey. But at the moment of death, we have to leave the steed behind. There are, therefore, certain spiritual exercises and practices in this life which lead to spiritual death and the soul distancing itself from the physical body, while refining and strengthening the subtle body, which accompanies the soul after physical death.

In addition to doctrine, Sufism is based on the practice of certain forms of prayer, accompanied on the higher levels with meditation, as well as the cultivation of virtues, which lie at the very heart of the effort towards integration. Putting doctrine aside, which is actually a metaphysical elaboration of the supreme formula of unity in Islam, that is, *lā ilāha illa'Llāh* (There is no divinity but God), I want to mention the last two elements briefly. First of all prayer. All devout Muslims pray five times a day. That is in itself a miraculous occurrence, to have so many hundreds of millions of people systematically breaking their daily routine of life—we call it life but it is really daydreaming—five times a day to stand before the Absolute, before the One. Those canonical prayers are the foundation of all other forms of prayer. But the soul can fall into forgetfulness, even if it turns five times a day to God. So the Sufis try to expand the experience of prayer to what can be called, in its highest form, the prayer of the heart, whose practice, ideally, is to fill all times of the day and even the night when one is asleep, in perpetual prayer. The final goal, however, is not only to pray at all moments, but to become prayer. The very substance of the soul must become prayer. It must become totally identified with prayer. That is why the Quran mentions so often the word *dhikr Allāh*, *dhikr* meaning remembrance and also invocation or quintessential prayer. To become fully integrated, one must remember God at the center of one's heart, where God Himself resides, where He is always present, even if we forget because we no longer live at our own center and are absent from our deeper self. It is we who have forgotten God because we have forgotten the center of our own being, having become scattered at the periphery of the circle of existence. I always like to recall a passage from Rūmī's *Mathnawī* where, referring to perfect prayer, which embraces all levels of one's being, even the most outward, he says (in paraphrase): "Go sit cross-legged in a corner, take a rosary into your hand and invoke the Name of God; say '*Allāh, Allāh*' until your very toe is invoking God's Name, for it is not sufficient that your tongue invoke it."

In Sufism prayer is essentially the remembrance of God, and the remembrance of God is quintessential and supreme prayer. It is impossible to pray without remembering God, and it is impossible to remember God without praying in one way or another. Sufism, like yoga, has extraordinary methods and spiritual techniques for making possible the penetration of prayer into all levels of human existence, from the physical body (of which I have just given an example) and the tongue (which is part of our body), to the air that comes out of our lungs, which represents the more subtle state of manifestation (like the Sanskrit *prana*), to the mind, and finally to the heart. The final goal of Sufism in prayer is that every time the heart beats it should repeat the Name of God. Every time we breathe we should invoke God. We take our breathing so much for granted, but every time we breathe in, we do not know if that breath will come out.

We never know which breath will be our last, therefore we must always be mindful of the preciousness of every moment of life (what Buddhism calls "right mindfulness"). Every breath we inhale should be identified with the remembrance of God, and every breath that we exhale should likewise be identified with the remembrance of Him. In the present cyclic condition, there is no greater and more efficacious means to integrate man than prayer, which ultimately penetrates into the whole of one's being and unifies the human state.

To individual practices that actualize the integration of the soul are added communal practices; invocation by groups, combined (sometimes) with beautiful music and poetry. All these elements help the soul to pay attention to its center and to become integrated. All these different means are used, because the fallen soul loves to do anything except pay attention to the "one thing necessary," to remember its own Origin and End. That is what makes continuous prayer with concentration difficult and also makes a second element, that is, meditation, necessary.

We are not only soul and body, but also spirit. As for the soul, there is a part of it which is like a mirror that reflects the intellect, but it is not the intellect itself. The intellect is not simply reason in the modern sense of this English word. According to a *ḥadīth*, *Awwalu mā khalaqa'Llāhu al-ʿaql* and also *Awwalu mā khalaqa'Llāhu al-rūḥ*, that is, "The first thing that God created was the Intellect" and "The first thing God created was the Spirit." These sayings refer ultimately to the same reality. Intellect resides at the center of our heart (*qalb*) at a point that is transcendent with respect to what is called the individual subject. It is reflected upon the mirror of the soul, what in modern thought is called the mind. It is interesting to note that, in French, the word for spirit and mind is the same, *l'esprit*. In German also the word *Geist* means both. In English we are in one sense fortunate in that we can make a distinction between spirit and mind, but this situation also makes it possible to forget the relation between the two. In any case we are not just minds, but we possess a mind which, as usually understood, refers to that part of our inner being where concepts are present, in which ideas arise, often in a manner that is beyond our control, and where the process of rational thinking takes place.

We also have another faculty in our soul which does not deal with concepts and ideas, but with forms and images. This faculty is the imagination, which can have both a negative and a positive function. The late Henry Corbin, basing himself mostly on major philosophical and mystical teachings of the great Andalusian Sufi Ibn ʿArabī and other Islamic masters such as Suhrawardī and Mullā Ṣadrā, has made the ontological status and spiritual and artistic significance of imagination known again to the modern West. What he calls the *mundus imaginalis*, the imaginal world, embraces the total imaginative function in all its positive and negative aspects. But we are not the masters of that world, any more than we are masters of concepts that flow into our mind this very minute. All of you sitting here are trying hard to follow what I am saying. My humble words may be of interest to you, but even so it is easy for your concentration to go astray after a few moments, so that you have to bring your mind back again and again to concentrate in order to follow what I am saying. It is extremely difficult to control the ever-flowing forms that the imagination creates, and the concepts and ideas that come into the mind. Again, to quote Rūmī, "You think you are the master of your mind but it is your mind that is the master of you, not you of it." So we have this very difficult problem of how to concentrate. All of these techniques you have heard about in Yoga, Zen, and Taoist practices, as well as the spiritual techniques of Sufism and Christianity especially as found in the great Hesychastic tradition, which is still alive on Mount Athos and elsewhere in the Orthodox world, are there to enable the disciple to concentrate.

Sufism, too, has very elaborate methods of meditation to make possible concentration, which must accompany inner prayer if that prayer is to become efficacious in being able to integrate our being. But in contrast to certain other traditions, such as Hinduism and Buddhism, little has been written in Sufism about this subject, its teachings having been passed down mostly through oral tradition, with each Sufi order having its own types of meditation. The goal of these various forms of meditation is, however, always the same. It is to control and integrate both aspects of the soul; what we call the mind, concerned with concepts and ideas, and what is known as imagination, dealing with forms and images. The methods of meditation within Sufism are too diverse for me to deal with here, but it is essential to remember their role in the integration of our inner being. Meditation (*fikr*) grows from and accompanies invocation (*dhikr*) and finally is reintegrated with it.

Then there is the question of embellishing the soul with virtues. The cultivation of virtues is so central that the early books of Sufism seem to be for the most part no more than books on virtue. Many people in the West who have fled from a kind of unintelligible moralism are put off by works that deal with virtue. They are attracted more to works on Oriental teachings that speak primarily about metaphysical and cosmological matters. But it is not possible to realize metaphysical truths without the possession of virtues. Truth belongs to God; it does not belong to us. What we have to ask is the question of how we can participate in the Truth. We can do so only by attaining virtue, although according to Sufism, virtues also come ultimately from God and belong to Him and it is He who has made it possible for us to attain them through the channel of His messengers and prophets. In the Islamic universe the virtues were embodied in the most palpable way in the character of the Prophet of Islam. For a Christian, all virtues belong to Christ and there is no virtue that a Christian can possess which was not possessed by Christ. It would be absurd and blasphemous to claim otherwise. Such is also the case in Islam. There is no virtue that any Muslim has possessed or will possess, anywhere from the southern Philippines to the Canary Islands, that was not possessed by the Prophet. This might seem astounding to many of you, because of the negative image of the Prophet that has been presented in the West via inaccurate biographies. The lack of an authentic account of the life of the Prophet in English was finally corrected by the wonderful biography of him by Dr. Martin Lings, my dear friend, published in England some years ago. Yet even now the inner, esoteric virtues of the Prophet are not well known to Western audiences. There is still a need for an "esoteric" biography of the Prophet in Western languages, such as exists in Arabic and Persian poetry, like the famous *Burdah* song of al-Būṣīrī in Arabic and its equivalents in Persian, Turkish, and other Islamic languages.

Now, how do we cultivate these inner, spiritual virtues and be successful in emulating the Prophet? That is a very difficult task indeed. It is easy to talk about virtues, but very difficult to attain them and cultivate them. God can give certain people the intelligence to understand doctrinally, that is, metaphysically. Such an understanding is already a gift from Heaven; it is a sacred science. But between the mental knowledge of metaphysics and its actualization in our being there is a great distance. I always compare the situation to seeing a mountain and climbing that mountain. If you come to the foot of the Himalayas, you can see the beautiful mountains before you. If, by the grace of God, you behold their majesty, that is a great gift and blessing. But how much more difficult it is to climb the mountains and to reach their exalted peaks. That is the difference between the mental understanding of doctrine, including the doctrine pertaining to virtue, and the realization of metaphysical truth, which means also the realization of the virtues with our whole being.

This third important element of Sufism is the one that makes possible the realization of Sufi doctrine and renders our prayers and meditations completely efficacious so as to transform the chaos of the soul into order and bring about unity within it, or, in other words, to integrate it. Once that is achieved, then the spirit (which is the only part of our being which is already integrated, being God's viceroy in us, as well as being identified with the heart/intellect) becomes wed to our soul, and the chaotic life of the soul becomes transmuted into that gold in which all the elements are integrated in perfect harmony. Inner integration enables that viceroy, the inner king, to rule within us, so that all of the chaos of the psyche and the various functions of the body, which we usually identify falsely as ourselves, become integrated into a center which is at once their center while itself belonging to a higher level of reality. Through the rule of this inner king each part of the soul is put into its proper place and made to function according to its proper nature, with the result that harmony and integration become established in the inner kingdom, and then by extension to the outer world.

8. The Throne of the All-Merciful

The heart is the center of the human microcosm, at once the center of the physical body, the vital energies, the emotions, and the soul, as well as the meeting place between the human and the celestial realms where the spirit resides. How remarkable is this reality of the heart, that mysterious center which from the point of view of our earthly existence seems so small, and yet as the Prophet has said, it is the Throne (*al-ʿarsh*) of God the All-Merciful (*al-Raḥmān*), the Throne that encompasses the whole universe. Or, as he uttered in a saying quoting God, "My Heaven containeth Me not, nor My Earth, but the heart of My faithful servant doth contain Me." . . .

There is a vast literature in Islam dealing with the heart and its intellectual and spiritual significance. Already in the Quran there are over one hundred thirty references to the heart (*qalb*; pl. *qulūb*), and numerous traditions of the Prophet (*aḥādīth*) also refer to this central subject. Likewise there is hardly a Sufi treatise that does not refer to the heart and what Sufis call "matters pertaining to the heart" (*al-umūr al-qalbiyyah*). One often finds titles of Islamic metaphysical and spiritual writings containing the term "heart," such as *Qūt al-qulūb* ("Nourishment for Hearts"), *Shifāʾ al-qulūb* ("Healing of Hearts"), and *Nūr al-fuʾād* ("Light of the Heart"). Moreover, there is not one but a series of terms referring to the heart on various levels of its reality, including, besides *qalb*, the terms *fuʾād*, *sirr*, and *lubb*, not to mention the Persian term *dil*.

To delineate the Islamic understanding of the heart on both a metaphysical and an operative level, it is best to start with the basic term in Arabic for heart, namely *qalb*. The root meaning of this term means change and transformation. The term *inqilāb*, which is used in modern Persian as a translation for the European concept of revolution, meant originally a change of state. One of the Names of God is in fact *Muqallib al-qulūb*, that is, the Transformer of Hearts, and Ibn ʿArabī uses the term *taqallub*, derived from the same root as *qalb*, to mean the constant transformative power inherent in the heart, a power which brings about integration in a dynamic mode. The root *QLB* also means to turn upside down. The heart on its corporeal level is in a sense suspended upside down, its traditional symbol being an inverted triangle. It has also the root meaning of mold (the Arabic word for mold being *qālab*), that is, what holds together the inner reality of man. There is here also an inversion of the "positive" and "negative" elements since the heart is moreover the isthmus (*barzakh*) and the principle of the microcosmic domain. The mutation of the root *QLB*, often carried out in the traditional Islamic science of *jafr*, gives *QBL*, which is the root of the word *qiblah*, or point to which one orients oneself during the daily canonical prayers, the *qiblah* (which is related in its root meaning to Kabbala) being the direction pointing to where the *Kaʿbah*, the House of God, is located. Esoterically the heart is the *Kaʿbah*, where the All-Merciful (*al-Raḥmān*) resides. That is why Rūmī, in reference to this inner identification between the *qalb* and the *Kaʿbah*, hence the *qiblah*, which is also the supreme goal of pilgrimage to Mecca, sings:

> O People who have gone to pilgrimage,
> where are you, where are you?
> The Beloved is here,
> come here, come here![1]

The expression "the *Kaʿbah* of the heart"—*Kaʿba-yi dil* in Persian—is very commonly used in Sufi literature. The root *QBL* also possesses the meaning of acceptance and receptivity, which are basic characteristics of the heart. The *qalb* is receiving evermore the theophanies which reach it from above and within, and it possesses not only the power of transformation or *taqallub*, but also receptivity, that is *qabūl* or *qābil*. It is to this reality that Ibn ʿArabī refers in his famous poem *Tarjumān al-ashwāq* ("The Interpreter of Desires") when he says, "My heart can take on any form" (*laqad ṣāra qalbī qābilan li kulli ṣūratin*), using the terms *qalb* and *qābil* in the verse.

The Quran, like other sacred scriptures, associates knowledge and understanding with the heart, and the blindness of the heart with loss of understanding, as for example when God, after complaining of man's not learning the appropriate lessons from earlier sacred history, asserts, "For indeed it is not the eyes that grow blind, but it is the hearts, which are within the bosoms, that grow blind" (22:46). This blindness of the heart so characteristic of fallen man is also described by the Quran as a hardening of the heart. "But their hearts were hardened, and the devil made all that they used to do seem fair unto them!" (6:43). Also, "Woe unto those whose hearts are hardened against remembrance of Allah. Such are in plain error" (39:22). Furthermore, the Quran identifies this hardening of the heart with

[1] *Kulliyyāt-i Shams*, ed. B. Forūzānfar, vol. 2 (Tehran: Sipihr Press, 1984), *ghazal* 648, p. 65.

a veil that God has cast over the heart of those who have turned away from the truth. "We have placed upon their hearts veils, lest they should understand, and in their ears a deafness" (6:25); also, "And We place upon their hearts veils lest they should understand it, and in their ears a deafness" (17:46).

The heart can, however, be softened and the veil removed with the help of God Himself, who has knowledge of our hearts, for "Allah knoweth what is in your hearts" (33:51), and "He knew what was in their [the believers'] hearts" (48:18). This melting or softening of the hardened heart can be achieved only with God's help through what He has revealed in His sacred scriptures and the grace that emanates from revelation. "Allah hath (now) revealed the fairest of statements, a Scripture consistent . . . so that their flesh and their hearts soften to Allah's reminder" (39:23). God wants man's heart to be at peace and rest, and although from one point of view God as *al-Raḥmān* resides in the heart of the faithful, from another point of view He comes between man and his heart. "Allah cometh in between the man and his own heart" (8:24), and it is only with the help of God that fallen man can gain access to his own heart. It is in this context that the famous Sufi description of the spiritual path as *takhliyah* (emptying), *taḥliyah* (embellishing), and *tajliyah* (receiving theophanies of and in the heart) must be understood.

Once one turns to God for help, He provides man with the possibility of having tranquility and peace in his heart. "Allah appointed it only as good tidings, and that your hearts thereby might be at rest" (8:10); also, "Verily in the remembrance (*al-dhikr*) of Allah do hearts find rest!" (13:28), a verse which relates peace and rest in the heart directly to *al-dhikr* or quintessential prayer, this verse serving as the scriptural basis for invocation in its relation to the heart. When God softens the heart and removes its veils, the heart becomes worthy of being the receptacle of the Divine Peace or *al-sakīnah* (*shekhinah* in Hebrew), for as the Quran says, "He it is who sends down peace of reassurance (*al-sakīnah*) into the hearts of believers" (48:4).

On the basis of these Quranic teachings and the prophetic *Sunnah* and *aḥādīth*, which serve as the first and most authoritative commentaries upon the word of God, Islamic sages developed an elaborate doctrine, at once metaphysical, cosmological, and anthropological—in the traditional sense of these terms—concerning the heart. They also continued and elaborated operative methods received from the Prophet and his earliest inheritors involving various modes of prayer and the means of reaching and penetrating the heart.

The answer to the question, "What is the heart?," is almost inexhaustible, but at least some of the major features of it can be mentioned here. The heart is first of all the center of our being on all the different levels of our existence, not only the corporeal and emotive, but also the intellectual and spiritual. It is what connects the individual to the supra-individual realms of being. In fact, if in modern society heart-knowledge is rejected, it is because modernism refuses to see man beyond his individual level of existence. The heart is not a center of our being; it is the supreme center, its uniqueness resulting from the metaphysical principle that for any specific realm of manifestation there must exist a principle of unity.

The heart is the *barzakh* or isthmus between this world and the next, between the visible and invisible worlds, between the human realm and the realm of the Spirit, between the horizontal and vertical dimensions of existence. In the same way that the vertical and horizontal lines of the cross, itself the symbol not only of Christ in Christianity but also of the Universal Man (*al-insān al-kāmil*) in Islam, meet at only one point, there can be only one heart for each human being, although this single reality partakes of gradations and levels of being. The heart, then, is our unique center, the place where the supreme axis penetrates our microcosmic existence, the place where the All-Merciful resides, and also the locus for the Breath of God. Hence the profound relation that exists between invocatory prayer carried out with the breath and the heart.

The heart is also a mirror, which must be polished by invocation (*al-dhikr*), according to the well known *ḥadīth*: "For everything there is a polish. The polish for the heart is invocation." Once this act of polishing has been carried out, the heart becomes the locus for the direct manifestations of God's Names and Qualities. The heart in fact is the locus *par excellence* for the theophanies (*tajalliyyāt*) which descend one after another upon it. This constant change in reflection of ever new Divine manifestations is related to the root meaning of *qalb*, to which allusion has already been made.

It might of course be asked, if the nature of the *qalb* is to be in constant transformation, what is permanent in the heart and how can the heart be at peace and rest? The answer lies in the quality itself of being a mirror. What is permanent is our nothingness (*al-fanāʾ*) before God; one is to become a perfect mirror which, in being nothing in itself, is able to reflect forms emanating from above. The peace of the heart is precisely our total surrender to God, not only on the level of the will, but also on the level of existence. To become "nothing" before God is to be at once "nothing" and "everything"—nothing as the surface of a mirror, and everything in reflecting the never-ending theophanies issuing from the Hidden Treasure of God, which according to the Quran is inexhaustible.

Once the heart has been softened and polished, it may be described not only as a mirror but also as an eye which has opened and which can now see the Invisible Realm, just as the physical eyes are able to see the external world. The symbol of the "eye of the heart" (*ʿayn al-qalb* in Arabic or *chashm-i dil* in Persian) is not confined to Islam but is universal, as we see in Plato's expression "eye of soul," St Augustine's *oculus cordis*, or the "third eye" of Hindu and Buddhist doctrines. But it is especially emphasized in Sufism. The reason that the symbol of vision is used rather than one of the other senses is that vision has an objective character and therefore better symbolizes the function of the heart-intellect. Nevertheless, the heart also has other inner faculties. With the ear of the heart man can hear the silent music of which Plato spoke, and with the olfactory faculty of the heart man can smell the perfumes of Paradise. But it is the "eye of the heart" that is of central importance. The eye of the heart, which is none other than the immanent intellect, is the faculty with which we are able to see the Invisible World and ultimately God, but it is also the eye with which God sees us. When we are *cordial* with God, then God is *cordial* with us, although principially the relation is reversed. Only when God loves us can we love God. The heart also has a face turned toward each world (*wajh al-qalb*), and the face that it turns to God is none other than the Face that God turns to man. That is why to seek to "efface" the Divine Reality from man's consciousness, as modern agnosticism and secularism attempt to do, leads ultimately to the "effacing" of man himself and his reduction to the subhuman.

In the depths of the heart resides *al-fuʾād* or the heart-center, in which two eyes, one meant to see God and the other the world, are unified. In contrast to the external eyes, which are also two in number and see multiplicity, the inner eye of the heart is essentially one, but is able to perceive both worlds. It therefore has the integrating power of unifying multiplicity in unity. When the eye of the heart has opened, man is able not only to see the One, but also to contemplate the One in the many and the many in the One, thereby achieving unity or *tawḥīd* in its highest sense.

Lest one forget the importance of the heart for faith and Divine Love, it must also be mentioned that first of all, according to the Quran and *aḥādīth*, real faith (*al-īmān*) is associated with the heart, and not with the mind or the tongue alone. To really believe we must believe in and with our heart where faith resides. Secondly, the heart is not only the seat of human love but also of Divine Love. The fire of love burns in the heart, and it is there that one is to find the Beloved. The heart of the saint is the source of a light resulting from his inner illumination and of a warmth issuing from the fire of the love of God. Knowledge and love at this level are united in a single reality, like the light and heat of a fire, the locus of this sacred fire being the heart.

Although the heart is a single reality, it partakes of many levels, as do the knowledge and love of God. Many Sufi masters, such as Rūmī, ʿAṭṭār, and al-Nūrī, have referred to the seven levels of the heart, for which various technical terms are used. Al-Ḥakīm al-Tirmidhī goes a step further to identify these levels with concentric castles of the soul, each with its own covering that defends the innermost heart and provides inner protection for the interior fortified castles, which can be penetrated only after great spiritual effort. As has been shown, this schema is very similar to that of St. Teresa of Ávila in her description of her interior castles, and we find the idea of concentric hearts made of fortified dwellings protected by walls in both Sufi and Christian sources.[2] These correspondences reveal both historical influences and morphological resemblance. But above all they point to the universal teachings of the *philosophia perennis* concerning the heart and the levels of its existence corresponding to the levels of microcosmic reality.

Returning to the word *qalb*, it is possible to point to another aspect of the reality of the heart by analyzing an Arabic term closely related to *qalb*, namely *qalīb*, which means a well. The heart is a well from which gushes forth the fountain of life and also of the knowledge and love which save. In Islam water is the most direct symbol of God's Mercy and Compassion. It might be said that since the All-Merciful resides in the heart of the faithful, once the veil of the heart is lifted, the water from the well of the heart gushes forth in correspondence to the outward flow of the Divine Compassion and Mercy, one of the most direct symbols of which in this world is water. That is why in the language of *ḥadīth* the heart is sometimes referred to as *yanbūʿ al-ḥikmah*, that is, "the source [or spring] of wisdom." According to a very famous *ḥadīth*, which is found in many versions and which is foundational to the operative aspect of Sufism, "When someone purifies himself for God for forty days, God makes the spring of wisdom

[2] Luce López-Baralt, *San Juan de la Cruz y el Islam* (Madrid: Hipérion, 1985); and "Saint John of the Cross and Ibn ʿArabi," *Journal of the Muhyiddin Ibn ʿArabi Society*, vol. 28 (2000), pp. 57-90.

(*al-ḥikmah*) to gush forth from his heart to his tongue." This *ḥadīth* also links spiritual practice directly to the means of access to the heart and indicates the way to remove the rust or crust from the heart so as to allow what one could call the water of wisdom to flow from the heart to the tongue.

If the heart is the reality described here, then all one would need to do in order to have spiritual realization would be to penetrate into the heart. The problem is that for the human being marked by the fall, the heart is no longer easily accessible, even though it remains the center of our being. For the men of the Golden Age or in the Edenic state, those who lived in the primordial condition (*al-fiṭrah*), the heart was directly accessible. They lived in the heart, that is, with God and in God. But through a series of falls the heart has become ever more inaccessible, covered by a hardened shell, which symbolizes powerful psychological forces. Long before modern times the heart had already become a crypt and a cave, to be found only with heroic effort and only after an arduous struggle to gain "knowledge of the mysteries" which reside in that cave. The symbolism of the heart as a cave hidden within the breast of man is in fact universal. In the context of Islam, the Prophet taking refuge with Abū Bakr in a cave on their way from Mecca to Medina, in that journey which is called the *hijrah* or migration, is understood by Sufis not only to signify an external historical event but also to point to the trans-historical and meta-individual reality of the heart where the Friend resides. It is in direct allusion to this truth that Rūmī sings in one of his *ghazals*:

> Consider this breast as the cave,
> the spiritual retreat of the Friend.
> If thou art the companion of the cave,
> enter the cave, enter the cave.[3]

But how does one enter the cave made inaccessible to fallen man? The answer resides in the reality of the All-Merciful (*al-Raḥmān*), whose Throne is the heart. Through His Qualities of Compassion and Mercy, God has sent revelations which provide the means of access to the heart. To accept a revelation means first of all to possess faith (*al-īmān*), which resides in the heart. Faith is the necessary element for participation in the revelation and the essential condition for the efficacy of the means provided by it to save man and to open the door to the inner kingdom. But in order to penetrate

[3] *Kulliyyāt-i Shams*, vol. 5, *ghazal* 2133, p. 12.

into the heart as the center of our being, we must also undertake the spiritual practices sanctioned and made efficacious by tradition. At the heart of those practices, as far as Islam is concerned, stands quintessential prayer or invocation (*al-dhikr*), which is ultimately the prayer of the heart. Invocation, sanctified by God Himself and combined with the meditation (*al-fikr*) needed to concentrate the mind and overcome its dispersing effects, is like an arrow which directly penetrates the heart. On a more operative level one could say that the soul of the invoker (*al-dhākir*), enwrapped as it is in the *dhikr*, is itself the arrow released by the hands of the master archer or the spiritual teacher toward the target of the heart. As for the energy or force which allows the arrow to travel toward the target and finally to penetrate it, it is the initiatic power (*al-walāyah* or *al-wilāyah* in Islam) without which the arrow would not be able to travel. That is why the practice of spiritual techniques made available by revelation is invalid unless they are carried out in the matrix of an orthodox religion and through the regularity of spiritual and initiatic transmission and guidance. Without orthodoxy and tradition, no one can overcome the obstacles which at once hide the heart and protect it from demonic forces, for there would be no force to propel the arrow toward its target.

The practice of spiritual techniques, made available to those who are qualified according to criteria established by the tradition, requires ample preparation of both a doctrinal and a practical nature. More specifically it requires the attainment of spiritual virtues, without which man has no right to penetrate the heart-center, and this attainment implies not only thinking about the virtues and speaking about them, but above all *being* the virtues, for the virtues, which ultimately belong to God, are the manner in which we participate existentially in the Sacred. The question of whether the spiritual practices make us virtuous or whether the virtues are necessary for a spiritual practice is a complicated matter with which we cannot deal here. As far as the heart is concerned, suffice it to say that to enter the heart as the spiritual center of our being, which is pure, one must oneself be pure and worthy of the sacred abode into which one is entering.

One might object that the heart of man is not always pure, as mentioned in so many sacred scriptures. The use of the term "heart" in the ordinary sense certainly warrants such an observation, but this ordinary understanding of the heart, which is available to us all, is not the same as the meaning of the heart in its purely spiritual sense, where the All-Merciful is to be found. Nevertheless the two are not totally unrelated. That is why the Prophet calls *dhikr* the "polish of the heart," meaning of course the heart which is covered by rust and not that inner heart or Throne which, having never been rusty, does not need to be polished. In any case, as far as the spiritual life is concerned, it is essential not only to polish or purify the heart, but also to keep it pure, to protect it (*ḥifẓ al-qalb*) from all defilement.

In Sufism, where the heart is compared to the Kaʿbah, it has been said that the heart of fallen man is like the Kaʿbah before the coming of Islam, when it was full of idols. When the Prophet entered Mecca triumphantly, he first went to the Kaʿbah and asked ʿAlī ibn Abī Ṭālib and Bilāl al-Ḥabashī to break all the idols therein and to purify the House of God built by Adam and rebuilt by Abraham to honor the one God. Through initiation and spiritual practice, the person who aspires to reach God must break all the idols in his heart and sweep away everything in it so that God alone can be present therein. God is one and therefore does not manifest His Presence where there are idols. Alas, the heart of how many of even believers is like the *Kaʿbah* during the Age of Ignorance (*al-jāhiliyyah*), full of all kinds of idols. Those who seek to follow the spiritual path in Sufism are taught at the time of initiation, when first embarking upon the path, that they must reserve their heart for God alone, for He alone is the master of the house of the heart. As the Arabic poem says, in response to someone knocking on the door of a Sufi's heart:

> There is no one in the house except the Master of the House.
> (*Laysa fi'l-dār ghayruhu'l-dayyār*)

The inner heart of man is itself the supreme Name of God (*al-ism al-aʿẓam*) by virtue of the mystery of the creation of man as a being at whose center resides the All-Merciful. That is why it is said in Islam that the saints are themselves the Names of God, men and women whose hearts are the theater of all of God's Names and Qualities. The invocation is the sacred means for the realization and actualization of this truth. The human microcosm is created in such a way that it can transform sound into light in the sense that the invocation performed by the tongue becomes ultimately transformed into light in the heart. Human speech in the form of prayer becomes the vision of the eye of the heart. He who invokes with sincerity, persistence, fervor, and total faith in God becomes the possessor of an illuminated heart. Thanks to the *dhikr*, he is able to break away the crust that veils the light of the inner heart, which is luminous by its own nature. Once this Inner Light is unveiled, it shines forth throughout the whole being of man, since the heart is the center of our being.

Ultimately the *dhikr* is itself the heart spiritually understood. Invocation as practiced in Sufism is at the highest level the prayer of the heart and by the heart. The spiritual itinerary of the Sufi is to penetrate the heart with help of the *dhikr* and finally to realize the identity of the two. It is not only to pray but to become prayer, to live at the heart-center, and to experience and to know all things from that center.

To know from the center is also to be able to go beyond the world of forms to the formless, for the heart is not only the center but also the abode of spiritual meaning (*maʿnā* in the terminology of Rūmī), which transcends external form (*ṣūrat*). The person who has reached the heart in its spiritual sense is also able to see the heart of things, especially sacred forms, and to realize their inner unity. He is able to attest to what Frithjof Schuon, who spoke so eloquently from the heart-center, has called the "transcendent unity of religions," which—from the point of view of the heart—could also be called the "immanent unity of religions," but an immanence which is also transcendent. Sufis have often spoken of the religion of the heart, which Schuon calls the *religio cordis*. Far from being a separate religion, the religion of the heart is that essential and supraformal reality which lies at the heart of all orthodox religions and which can be reached only through the orthodox and traditional religions. It was to this *religio cordis* that Rūmī referred in the following lines:

> The creed of love is separate from all religions;
> The creed and the religion of the lovers of God is God himself.[4]

Furthermore, being open to the reception of theophanies and residing at the same time on the level of the formless, the heart once cleansed becomes the theater for the manifestation of different sacred forms, and the gnostic is able to discern, through his heart-knowledge, the inner unity of religions, while at the same time being aware of their outward differences and the inviolability of their sacred forms. The famous poem of Ibn ʿArabī, to which allusion was made above, recapitulates these truths in verses of haunting beauty:

> Wonder,
> A garden among the flames!

[4] *Mathnawī*, ed. R. Nicholson (London: Luzac, 1925-40), Book 2, verse 1770.

My heart can take on any form:
A meadow for gazelles,
A cloister for monks,
For the idols, sacred ground,
Kaʿbah for the circling pilgrim,
The tables of Torah,
The scrolls of the Quran.

My creed is love;
Wherever its caravan turns along the way,
That is my belief,
My faith.[5]

Through quintessential prayer, within the framework of an orthodox tradition, one reaches the inner heart, where God as the All-Merciful resides, and by penetration into the heart-center, man moves beyond the realm of outwardness and the domain of individual existence to reach the abode of inwardness and the universal order. In that state his heart becomes the eye with which he sees God and also the eye with which God sees him. In that presence he is nothing in himself, as separate existence. He is but a mirror whose surface is nothing, and yet reflects everything. In the heart, the spiritual man lives in intimacy with God, with the Origin of all those theophanies whose outward manifestations constitute all the beauty that is reflected in the world around us. He lives in that inner garden, that inner paradise, constantly aware of the ubiquitous Gardener. On the highest level of realization, man becomes aware that all theophanies are nothing but the Source of those theophanies, that the house itself is nothing but the reflection of the Master of the house, that there is in fact but one Reality which, through its infinite manifestations and reflections upon the mirrors of cosmic existence, has brought about all that appears to us as multiplicity and otherness, and all the apparent distinctions between I and thou, he and they, we and you. At the center of the heart, there resides but one Reality above and beyond all forms. It was to this Reality, far beyond all individual manifestations, that Manṣūr al-Ḥallāj was referring when he sang:

I saw my Lord with the eyes of my heart;
I asked Him, Who art Thou? He said, Thou.[6]

[5] Michael Sells, *Mystical Languages of Unsaying* (Chicago: University of Chicago Press, 1994), p. 90.

[6] *Le Dīwān d'al-Hallāj*, ed. L. Massignon (Paris: Paul Geuthner, 1955), p. 46.

Happy is the man who can open the eyes of his heart with the aid of Heaven before his earthly eyes become shut at the moment of death, and who is able to see the countenance of the Beloved while still possessing the precious gift of human life.

9. The Role of Philosophy

In discussing the meaning and role of philosophy in Islam we must turn before everything else to the exact meaning of the term "philosophy" and also to the structure of Islam in its essence and historical deployment. Islam is hierarchic in its essential structure and also in the way it has manifested itself in history. The Islamic revelation possesses within itself several dimensions and has been manifested to mankind on the basic levels of *al-islām*, *al-īmān*, and *al-iḥsān* and from another perspective as *Sharīʿah*, *Ṭarīqah*, and *Ḥaqīqah*. When we speak of the role of philosophy in Islam we must first of all ask which aspect of Islam we are dealing with. In any case we must avoid the mistake made only too often by many Orientalists during the past century of identifying Islam with only the *Sharīʿah* or *kalām* and then studying the relationship of "philosophy" or metaphysics with that particular dimension of Islam. Rather, in order to understand the real role of "philosophy" in Islam we must consider Islam in all its amplitude and depth, including especially the dimension of *al-Ḥaqīqah*, where precisely one will find the point of intersection between "traditional philosophy" and metaphysics and that aspect of the Islamic perspective into which *sapientia* in all its forms has been integrated throughout Islamic history. Likewise, the whole of Islamic civilization must be considered in its width and breadth, not only a single part of *dār al-islām*, for it is one of the characteristics of Islamic civilization that the totality of its life and the richness of its arts and sciences can only be gauged by studying all of its parts. Only in unison do these parts reveal the complete unity that lies within all the genuine manifestations of Islam. One cannot understand the role of "philosophy" or any other intellectual discipline in Islam by selecting only one dimension of Islam or one particular geographical area, no matter how important that dimension or that area may be in itself.

As for "philosophy," the sense in which we intend to use it in this discussion must be defined with precision, for here we are dealing with a question of some complexity. First of all it must be remembered that terms have a precise meaning in the sciences of traditional civilizations such as the Islamic. We can use the term "philosophy" as the translation of the Arabic *al-falsafah* and inquire into the meaning of the latter term in Islam and its civilization. Or we can seek to discover how the term "philosophy" as used today must be understood within the context of Islamic civilization. Or again we can seek to find all those Islamic sciences and intellectual disciplines which possess a "philosophical" aspect in the sense of dealing with the general world view of man and his position in the Universe. For our own part, we must begin by making the basic affirmation that if by philosophy we mean profane philosophy as currently understood in the West, that is, the attempt of man to reach ultimate knowledge of things through the use of his own rational and sensuous faculties and cut off completely from both the effusion of grace and the light of the Divine Intellect, then such an activity is alien to the Islamic perspective. It is a fruit of a humanism which did not manifest itself in Islam except for a very few instances of a completely peripheral and unimportant nature. It is what the Persian philosophers themselves have called mental acrobatics or literally "weaving" (*bāftan*), in contrast to philosophy as the gaining of certainty, or literally the discovery of truth (*yāftan*). But if by philosophy we mean a traditional philosophy based on certainty rather than doubt, where man's mind is continuously illuminated by the light of the Divine Intellect and protected from error by the grace provided by a traditional world in which man breathes, then we certainly do have an Islamic philosophy which possesses illimitable horizons and is one of the richest intellectual traditions in the world, a philosophy that is always related to religious realities and has been most often wedded to illumination (*ishrāq*) and gnosis (*ʿirfān*). If we view philosophy in this light, then the title of "philosopher" cannot be refused to those in Islam who are called the *falāsifah*, *ḥukamāʾ*, and *ʿurafāʾ*.

Moreover, if one takes the whole of the Islamic world into account, including the Persian and the Indian parts of it, one certainly cannot call Islamic philosophy a transient phenomenon which had a short-lived existence in a civilization whose intellectual structure did not permit its survival. One can no longer speak of Christian and Jewish philosophy and then refuse to accept the reality of Islamic philosophy.[1] One can with some logic assert, as has been done by F. Van Steenberghen and certain others, that philosophy, as understood by the scholastics, was not called specifically Christian by them but was conceived of as philosophy as such.[2] In the same way in classical Islamic texts one reads usually of the term *al-falsafah*, *the* philosophy, but not *al-falsafat al-islāmiyyah* which is of a more cur-

[1] As does L. Gardet in "Le problème de la philosophie musulmane," *Mélanges offerts à Étienne Gilson* (Paris, 1959), p. 282.

[2] F. van Steenberghen, *La philosophie au XIIIe siècle* (Louvain, 1966), pp. 533-40.

rent usage, just as most classical authors have usually written of *al-dīn, the* religion in itself, rather than of *al-islām* as a distinct religion. The homogeneity and unity of traditional civilization was such that for its members their world was *the* world. Western man certainly produced Christian art during the Middle Ages but this art was usually called art as such. Islam produced some of the greatest architectural marvels in the world, which were, however, very rarely referred to as Islamic architecture by their own makers. They simply called them architecture. This characteristic is a profound aspect of the medieval world and of traditional civilization in general which must be taken into full consideration in the present discussion. But if we stand "outside" of these worlds and study them in comparison with the secular modern world or with other sacred civilizations, then in the same way that we can call Chartres Christian architecture and St. Thomas a Christian philosopher we can refer to the Alhambra as Islamic architecture and Ibn Sīnā and Suhrawardī as Islamic philosophers.

In all honesty and taking into consideration the long tradition and the still living character of Islamic philosophy we cannot refuse to recognize the reality of this distinct type of traditional philosophy as being just as closely allied to the structure of Islam, and just as closely related to a particular dimension of it, as other traditional philosophies are related to the tradition in whose bosoms they have been cultivated. For the Islamic philosophers, especially those of the later period, traditional philosophy has always been a way in which the truths of religion have been expressed in the language of intellectual and rational discourse. The truth reached by traditional philosophy is for the *ḥukamā'* an aspect of the Truth itself, of *al-Ḥaqq*, which is a Divine Name and therefore the source of all revealed truth. For the Islamic *ḥukamā'*, as for Philo, philosophy was originally a form of revealed Truth, closely allied to revelation and connected with the name of Hermes, who became identified by them with Idris, who was entitled "The Father of Philosophers" (Abu'l-Ḥukamā'). The identification of the chain of philosophy with an antediluvian prophet reveals a profound aspect of the concept of philosophy in Islam—far more profound than that any historical criticism could claim to negate it. It was a means of confirming the legitimacy of *ḥikmah* in the Islamic intellectual world.

Having established the existence of Islamic philosophy as a distinct type of traditional philosophy, we must now probe into its meaning and definition. We must first of all make a distinction between philosophy in the general sense as *Weltanschauung* and philosophy as a distinct intellectual discipline in the technical sense. If we think of philosophy in the general sense of *Weltanschauung*, then outside of *al-falsafah* and *al-ḥikmah*, with which philosophy has been identified by most schools, we must search within several other traditional Islamic disciplines for "philosophy," these disciplines including *kalām* or theology, *uṣūl al-fiqh*, or principles of jurisprudence, and especially Sufism, in particular its intellectual expression which is also called *al-ʿirfān* or gnosis. This fact is especially true of the later period of Islamic history when in most of the Arab world *falsafah* as a distinct school disappeared and the intellectual needs corresponding to it found their fulfillment in *kalām* and Sufism. As for philosophy in the technical sense, it embraces not only Peripatetic philosophy in its early phase, known in the West thanks to medieval translations and modern research following the earlier tradition, but also later Peripatetic philosophy after Ibn Rushd and beginning with Khwājah Naṣīr al-Dīn al-Ṭūsī, the School of Illumination (*ishrāq*) founded by Suhrawardī, metaphysical and gnostic forms of Sufism identified closely with the school of Ibn ʿArabī, and the "transcendent theosophy" (*al-ḥikmat al-mutaʿāliyah*) of Mullā Ṣadrā, not to speak of philosophies with specific religious forms such as Isma'ili philosophy, which possesses its own long and rich history.

Because of the vastness of the subject we shall confine ourselves in this essay to the role and meaning of *falsafah* or *ḥikmah*, or philosophy in its technical sense, in Islam, always keeping in mind, however, the richness of Sufism and *kalām* in the domain of ideas which concern the Islamic *Weltanschauung* and man's position in the Universe and vis-à-vis God. The most profound metaphysics in Islam is to be found in the writings of the Sufi masters, especially those who have chosen to deal with the theoretical aspects of the spiritual way, or with that *scientia sacra* called gnosis (*al-ʿirfān*). A more general treatment of the meaning of philosophy in Islam would have to include Sufism, *kalām*, *uṣūl*, and some of the other Islamic sciences as well, but as already mentioned, these lie outside the boundaries of the present discussion, which concerns only *falsafah* or *ḥikmah* as these terms have been understood by the traditional Islamic authorities themselves.

To understand the meaning of Islamic philosophy it is best to examine the use of the terms *falsafah* and *ḥikmah* in various traditional sources and the definitions provided for them by the Islamic philosophers themselves. The term *ḥikmah* appears in several places in the Quran, of which perhaps the most often cited is, "He giveth wisdom [*ḥikmah*] unto whom He will, and he unto whom wisdom is given, he truly hath received abundant good" (2:269). It also appears in the *Ḥadīth* literature in such sayings as "The acquisition of *ḥikmah* is incumbent upon thee: verily the good resides in *ḥikmah*" and "Speak not of *ḥikmah* to fools."[3]

Different Muslim authorities have debated as to what *ḥikmah* means in such verses and sayings and many theologians such as Fakhr al-Dīn al-Rāzī have identified it with *kalām*. But also throughout Islamic history many have identified it with the intellectual sciences (*al-ʿulūm al-ʿaqliyyah*) in general and traditional philosophy in particular. In fact traditional philosophy came to be known, especially in Persia, as *al-ḥikmat al-ilāhiyyah*, or "*theosophia*" in its original sense. Even early in Islamic history certain authorities used the term *ḥikmah* in the sense of the intellectual sciences and philosophy, as for example Jāḥiẓ, who in *al-Bayān wa'l-tabyīn* refers to it in connection with Sahl ibn Hārūn,[4] and Ibn Nadīm, who calls Khālid ibn Yazīd, known for his interest in the "pre-Islamic" or *awāʾil* sciences, the *ḥakīm* of Āl al-Marwān.[5]

The definitions given by the Islamic philosophers themselves are more revealing than those of literary figures in elucidating the meaning of philosophy for Islam. In his well-known definition of *falsafah*, the first of the great Muslim Peripatetics, al-Kindī, writes: "Philosophy is the knowledge of the reality of things within man's possibility, because the philosopher's end in his theoretical knowledge is to gain truth and in his practical knowledge to behave in accordance with truth."[6] His successor al-Fārābī accepted this definition in principle, making in addition a distinction between "philosophy rooted in certainty" (*falsafah yaqīniyyah*), which is based on demonstration (*burhān*), and "philosophy deriving from opinion" (*falsafah maẓnūnah*), based upon dialectics and sophistry.[7] He also gives the well-known definition of philosophy as "the knowledge of existents *qua* existents" and adds that "there is nothing among existing things with which philosophy is not concerned."[8]

[3] Both are found in al-Dārimī, *Muqaddimah*, 34.

[4] M. ʿAbd al-Rāziq, *Tamhīd li-taʾrīkh al-falsafat al-islāmiyyah*, p. 45, where reference is also made to various other Islamic sources using the term *ḥikmah*.

[5] *The Fihrist of al-Nadīm*, trans. by B. Dodge (New York, 1970), vol. 2, p. 581.

[6] From his *On First Philosophy*, quoted by A. F. El-Ehwany, "Al-Kindi," in *A History of Muslim Philosophy*, ed. by M. M. Sharif, vol. I (Wiesbaden, 1963), p. 424.

[7] Al-Fārābī, *Kilāb al-ḥurūf* (*Book of Letters*), ed. by M. Mahdi (Beirut, 1968), pp. 153-57.

[8] *Al-Jamʿ bayn raʾyay al-ḥakimayn Aflāṭūn al-ilāhī wa Arisṭū* (Hyderabad, Daccan), pp. 36-37.

The master of Peripatetics, Ibn Sīnā, again adds an element to the definition of *ḥikmah* and relates it more closely to realization and perfection of the being of man when he writes: "*Ḥikmah* is the perfecting of the human soul through the conceptualization of things and the judgment of theoretical and practical truths to the measure of human capability."[9] This close accordance between knowledge and its practice, so important for later Islamic philosophy, is repeated in the definition of the Ikhwān al-Ṣafā' when they say, "The beginning of philosophy is the love of the sciences; its middle is knowledge of the reality of things to the extent to which man is capable; and its end is speech and action in conformity with this knowledge."[10]

With Suhrawardī and the *ishrāqī* school, the close rapport between philosophy and religion or more precisely between philosophy as an aspect of the esoteric dimension of revelation and the ascetic and spiritual practices related to religious discipline, which in Islam are connected with Sufism, becomes fully established. Not only was Suhrawardī himself a Sufi and a *ḥakīm* at the same time, but also he conceived of a true *faylasūf* or *ḥakīm* as one who possesses both theoretical knowledge and spiritual vision. He calls such a person *muta'allih*, literally he who has become "God-like," and speaks in his *Partaw-nāmah* of *ḥikmah* as "The act of the soul's becoming imprinted by the spiritual truths and the intelligibles."[11] After him philosophy and spiritual realization were always wedded together and *al-ḥikmat al-ilāhiyyah* became, especially in Persia and other eastern lands of Islam, the bridge between the formal religious sciences and the verities of pure gnosis.

The Safavid *ḥakīms*, who brought many trends of Islamic philosophy to their full fruition and flowering, continued to relate philosophy closely to the esoteric dimension of religion and considered the traditional philosopher as the person who possesses not only theoretical knowledge but also a direct vision of the truth, so that he speaks to mankind as a sage fulfilling a certain aspect of the prophetic function after the close of the cycle of prophecy. In the Shi'ite world many an authority has identified the term "scholars" (*'ulamā'*) in the famous prophetic saying, "The scholars of my community are like the prophets of the Children of Israel," with the *ḥukamā'*, who in

[9] *'Uyūn al-ḥikmah* (Cairo, 1326), p. 30.

[10] *Rasā'il*, vol. I (Cairo, 1928), p. 23.

[11] *Opera Metaphysica et Mystica*, vol. 3, ed. by S. H. Nasr (Tehran, 1970), p. 69.

the later period were mostly also Sufis and gnostics. *Ḥikmah*, therefore, continued its close relation with Islamic esotericism and became identified in the context of Shi'ism with the "cycle of initiation" (*dā'irat al-walāyah*) following the cycle of prophecy (*dā'irat al-nubuwwah*). Mīr Findiriskī, for example, considers the *hukamā'* as standing in the class immediately below the prophets and writes, "The utmost extremity reached by the *falāsifah* is the point of departure for prophecy."[12]

With Ṣadr al-Dīn Shīrāzī (Mullā Ṣadrā), who achieved a vast synthesis of the various schools of Islamic philosophy and intellectuality, the definition of *ḥikmah* also reaches a fullness and synthetic quality that embraces much that came before him. In one of his famous definitions, which echoes in part the words of Plato, he writes, "*Falsafah* is the perfecting of the human soul to the extent of human possibility through knowledge of the essential realities of things as they are in themselves and through judgment concerning their existence established upon demonstration and not derived from opinion or through imitation. Or if thou liketh thou canst say it is to give intelligible order to the world to the extent of human possibility in order to gain 'resemblance' to the Divine."[13] Similarly in another definition he considers *ḥikmah* as the means whereby "man becomes an intelligible world resembling the objective world and similar to the order of universal existence."[14] Referring to the first principles discussed in *ḥikmah*, Mullā Ṣadrā says, "It is this *ḥikmah* which the Holy Prophet had in mind in his prayer to his Lord when he said: 'O Lord! Show us things as they really are.'"[15] Moreover, he gives a spiritual exegesis of the Quranic verse "Surely We created man of the best stature, then We reduced him to the lowest of the low, save those who believe and do good works" (95:4-6) in this way: "of the best stature" refers to the spiritual world and the angelic part of the soul, "the lowest of the low" to the material world and the animal part of the soul, "those who believe" to theoretical *ḥikmah* and those who "do good works" to practical *ḥikmah*. Seen in this light *ḥikmah*, in its two aspects of knowledge and action, becomes the means whereby man is saved

[12] *Risāla-yi ṣinā'iyyah* in *Anthologie des philosophes iraniens* (Tehran, 1972), vol. 1, p. 73.

[13] *Al-Ḥikmat al-muta'āliyah fi'l-asfār al-arba'ah,* vol. 1, part 1 (Tehran, 1387 lunar), p. 20.

[14] Introduction of S. J. Āshtiyānī to Ṣadr al-Dīn Shīrāzī, *al-Shawāhid al-rubūbiyyah* (Mashhad, 1346), p. vii.

[15] *Al-Ḥikmat al-muta'āliyah*, p. 21.

from his wretched state of the lowest of the low and enabled to regain the angelic and paradisial state in which he was originally made. *Ḥikmah* is, in his view, completely wedded to religion and the spiritual life and is far removed from purely mental activity connected with the rationalistic conception of philosophy that has become prevalent in the West since the post-Renaissance period.

Having surveyed the meaning of philosophy through the eyes of its supporters, we need to say a few words about the different forms of "opposition" to it, before turning to its role and function in Islam. It must, however, be remembered that "opposition" in the context of a traditional civilization is very different from the opposition of contending philosophical schools that have no principles in common. In Islam there has often been a tension between the various components and dimensions of the tradition, but a tension that has been almost always creative and has never destroyed the unity of Islam and its civilization. With this reserve in mind it can be said that "opposition" to *falsafah* in Islam came mainly from three groups, but for different reasons: the purely religious scholars dealing with *fiqh* and *uṣūl*, the theologians (*mutakallimūn*), especially of the Ash'arite school, and certain of the Sufis.

Some of the scholars of the religious sciences criticized *falsafah* simply because it stood outside of the domain of the *Sharīʿah* with which they were solely concerned. Some like Ibn Taymiyyah in Sunnism and Mullā Bāqir Majlisī in Shi'ism wrote specifically against the *falāsifah* and in the case of the former against logic, although he himself made use of logical discourse. Their opposition to *falsafah* is related to their mission to preserve the purely transmitted sciences on the exoteric level. Thus they refused to be concerned with either the intellectual sciences or the esoteric dimension of Islam which alone could integrate these sciences, and chief among them philosophy, into the Islamic perspective.

As for the theologians, the opposition of the Ash'arites to *falsafah* was of course much greater than that of the Mu'tazilites, while in the Shi'ite world, Isma'ili *kalām* was always close to Isma'ili philosophy and Shi'ite *kalām* became closely wed to *falsafah* with the *Tajrīd* of Naṣīr al-Dīn al-Ṭūsī. In fact later *falsafah* or *al-ḥikmat al-ilāhiyyah* in Shi'ism itself claimed to fulfill the true role of theology and in reality contains much that in Western terms would be considered as theology. The well-known attack of al-Ghazzālī against *falsafah* was not simply a negative act of demolishing *falsafah*. First of all it attacked only Peripatetic philosophy and moreover the rationalistic tendencies within it. Secondly the criticism was of such a positive nature that it changed the direction of the flow of Islamic intellectual life rather than put an end to it. The background which made possible the spread of the sapiential teachings of Suhrawardī and Ibn ʿArabī owes much to al-Ghazzalī, while the later revival of Peripatetic philosophy by al-Ṭūsī is related closely to the criticism of Ibn Sīnā by another Ash'arite critic of *falsafah*, Fakhr al-Dīn al-Rāzī. The criticism of *falsafah* by the *mutakallimūn*, therefore, was more than anything else a creative interplay between *falsafah* and *kalām* which left an indelible mark upon both of them. *Kalām* forced *falsafah*, even the Peripatetic school, to deal with certain specifically religious issues, while *falsafah* influenced ever more the formulation and argumentation of *kalām* itself, starting with Imām al-Ḥaramayn al-Juwaynī, continuing with al-Ghazzālī and al-Rāzī, and in a sense culminating with ʿAḍud al-Dīn al-Ījī and his *Kitāb al-mawāqif*, which is almost as much *falsafah* as *kalām*. In Shi'ism also it is difficult to distinguish some of the later commentaries upon the *Tajrīd* from works on *falsafah*. The "opposition" of *kalām* to *falsafah*, therefore, far from destroying *falsafah*, influenced its later course and in much of the Sunni world absorbed it into itself after the seventh/thirteenth century, with the result that, as already mentioned, such a figure as Ibn Khaldūn was to call this late *kalām* a form of philosophy.

As for the criticism of *falsafah* made by certain Sufis, it too must be taken in the light of the nature of Islamic esotericism. Sufi metaphysics could not become bound to the "lesser truth" of Aristotelianism against whose inherent limitations it reacted and whose limits it criticized. But the criticism against the substance of *falsafah* came, not from the whole of Sufism, but from a particular tendency within it. In general one can distinguish two tendencies in Sufi spirituality, one which takes the human intellect to be a ladder to the luminous world of the spirit and the other which emphasizes more the discontinuity between the human reason and the Divine Intellect and seeks to reach the world of the spirit by breaking completely the power of ratiocination within the mind. The final result, which is union with God, is the same in both cases, but the role played by reason is somewhat different in the two instances. The first tendency can be seen in Ibn ʿArabī, ʿAbd al-Karīm al-Jīlī, Ṣadr al-Dīn al-Qūnawī and the like, and the second in some of the famous Persian Sufi poets such as Sanāʾī and Mawlānā Jalāl al-Dīn Rūmī and in the Arab world in certain early Sufi poets, as well as in Shaykh Bahāʾ al-Dīn ʿĀmilī, who wrote in both Arabic and Persian. In the case of those following the first tendency many sapiential doctrines belonging to ancient schools of philosophy such as Hermeticism, Neopythagoreanism, and Neoplatonism were integrated into Islamic esotericism through the light of Islamic gnosis. It must be remembered that one of the titles of Ibn ʿArabī was "The Plato of his time" (*Aflāṭūnu zamānihi*). In the second case there is a greater criticism of ratiocination (*istidlāl*) for spiritual reasons, and throughout Islamic history followers of this type of Sufism have severely criticized *falsafah*, particularly of the Peripatetic kind, in order to open before man the luminous skies of illumination and gnosis. Without Sufism and other aspects of Islamic esotericism contained in Shi'ism the rise of a Suhrawardī or Mullā Ṣadrā would be inconceivable. In fact the tendencies within Sufism have played a critical role in the later history of *falsafah*, one more positive and the other in a sense more negative, while both aspects of Sufism have remained the guardians and expositors of traditional *falsafah* or *ḥikmah* in its profoundest and most immutable sense or what in Western parlance is called *philosophia perennis*. *Falsafah* for its part benefited immensely from this interaction with Sufism and gradually became itself the outer courtyard leading the qualified to the inner garden of gnosis and beatitude. . . .

The criticism made by Sufis of *falsafah* and their influence upon its development was like the transformation brought about by the alchemist through the presence of the philosopher's stone: The very substance of *falsafah* was changed during later Islamic history from simply a rational system of thought with an Islamic form to an ancillary of esotericism closely wedded to illumination and gnosis. Likewise Islamic philosophy was saved from the deadlock it had reached with the type of excessive Aristotelianism of an Ibn Rushd and was enabled to channel itself into a new direction, a direction which bestowed upon it renewed vigor and made it a major aspect of Islamic intellectual life in the Eastern lands of Islam during the eight centuries following the death of the Andalusian master of Aristotelianism with whom the earlier chapter of Islamic philosophy had drawn to a close.

In discussing the role and function of *falsafah* in Islam and Islamic civilization we must note the change that took place to some degree after the period leading to Ibn Sīnā in the East and Ibn Rushd in the West. During the early period, which is also the formative period of the Islamic intellectual sciences, *falsafah* performed an important role in the process of the absorption and synthesis of the pre-Islamic sciences and the formulation of the Islamic sciences. The science of logic, the problem of the classification of the sciences, the methodology of the sciences, and their interaction with the rest of Islamic culture were all deeply influenced by *falsafah* and its particular elaboration in Islam. Moreover, during this early period most of the great scientists were also philosophers, so that we can speak during the early centuries, and even later, of a single type of Muslim savant who was both philosopher and scientist and whom we have already called philosopher-scientist. The development of Islamic science in the early period is related to that of Peripatetic philosophy as well as to the philosophical trends of an anti-Peripatetic nature. Not only al-Fārābī and Ibn Sīnā, but also Muḥammad ibn Zakariyyā' al-Rāzī and al-Bīrūnī, were all prominent figures of Islamic science. In fact the anti-Peripatetic view, which is nevertheless *falsafah*, is particularly significant in the development of many new ideas in the sciences. In any case during early Islamic history the cultivation and the development of the sciences would have been inconceivable without those of *falsafah*. The meaning of the term *ḥakīm*, which denotes at once a physician, scientist, and philosopher, is the best proof of this close connection.

Not only did *falsafah* aid closely in the development of the intellectual sciences, but also it was the major discipline in which tools and instruments of analysis, logic, and rational inquiry were developed for the transmitted sciences and other aspects of Islamic culture as well. The tools of logic developed mostly by the *falāsifah* and in conformity with the particular genius of Islam, in which logic plays a positive role and prepares the mind for illumination and contemplation, were applied to fields ranging far and wide, from grammar and rhetoric to even the classification and categorization of *Ḥadīth*, from organizing economic activity in the bazaar to developing the geometry and arithmetic required to construct the great monuments of Islamic architecture. To be sure the function of the *falsafah* with which we are concerned here does not involve only the rationalizing tendencies of the Graeco-Alexandrian doctrines adopted by the Muslim Peripatetics or specific Aristotelian teachings. It concerns more generally the development of a climate of rational thought and the instrument of logic and logical reasoning which, once developed, were adopted by the various Islamic arts and sciences for their own ends and in accordance with the nature of Islam and its teachings.

Also during this early period when Islam made its first contacts with the arts and sciences of other civilizations, *falsafah* played an important role in enabling the Muslims to integrate the pre-Islamic sciences into their own perspective. Its role on the formal level complements that of Islamic esotericism, whose insistence on the universality of revelation on the supra-formal level made possible positive contact with other religions and traditions. For the *falāsifah*, as al-Kindī asserted so clearly from the beginning, the truth was one; therefore they were certain that the truth, wherever and whenever it might be discovered, would conform to the inner teachings of Islam, simply because the instrument of knowledge for both *falsafah* or *ḥikmah* and religion was the same, namely the Universal Intellect or Logos, which plays such an important role in the theory of knowledge of the Islamic philosophers. Such facts as the attention paid to Hermes as Idris and the identification of the Sabaeans with the followers of Hermes, the belief that the early philosophers of Greece learned their *sophia* from Solomon and, looking eastward, the open interest shown by the *falāsifah* in the wisdom of India and ancient Persia, all attest to the important role of *falsafah* in early Islam in providing the appropriate intellectual background for the encounter of Muslims with the arts, sciences, and philosophies of other civilizations. This role was in fact crucial during the early period of Islamic history when Muslims were translating the heritage of the great civilizations which had preceded them into their own world of thought and were laying the foundations for the rise of the Islamic sciences. This role was particularly important then, but it did not cease to manifest itself even later. The translation of the Chinese sciences during the IlKhanid period was supported by men whose background was that of *ḥikmah*, such men as Rashīd al-Dīn Faḍlallāh, who was both vizier and philosopher-scientist. And during the Mogul period in India the movement of translation of Sanskrit works into Persian incited by Akbar and reaching its culmination with Dārā Shukūh, a movement whose great religious and cultural significance is not as yet generally recognized outside the Indo-Pakistani subcontinent, is again closely connected with the later tradition of *falsafah* and *ḥikmah* as it spread from Persia, starting mostly with the reign of Skandar Lodi, to the Indian subcontinent. Finally it must be re-asserted that during this earlier phase of Islamic history one of the important and enduring roles of *falsafah* was its struggle with *kalām* and the particularly "philosophical" structure it finally bestowed upon *kalām*. The difference between the treatises of *kalām* of al-Ashʿarī himself or his student Abū Bakr al-Bāqillānī and Rāzī, Ījī, and Sayyid Sharīf al-Jurjānī is due solely to the long struggle with *falsafah*. Through *kalām*, therefore, *falsafah*, as an *Islamic* discipline, left its indelible mark upon the Sunni world.

Something must also be said about the position of *falsafah* in Islamic universities during this early period. The official position accorded to *falsafah* in the curriculum of the Islamic universities varied greatly from land to land and period to period, depending upon theological and political factors of a complex kind which we cannot analyze here. In Jundishapur and the Bayt al-Ḥikmah in Baghdad, *falsafah* was respected and taught, as it was also in al-Azhar, established by the Fatimids. But its teaching in official *madrasahs* came to be banned with the rise of Ash'arite power among the Abbasids and Seljuqs, to the extent that in his will and testament for the trust (*waqf*) of the Niẓāmiyyah school system, Khwājah Niẓām al-Mulk ordered specifically that the teaching of *falsafah* be banned from the university system founded by him. This ban in fact continued in most of the Sunni world afterwards except for logic, which was always taught there. But later in Islamic history the teaching of *falsafah* was made once again a part of the curriculum by Khwājah Naṣīr al-Dīn al-Ṭūsī at Maraghah and Rashīd al-Dīn Faḍlallāh in the Rabʿ al-Rashīdī in Tabriz, and, despite a checkered career, it has continued as a part of the *madrasah* curricula in Persia and many schools of the Indo-Pakistani subcontinent and Iraq to this day. In any case, however, the extent of the role of *falsafah* must not be judged solely by whether it was taught in universities or not, thus making a comparison with the situation in the West. In Islam, because of the very informal structure of traditional education, much of the instruction in *falsafah* as well as in the esoteric sciences has always been carried out in private circles and continues so to this day.

When we come to later Islamic history, or what we might call the post-Ibn Rushdian phase of Islamic philosophy, the role and function of *falsafah* is seen to be somewhat different from what it had been until then. The Islamic sciences, both the intellectual and transmitted, had by now already become elaborated and were following their own course of development. Peripatetic philosophy, moreover, had reached an impasse, as seen in the far-reaching attacks of al-Ghazzāli and the much less influential rebuttal of Ibn Rushd. New intellectual forces had appeared upon the scene, of which the most important were those identified with the names of Ibn ʿArabī and Suhrawardī. Politically also the symbolic unity of the Islamic world was soon brought to an end by the destruction of the Abbasid caliphate by the Mongols and the emerging of a new pattern, which finally led to the establishment of the three major Muslim empires of the Ottomans, Safavids, and Moguls. In this new situation *falsafah* was to have a different function and role in the Western and the Eastern lands of Islam.

In the Western lands of Islam, after Ibn Rushd *falsafah* ceased to exist as an independent and rigorously followed discipline, with a few exceptions in the Arab world like Ibn Sabʿīn and Ibn Khaldūn. Also, among the Turks and the Arabs of Syria and Iraq a certain amount of philosophic activity continued, associated mostly with the school of Suhrawardī and the metaphysical doctrines of Ibn ʿArabī, but unfortunately this tradition has not been investigated thoroughly until now. In the Western lands of Islam the life of the main substance of *falsafah*, however, both in its logical aspects and cosmological and metaphysical doctrines, continued to pulsate within *kalām* and also within Sufism of the gnostic and metaphysical type, associated with Ibn ʿArabī and his commentators such as al-Qūnawī, Dāʾūd al-Qayṣarī, ʿAbd al-Wahhāb al-Shaʿrānī, Bālī Afandī, and ʿAbd al-Salām al-Nābulusī. The continuation of the intellectual life of the Muslims of the Western regions, a life which manifested itself in *falsafah* as well as *kalām* and *taṣawwuf* in the early centuries, is to be found during the later period only in *kalām* and Sufism. One would, therefore, have to say that although until the revival of Islamic philosophy in Egypt by Jamāl al-Dīn al-Astarābādī (known as al-Afghānī) in the thirteenth/nineteenth century *falsafah* or *ḥikmah* was only pursued sparsely and was not cultivated avidly in the Western lands of Islam, it nevertheless continued to possess a certain mode of life within the matrix of *kalām* and Sufism.

In the Eastern lands of Islam and particularly in Persia the role of *falsafah* was quite different. Thanks to Suhrawardī and Ibn ʿArabī new schools of *ḥikmah* grew up while the teachings of Ibn Sīnā were revived by al-Ṭūsī. As a result, a rich intellectual life came into being which reached its apogee in many ways in the Safavid period with Mīr Dāmād and Mullā Ṣadrā and which also played a major role among the Muslims of the Indian subcontinent. Besides its function to sustain the intellectual sciences, which continued to be cultivated in Persia and India—and also to a certain degree among the Ottomans—up to the twelfth/eighteenth century, and its role in the various aspects of the religious life of the community, *falsafah* or *ḥikmah*, which by now had come closer to the heart of the Islamic message and had left the limitative confines of Peripatetic philosophy, became for many men the door to Sufism and Sufi metaphysics. In the same way that in the Sunni world one observes in many circles today a certain wedding between Ash'arite *kalām* and Sufism, in Persia and to a certain extent in the Indian subcontinent there came into being a notable wedding between *ḥikmah* and *ʿirfān* and many masters appeared who were both *ḥakīms* and *ʿārifs* (gnostics). On the one hand *ḥikmah* became profoundly imbued with the gnostic teachings of Ibn ʿArabī and his school and was able to present in such cases as Mullā Ṣadrā a more systematic and logical interpretation of Sufi metaphysics than found in many of the Sufi texts themselves, and on the other hand it became in turn the major point of access to the teachings of Sufism for many men of intellectual inclination who were engaged in the cultivation of the official religious sciences. As a result of the transformation it received and the role it fulfilled, *falsafah* or *ḥikmah* continued its own life and remains to this day in Persia and certain adjacent lands as a living intellectual tradition.

10. Suhrawardī

The complete harmonization of spirituality and philosophy in Islam was achieved in the School of Illumination (*al-ishrāq*) founded by Shaykh al-Ishrāq Shihāb al-Dīn Suhrawardī. Born in the small village of Suhraward in Western Persia in 549/1153, he studied in Zanjan and Isfahan, where he completed his formal education in the religious and philosophical sciences and entered into Sufism. He then set out for Anatolia and settled in Aleppo, where as a result of the opposition of certain jurists he met his death at a young age in 587/1191. Suhrawardī was a great mystic and philosopher and the restorer within the bosom of Islam of the perennial philosophy, which he called *al-ḥikmat al-ʿatīqah*, the *philosophia priscorium* referred to by certain Renaissance philosophers, whose origin he considered to be divine. He saw veritable philosophy—or one should rather say theosophy, if this word is understood in its original sense and as used by Jakob Boehme—as resulting from the wedding between the training of the theoretical intellect through philosophy and the purification of the heart through Sufism. The means of attaining supreme knowledge he considered to be illumination, which at once transforms one's being and bestows knowledge.

During his short and tragic life, Suhrawardī wrote more than forty treatises, the doctrinal ones almost all in Arabic, and the symbolic or visionary recitals almost all in Persian. Both his Arabic and Persian works are among the literary masterpieces of Islamic philosophy. His doctrinal writings, which begin with an elaboration and gradual transformation of Avicennan Peripatetic philosophy, culminate in the *Ḥikmat al-ishrāq* (*The Theosophy of the Orient of Light*), which is one of the most important works in the tradition of Islamic philosophy. His recitals include some of the most beautiful prose writings of the Persian language, including such masterpieces as *Fī ḥaqīqat al-ʿishq* (*On the Reality of Love*) and *Āwāz-i par-i Jibraʾīl* (*The Chant of the Wing of Gabriel*). Few other Islamic philosophers were able to combine metaphysics of the highest order with a poetic prose of almost incomparable richness and literary quality.

Suhrawardī integrated Platonism and Mazdaean angelology in the matrix of Islamic gnosis. He believed that there existed in antiquity two traditions of wisdom (*al-ḥikmah*), both of divine origin. One of these reached Pythagoras, Plato, and other Greek philosophers and created the authentic Greek philosophical tradition which terminated with Aristotle. The other was disseminated among the sages of ancient Persia whom he calls the *khusrawāniyyūn*, or sages who were followers of the Persian philosopher-king Kay Khusraw. Finally, these traditions became united in Suhrawardī. Like many Islamic philosophers, he identified Hermes with the prophet Idris, who was given the title Father of Philosophers (*wālid al-ḥukamā'*) and was considered to be the recipient of the celestial wisdom which was the origin of philosophy. It was finally in Islam, the last and primordial religion, that this primordial tradition became restored by Suhrawardī as the school of Illumination (*al-ishrāq*).

The Master of Illumination insisted that there existed from the beginning an "eternal dough" (*al-khamīrat al-azaliyyah*), which is none other than eternal wisdom or *sophia perennis*. It is hidden in the very substance of man ready to be "leavened" and actualized through intellectual training and inner purification. It is this "eternal dough" which was actualized and transmitted by the Pythagoreans and Plato to the Sufis Dhu'l-Nūn al-Miṣrī and Sahl al-Tustarī and through the Persian sages to Bāyazīd al-Basṭāmi and Manṣūr al-Ḥallāj and which was restored in its full glory by Suhrawardī, who combined the inner knowledge of these masters with the intellectual discipline of such philosophers as al-Fārābī and Ibn Sīnā. Suhrawardī, however, never mentions historical chains connecting him to this long tradition of wisdom but insists that the real means of attainment of this knowledge is through God and His revealed Book. That is why he bases himself so much on the Quran and is the first major Muslim philosopher to quote the Quran extensively in his philosophical writings.

Suhrawardī created a vast philosophical synthesis, which draws from many sources and especially the nearly six centuries of Islamic thought before him. But this synthesis is unified by a metaphysics and an epistemology that are able to relate all the different strands of thought to each other in a unified pattern. What is most significant from the point of view of spirituality is the insistence of *ishrāqī* philosophy on the organic nexus between intellectual activity and inner purification. Henceforth in the Islamic world, wherever philosophy survived, it was seen as lived wisdom. The philosopher or *ḥakīm* was expected to be not only a person possessing cerebral knowledge but a saintly person transformed by his knowledge. Philosophy as a mental activity divorced from spiritual realization and the inner life ceased to be accepted as a legitimate intellectual category, and Islamic philosophy became henceforth what *sophia* has always been in Oriental traditions, namely, a wisdom lived and experienced as well as thought and reasoned.

Although as a result of his violent death Suhrawardī and his doctrines were not visible for a generation, the teachings of the School of Illumination reappeared in the middle part of the seventh/thirteenth century in the major commentary by Muḥammad al-Shahrazūrī (d. after 687/1288) on the *Ḥikmat al-ishrāq*. This was followed by the second major commentary on this work by Quṭb al-Dīn al-Shīrāzī (d. 710/1311). The latter must be considered one of the major intellectual figures of Islam, at once physicist and astronomer, authority in logic and medicine, commentator on Ibn Sīnā and Suhrawardī. His *Durrat al-tāj* (*Jewel of the Crown*), which is a vast philosophical encyclopedia mostly along Peripatetic lines, is well known, as is his commentary on the *Canon of Medicine* of Ibn Sīnā and several major astronomical treatises. But Quṭb al-Dīn al-Shīrāzī's most enduring philosophical work is his commentary on the *Ḥikmat al-ishrāq*, which resuscitated the teachings of Suhrawardī and is read and studied in Persia and Muslim India to this day. After him a long line of *ishrāqī* philosophers appeared in both Persia and the Indian subcontinent, where the influence of Suhrawardī has been very extensive. Suhrawardī established a new and at the same time primordial intellectual dimension in Islam, which became a permanent aspect of the Islamic intellectual scene and survives to this day.

Ishrāqī philosophy—or theosophy, to be more precise—is based on the metaphysics of light. The origin and source of all things is the Light of lights (*nūr al-anwār*), which is infinite and absolute Light above and beyond all the rays which it emanates. All levels of reality, however, are also degrees and levels of light distinguished from each other by their degrees of intensity and weakness and by nothing other than light. There is, in fact, nothing in the whole universe but light. From the Light of lights there issues a vertical or longitudinal hierarchy of lights which comprises the levels of universal existence and a horizontal or latitudinal order which contains the archetypes (sg. *rabb al-nawʿ*) or Platonic ideas of all that appears here below as objects and things. These lights are none other than what in the language of religion are called angels. Suhrawardī gives names of Mazdaean angels as well as Islamic ones to these lights and brings out the central role of the angels in cosmology as well as in epistemology and soteriology.

The word *ishrāq* in Arabic itself means at once illumination and the first light of the early morning as it shines from the east (*sharq*). The Orient is not only the geographical east but the origin of light, of reality. *Ishrāqī* philosophy is both "Oriental" and "illuminative." It illuminates because it is Oriental and is Oriental because it is illuminative. It is the knowledge with the help of which man can orient himself in the universe and finally reach that Orient which is his original abode, while in the shadow and darkness of terrestrial existence man lives in the "occident" of the world of being no matter where he lives geographically. The spiritual or illuminated man who is aware of his "Oriental" origin, is therefore a stranger and an exile in this world, as described in one of Suhrawardī's most eloquent symbolic recitals *Qiṣṣat al-ghurbat al-gharbiyyah* (*The Story of the Occidental Exile*). It is through reminiscence of his original abode that man begins to have a nostalgia for his veritable home, and with the help of illuminative knowledge he is able to reach that abode. Illuminative knowledge, which is made possible by contact with the angelic orders, transforms man's being and saves him. The angel is the instrument of illumination and hence salvation. Man has descended from the world of the "seigneurial lights" and it is by returning to this world and reunifying with his angelic "alter-ego" that man finds his wholeness once again.

Ishrāqī philosophy depicts in an eminently symbolic language a vast universe based on the symbolism of light and the "Orient." It breaks the boundaries of Aristotelian cosmology as well as the confines of *ratio* defined by the Aristotelians. Suhrawardī was able to create an essentialistic metaphysics of light and a cosmology of rarely paralleled grandeur and beauty which "orients" the veritable seeker through the cosmic crypt and guides him to the realm of pure light, which is none other than the Orient of being. In this journey, which is at once philosophical and spiritual, man is led by a knowledge which is itself light, according to the saying of the Prophet who said *al-ʿilm nūr* (Knowledge is light). That is why this philosophy, according to Suhrawardī's last will and testament at the end of his *Ḥikmat al-ishrāq*, is not to be taught to everyone. It is for those whose minds have been trained by rigorous philosophical training and whose hearts have been purified through inner effort to subdue that interior dragon which is the carnal soul. For such people, the teachings of *ishrāq* reveal an inner knowledge that is none other than the eternal wisdom or *sophia perennis* which illuminates and transforms, obliterates and resurrects until man reaches the pleroma of the world of lights and the original abode from which he began his cosmic wayfaring.

11. Mullā Ṣadrā

This remarkable figure was born in Shiraz about 979/1571, studied with Mir Dāmād and other masters of the day in Isfahan, then retired for some ten years to a village near Qum, and finally returned to Shiraz, where he spent the last thirty years of his life writing and training students who came to him from as far away as North Africa and Tibet. He died in Basra in 1050/1640 while returning from his seventh pilgrimage on foot to Mecca.

Mullā Ṣadrā incorporates that Suhrawardian ideal according to which the perfect philosopher or theosopher (*ḥakīm muta'allih*) must have undergone both intellectual training and inner purification. Later Islamic philosophy in fact bestowed the title of *Ṣadr al-muta'allihīn* upon Mullā Ṣadrā, meaning foremost among theosophers. Indeed, he does represent the perfection of his Suhrawardian norm. A master dialectician and logician as well as a visionary and seer, Mullā Ṣadrā created a perfect harmony between the poles of ratiocination and mystical perception. Through the intellect wed to revelation he reached a *coincidentia oppositorum* that embraces the vigor of logic and the immediacy of spiritual unveiling. Like the *Ḥikmat al-ishrāq*, which begins with logic and ends with mystical ecstasy, Mullā Ṣadrā wove a pattern of thought that is logical and immersed in the ocean of the light of gnosis. He called this synthesis—which he considered to be based specifically on the three grand paths to the truth open to man, namely, revelation (*waḥy* or *shar'*), intellection (*'aql*), and mystical unveiling (*kashf*)—*al-ḥikmat al-muta'āliyah* or "the transcendent theosophy." His synthesis represented a new intellectual perspective in Islamic philosophy, a perspective which has had numerous followers especially in Persia and India but also in Iraq and certain other Arab lands over the centuries.

Mullā Ṣadrā composed some fifty books, almost all in Arabic, of which the most important is *al-Asfār al-arba'ah* (*The Four Journeys*), which remains the most advanced text of traditional Islamic philosophy in the *madrasahs* to this day. It includes not only his own metaphysical and cosmological views and the most extensive treatment of eschatology found in any Islamic philosophical text, but also the views of various schools of thought both Islamic and pre-Islamic. It is a veritable philosophical encyclopedia in which the influence of the Avicennan school, of Suhrawardī and Ibn 'Arabī, and of *kalām* both Sunni and Shi'ite is clearly discernible. But above and beyond these sources one can detect in this work, as in Mullā Ṣadrā's other writings, the great influence of the Quran and the sayings of the Prophet and the Shi'ite Imams. His Quranic commentaries such as the *Asrār al-āyāt* (*The Secrets of the Verses of the Quran*) are the most important contributions made to Quranic studies by an Islamic philosopher, and his commentary on the Shi'ite collection of *Ḥadīth*, the *Uṣūl al-kāfī* of Kulaynī, is one of his philosophical masterpieces. But these works also reveal the central significance of the Quran as the source of philosophical meditation for Islamic philosophers and of the sayings of the Prophet and the Imams as sources of inspiration for later Islamic philosophy. Among Mullā Ṣadrā's major achievements is the creation of a perfect harmony between faith and reason, religion and philosophy, a harmony which is the achievement of the goal of some nine centuries of Islamic theology and philosophy.

No other Islamic philosopher has dealt in depth with matters of faith ranging from the basis of ethics to eschatological imagery depicted in the Quran and *Ḥadīth* as has Mullā Ṣadrā. Nor have any of the philosophers dealt as thoroughly as he with all the questions which concerned the scholars of *kalām*. In fact, Mullā Ṣadrā claims that the *mutakallimūn* did not possess the divine knowledge (*al-maʿrifah*) necessary to deal with the questions they were treating and that therefore their activity was illegitimate. It was for the *ḥukamā-yi ilāhī* (literally, "the theosophers") to deal with such questions and to provide the answers for the enigmas and complex problems contained in religious teachings. Much of what Christians understand by theology would find its counterpart in Islamic thought in the writings of Mullā Ṣadrā rather than the Ash'arites, except that his is a "theology" always immersed in the light of divine knowledge, of gnosis, and not only of rational arguments concerning the tenets of the faith. Mullā Ṣadrā's "transcendent theosophy" is in fact philosophy, theology, and gnosis and draws from all these schools as they developed during the earlier centuries of Islamic intellectual history.

In his youth Mullā Ṣadrā followed the "essentialist metaphysics" of Suhrawardī, but as a result of a spiritual experience combined with intellectual vision he brought about what Corbin has called "a revolution in Islamic philosophy" and formulated the "existential metaphysics" by which he has come to be known. This metaphysical edifice, which is incomprehensible without a knowledge of Avicennan ontology and Suhrawardian cosmology and noetics, is based on the unity (*waḥdah*), principiality (*aṣālah*), and gradation (*tashkīk*) of being (*wujūd*). There is only one reality, which participates in grades and levels. The reality of each thing comes from its *wujūd* and not its quiddity or essence (*māhiyyah*). The quiddities are nothing but limitations imposed on *wujūd*, which extends in a hierarchy from dust to the Divine Throne. God Himself is the Absolute

Being (*al-wujūd al-muṭlaq*) who is the origin of all realms of existence and yet transcendent vis-à-vis the chain of being. Moreover, there is unity of all being not so much in the general *waḥdat al-wujūd* sense according to which there is only One Being, God, and nothing else even exists. Rather, Mullā Ṣadrā speaks of a unity that is more similar to the unity between the sun and the rays that emanate from it.

This vast ocean of being—or rather becoming—moreover, is in constant movement toward its Divine Origin in what Mullā Ṣadrā calls trans-substantial motion (*al-ḥarakat al-jawhariyyah*). He has the vision of a cosmos in constant becoming moving toward its entelechy or perfection (*kamāl*). This movement must not, however, be construed in an evolutionary sense, for Mullā Ṣadrā asserts categorically the reality of the Platonic ideas or the immutable archetypes of all things existing in the world below. The higher states of being do not belong to a future time. They are real and present here and now to be realized by man, who forms the vertical axis of cosmic existence.

This vertical progression in the scales of being is achieved most of all through knowledge. Knowledge transforms the being of the knower, as from another point of view knowledge depends on the mode of the knower. Mullā Ṣadrā points to the principle of the identity of the intellect and the intelligible (*ittiḥād al-ʿāqil wa'l-maʿqūl*) to emphasize the inner link between knowing and being. In fact, in the supreme form of knowledge, being is knowledge and knowledge being, as the dichotomy between the object and the subject is transcended.

In ascending the scales of being, man not only traverses the physical and spiritual or intelligible realms of reality but also the realm between the two, which Islamic metaphysicians have called the "world of imagination." Mullā Ṣadrā insists on the reality of this world both macrocosmically and microcosmically and insists on its survival after man's death. He provides an ontological status for a realm spoken of already by Suhrawardī in its microcosmic aspect and emphasized greatly by Ibn ʿArabī, who speaks of the creative power of imagination. It was, however, Mullā Ṣadrā who treated this world in a thoroughly metaphysical and cosmological manner, bringing out its significance in both the descending and the ascending arcs of universal existence.

It is in fact in this intermediate realm that eschatological events referred to in the Quran and *Ḥadīth* take place. Mullā Ṣadrā dealt extensively with this issue in many of his works. Not only did he devote independent treatises to this subject, such as the *Risālah fi'l-ḥashr* (*Treatise on Resurrection*), but also the extensive fourth "journey" or *safar* of his masterpiece, the *Asfār al-arbaʿah* is devoted to the soul (*nafs*) and its journey from the womb to its resurrection in the Divine Presence. No Islamic philosopher has ever dealt with the vast ocean of the soul and its posthumous development with such thoroughness as Mullā Ṣadrā. Those who search for an Islamic counterpart to the major treatises on eschatology found in other religions such as Hinduism and Buddhism must turn to later Islamic philosophy, especially the teachings of Mullā Ṣadrā and his students. They bring out the inner meaning of the teachings of the Quran, *Ḥadīth*, the sayings of the Shi'ite Imams concerning eschatology, and also of such earlier Sufis as Ibn ʿArabī, who also wrote extensively on the subject.

Mullā Ṣadrā created a vast metaphysical synthesis in which strands from many earlier schools of Islamic thought were woven together in a rich tapestry of many hues and shades, dominated by the unity of Sadrian ontology and metaphysics. In Mullā Ṣadrā one finds not only peaceful coexistence, but complementarity and harmony, between the tenets of faith or revelation, intellection, and mystical vision or unveiling. This last major school of Islamic philosophy achieved in a sense the final elaboration of the synthesis of modes of knowledge toward which Islamic philosophy had been moving since its earliest patriarchs such as al-Kindī began to philosophize in a world dominated by the reality of prophetic revelation and characterized by the inalienable wedding between the intellect as the instrument of inner illumination and the reasoning faculty of the human mind.

12. Existence and Quiddity

There is nothing more central to Islamic philosophy and especially metaphysics than *wujūd* (at once Being and existence), in itself and in its relation to *māhiyyah* (quiddity or essence). For eleven centuries Islamic philosophers and even certain Sufis and theologians (*mutakallimūn*) have been concerned with this subject and have developed on the basis of their study of *wujūd* world views which have dominated Islamic thought and have also had a deep influence upon Christian and Jewish philosophy. Islamic philosophy is most of all a philosophy concerned with *wujūd* and hence with its distinction from *māhiyyah.* To understand the meaning of these basic concepts, their distinction and relationship, is, therefore, to grasp the very basis of Islamic philosophical thought.

It is true that Islamic metaphysics places the Absolute above all limitations, even beyond the ontological principle as usually understood. It knows that the Divine Essence (*al-dhāt al-ilāhiyyah*) stands above even Being, that it is Non-Being or Beyond-Being in that it stands beyond all limitation and even beyond the qualification of being beyond all limitation. Nevertheless, the language of this metaphysical doctrine remains in most schools of Islamic thought that of *wujūd.* Hence, the discussion concerning the choice between *wujūd* and *māhiyyah* remains central to Islamic metaphysical thought, even if the Muslim gnostics and metaphysicians have remained fully aware of the supra-ontological nature of the Supreme Reality and have not limited metaphysics to ontology.

Only too often the concern of Islamic philosophers with *wujūd* and *māhiyyah* has been traced back solely to Greek philosophy and especially to Aristotle. There is, of course, no doubt concerning the debt of al-Fārābī, who was the first Muslim philosopher to discuss fully the distinction between *wujūd* and *māhiyyah,* to the Stagirite. The manner, however, in which he and especially Ibn Sīnā, who has been called the "philosopher of being" *par excellence,* approached the subject and the centrality that the study of *wujūd* gained in Islamic thought have very much to do with the Islamic revelation itself. The Quran states explicitly, "But His command, when He intendeth a thing, is only that He saith unto it: Be! and it is (*kun fa-yakūn*)" (36:82); it also speaks over and over of the creation and destruction of the world. This world as experienced by the *homo islamicus* is, therefore, not synonymous with *wujūd*. It is not "an ontological block without fissure in which essence, existence and unity are but one."[1]

Moreover, the origin of the "chain of being" is not simply the first link in the chain but is transcendent vis-à-vis the chain. The levels of existence (*marātib al-wujūd*) to which Aristotle and Theophrastus and before them Plato refer are, therefore, from the Islamic point of view discontinuous with respect to their Source, which is above and beyond them. The Quranic teachings about Allah as Creator of the world played a most crucial role in the development of Islamic philosophy as far as the study of *wujūd* is concerned. On the one hand, it made central the importance of the ontological hiatus between Being and existents and, on the other hand, bestowed another significance on the distinction between *wujūd* and *māhiyyah* by providing a meaning to the act of existentiation or the bestowal of *wujūd* upon *māhiyyah* other than what one finds in Aristotelian philosophy as it developed among the Greeks.

* * *

Traditional teachers of Islamic philosophy begin the teaching of natural theology, or *ḥikmat-i ilāhī* (literally *theosophia*) as it is called in Persian, by instilling in the mind of the student a way of thinking based upon the distinction between *wujūd* and *māhiyyah*. They appeal to the immediate perception of things and assert that man in seeking to understand the nature of the reality he perceives can ask two questions about it: 1) Is it (*hal huwa*)? and 2) What is it (*mā huwa*)? The answer to the first question is *wujūd* or its opposite (*ʿadam* or nonexistence) while the answer to the second question is *māhiyyah* (from the word *mā huwa* or *mā hiya*, which is its feminine form).

Usually in Islamic philosophy terms are carefully defined, but in the case of *wujūd* it is impossible to define it in the usual meaning of definition as used in logic, which consists of genus and specific difference. Moreover, every unknown is defined by that which is known, but there is nothing more universally known than *wujūd* and therefore nothing else in terms of which *wujūd* can be defined. In traditional circles it is said that everyone,

[1] E. Gilson, *L'Être et l'essence* (Paris: J. Vrin, 1948), p. 90; also quoted in Izutsu, "The Fundamental Structure of Sabzavārī's Metaphysics," introduction to the Arabic text of Sabzawārī's *Sharḥ-i manẓūmah*, ed. by M. Mohaghegh and T. Izutsu (Tehran: McGill University Institute of Islamic Studies, Tehran Branch, 1969), pp. 54-55.

even a small baby, knows intuitively the difference between *wujūd* and its opposite, as can be seen by the fact that when a baby is crying, to speak to it about milk is of no avail, but as soon as "real" milk, that is, milk possessing *wujūd*, is given to it, it stops crying.

Rather than define *wujūd*, therefore, Islamic philosophers allude to its meaning through such assertions as "*Wujūd* is that by virtue of which it is possible to give knowledge about something" or "*Wujūd* is that which is the source of all effects." As for *māhiyyah*, it is possible to define it clearly and precisely as that which provides an answer to the question "What is it?" There is, however, a further development of this concept in later Islamic philosophy, which distinguishes between *māhiyyah* in its particular sense (*bi'l-maʿna'l-akhaṣṣ*), which is the response to the question "What is it?," and *māhiyyah* in its general sense (*bi'l-maʿna'l-aʿamm*), which means that by which a thing is what it is. It is said that *māhiyyah* in this second sense is derived from the Arabic phrase *mā bihi huwa huwa* (that by which something is what it is). This second meaning refers to the reality (*ḥaqīqah*) of a thing and is not opposed to *wujūd*, as is the first meaning of *māhiyyah*.

As far as the etymological derivation of the term *wujūd* is concerned, it is an Arabic term related to the root *WJD* which possesses the basic meaning to find or come to know about something. It is etymologically related to the term *wijdān*, which means consciousness, awareness, or knowledge, as well as to *wajd*, which means ecstasy or bliss.[2] The Islamic philosophers who were Persian or used that language also employed the Persian term *hastī*, which is of Iranian origin and is related to the Indo-European terms denoting being, such as "*ist*" in German and "is" in English.

Wujūd as used in traditional Islamic philosophy cannot be rendered simply as existence. Rather, it denotes at once Being, being, Existence, and existence, each of these terms having a specific meaning in the context of Islamic metaphysics. The term "Being" refers to the Absolute or Necessary Being (*wājib al-wujūd*); "being" is a universal concept encompassing all levels of reality, both that of creatures and that of the Necessary Being Itself. The term "Existence" refers to the first emanation or effusion from the Pure or Absolute Being, or what is called *al-fayḍ al-aqdas*, the Most

[2] It is remarkable how the three terms *wujūd*, *wijdān*, and *wajd* resemble so closely the famous *sat*, *chit*, and *ananda* in Hinduism, where their combination *satchitananda* is considered as a name of God and the metaphysical characterization of Reality.

Sacred Effusion in later Islamic philosophy, while "existence" refers to the reality of all things other than the Necessary Being.

Technically speaking, God is, but He cannot be said to exist, for one must remember that existence is derived from the Latin *ex-sistere*, which implies a pulling away or drawing away from the substance or ground of reality. The very rich vocabulary of Islamic philosophy differentiates all these usages by using the term *wujūd* with various modifiers and connotations based upon the context, whereas the single English term "existence," for example, cannot render justice to all the nuances of meaning contained in the Arabic term. Thus throughout this essay we have used the Arabic term *wujūd* rather than a particular English translation. There are also terms derived from *wujūd* which are of great philosophical importance, especially the term *mawjūd* or existent which Islamic philosophy, especially of the later period, clearly distinguished from *wujūd* as the "act of existence." Muslim metaphysicians knew fully well the difference between *ens* and *actus essendi* or *Sein* and *Dasein*, and therefore followed a path which led to conclusions very different from those in the West that finally led to modern Western *Existenz Philosophie* and existentialism.

The starting point of Islamic ontology is not the world of existents in which the existence of something, that something as existent, and the unity of that thing are the same, as is the case with Aristotelian metaphysics. For Aristotle the world could not not exist. It is an ontological block which cannot conceivably be broken; thus the distinction between *wujūd* and *māhiyyah* is not of any great consequence. For Islamic thought, on the contrary, the world is not synonymous with *wujūd*. There is an ontological poverty (*faqr*) of the world in the sense that *wujūd* is given by God Who alone is the abiding Reality, all "other" existents coming into being and passing away. The conceptual distinction between *wujūd* and *māhiyyah*, therefore, gains great significance and, far from being inconsequential, becomes in fact the key for understanding the nature of reality.

According to traditional Islamic philosophy, the intellect (*al-ʿaql*) is able to distinguish clearly between the *wujūd* and *māhiyyah* of anything, not as they are externally, where there is but one existent object, but in the "container of the mind." When man asks himself the question "What is it?" with respect to a particular object, the answer given is totally distinct from concern for its existence or nonexistence. The "mind" has the power to conceive of the quiddity of something, let us say man, purely and completely as *māhiyyah* and totally distinct from any form of *wujūd*. *Māhiyyah* thus considered in itself and in so far as it is itself (*min ḥaythu hiya hiya*) is called in Islamic philosophy, and following the terminology of Ibn Sīnā, "natural universal" (*al-kullī al-ṭabīʿī*). *Māhiyyah* can also appear in the mind, possessing "mental existence," and in the external world *in concreto*, possessing external existence; but in itself it can be conceived completely shorn of any concern with *wujūd*, such as when the "mind" conceives of the *māhiyyah* of man which includes the definition of man without any consideration as to whether man exists or not.

Moreover, *māhiyyah* excludes *wujūd* as one of its constituent elements. Or to use traditional terminology, *wujūd* is not a *muqawwim* of *māhiyyah* in the sense that animal, which is contained in the definition of man as rational animal, is a constituent or *muqawwim* of the *māhiyyah* of man. There is nothing in a *māhiyyah* which would relate it to *wujūd* or necessitate the existence of that *māhiyyah*. The two concepts are totally distinct as are their causes. The causes of a *māhiyyah* are the elements that constitute its definition, namely, the genus and specific difference, while the causes of the *wujūd* of a particular existent are its efficient and final causes as well as its substratum. For a *māhiyyah* to exist, therefore, *wujūd* must be "added to it," that is, become wedded to it from "outside" itself.

In the history of Islamic thought, not to speak of modern studies of Islamic philosophy, there has often been a misunderstanding about this distinction and about the relation between *wujūd* and *māhiyyah*. It is essential, therefore, to emphasize that Ibn Sīnā and those who followed him did not begin with two "realities," one *māhiyyah* and the other *wujūd*, which became wedded in concrete, external objects, even if certain philosophers have referred to existents as "combined pairs" (*zawj tarkībī*). Rather, they began with the single, concrete external object, the *ens* or *mawjūd*, and analyzed them conceptually in terms of *māhiyyah* and *wujūd*, which they studied separately in their philosophical treatises. These concepts, however, were to provide a key for the understanding of not only the relation between the "suchness" and "is-ness" of existents, but also the ontological origin of things and their interrelatedness, as we see in the "transcendent theosophy" of Ṣadr al-Dīn Shīrāzī.

* * *

One of the fundamental distinctions in the Islamic philosophy of being is that between necessity (*wujūb*), contingency or possibility (*imkān*), and impossibility (*imtināʿ*). This distinction, which, again, was formulated in its perfected form for the first time by Ibn Sīnā and stated in many of his works, is traditionally called "the three directions" (*al-jihāt al-thalāth*) and is basic to the understanding of Islamic metaphysics. It possesses, in fact, at once a philosophical and a theological significance to the extent that the term *wājib al-wujūd*, the Necessary Being, which is a philosophical term for

God, has been used throughout the centuries extensively by theologians, Sufis, and even jurists and ordinary preachers.

If one were to consider a *māhiyyah* in itself in the "container of the mind," one of three conditions would hold true:

1. It could exist or not exist. In either case there would be no logical contradiction.

2. It must exist because if it were not to exist, there would follow a logical contradiction.

3. It cannot exist because if it were to exist, there would follow a logical contradiction.

The first category is called *mumkin*, the second *wājib*, and the third *mumtaniʿ*. The vast majority of *māhiyyāt* are *mumkin*, such as the *māhiyyah* of man, horse, or star. Once one considers the *māhiyyah* of man in itself in the mind, there is no logical contradiction, whether it possesses *wujūd* or not. Everything in the created order in fact participates in the condition of contingency so that the universe, or all that is other than God (*mā siwa'Llāh*), is often called the world of contingencies (*ʿālam al-mumkināt*).

It is also possible for the mind (or strictly speaking *al-ʿaql*) to conceive of certain *māhiyyāt*, the supposition of whose existence would involve a logical contradiction. In traditional Islamic thought the example usually given is *sharīk al-bāriʾ*, that is, a partner taken unto God. Such an example might not be so obvious to the modern mind, but numerous other examples could be given, such as a quantity which would be greater than the sum of its parts, for the supposition of that which is impossible in reality is not itself impossible.

Finally, the mind can conceive of a *māhiyyah* which must possess *wujūd* of necessity, that *māhiyyah* being one which is itself *wujūd*. That Reality whose *māhiyyah* is *wujūd* cannot not be; it is called the Necessary Being or *wājib al-wujūd*. Furthermore, numerous arguments have been provided to prove that there can be but one *wājib al-wujūd* in harmony with the Quranic doctrine of the Oneness of God. The quality of necessity in the ultimate sense belongs to God alone, as does that of freedom. One of the great masters of traditional Islamic philosophy at the beginning of this century, who was devoted to the school of the "transcendent unity of being," in fact asserted that after a lifetime of study he had finally discovered that *wujūb* or necessity is none other than *wujūd* itself.

This analysis in the "container of the mind" might seem to be contradicted by the external world in which objects already possess *wujūd*. Can one say in their case that they are still contingent? This question becomes particularly pertinent when one remembers that according to most schools of Islamic philosophy what exists must exist and cannot not exist. Naṣīr al-Dīn al-Ṭūsī summarizes this doctrine in his famous poem:

> That which exists is as it should be,
> That which should not exist does not.

The answer to this problem resides in the distinction between an object in its essence and as it exists in the external world. In itself, as a *māhiyyah*, every object save God is contingent, a *mumkin al-wujūd*. It has gained *wujūd*, and so for it to exist necessarily requires the agency of reality other than itself. Existents are, therefore, *wājib bi'l-ghayr*, necessary through an agent other than themselves. They are necessary as existents by the very fact that they possess *wujūd*, but are contingent in their essence in contrast to the Necessary Being which is necessary in Its own Essence and not through an agent outside Itself.

The distinction between necessity and contingency makes possible a vision of the universe in perfect accord with the Islamic perspective where to God alone belongs the power of creation and existentiation (*ījād*). It is He who said "Be!" and it was. Everything in the universe is "poor" in the sense of not possessing any *wujūd* of its own. It is the Necessary Being alone which bestows *wujūd* upon the *māhiyyāt* and brings them from the darkness of nonexistence into the light of *wujūd*, covering them with the robe of necessity while in themselves they remain forever in the nakedness of contingency.

* * *

Islamic philosophy followed a different course from Western philosophy in nearly every domain despite their common roots and the considerable influence of Islamic philosophy upon Latin Scholasticism. In the subject of ontology most of the differences belong to later centuries when Islamic and Western thought had parted ways. One of these important differences concerns the distinction between the concept (*mafhūm*) and reality (*ḥaqīqah*) of *wujūd* which is discussed in later Islamic metaphysics in a manner very different from that found in later Western thought.

There are some schools of Islamic philosophy, similar to certain Western schools of philosophy, which consider *wujūd* to be merely an abstraction not corresponding to any external reality, which consists solely of existents. The most important school of Islamic philosophy, however, which flowered during the later centuries under the influence of Ṣadr al-Dīn Shīrāzī, distinguishes clearly between the concept of *wujūd* and the

Reality to which it corresponds. The concept "being" is the most universal and known of all concepts, while the Reality of *wujūd* is the most inaccessible of all realities although it is the most manifest. In fact, it is the only Reality for those who possess the knowledge that results from illumination and "unveiling."

All later discussions of *wujūd* and *māhiyyah* must be understood in light of the distinction between the concept of *wujūd*, which exists in the "mind," and the Reality of *wujūd*, which exists externally and can be known and experienced provided man is willing to conform himself to what Being demands of him. Here, philosophy and gnosis meet and the supreme experience made possible through spiritual practice becomes the ever present reality that underlies the conceptualizations of the philosophers.

It is also in the light of this experience of *wujūd* that Islamic metaphysics has remained always aware of the distinction between *ens* and *actu essendi* and has seen things not merely as objects which exist but as acts of *wujūd*, as *esto*. If Islamic philosophy did not move, as did Western philosophy, towards an ever greater concern with a world of solidified objects, or what certain French philosophers have called "la chosification du monde," it was because the experience of the Reality of Being as an ever present element has prevented the speculative mind of the majority of Muslim philosophers either from mistaking the act of *wujūd* for the existent that appears to possess *wujūd* on its own while being cut off from the Absolute Being, or from failing to distinguish between the concept of *wujūd* and its blinding Reality.

* * *

Man lives in the world of multiplicity; his immediate experience is of objects and forms, of existents. Yet he yearns for unity, for the Reality which stands beyond and behind this veil of the manifold. One might say that the *māhiyyah* of man is such that he yearns for the experience of *wujūd*. It is in the nature of man, and in this realm of terrestrial existence of man alone, to seek to transcend himself and to go beyond what he "is" in order to become what he really is. Man's mode of existence, his acts, his way of living his life, his inner discipline, his attainment of knowledge, and his living according to the dictates of Being affect his own mode of being. Man can perfect himself in such a manner that the act of *wujūd* in him is intensified until he ceases to exist as a separate ego and experiences the Supreme Being, becoming completely drowned in the ocean of the Reality of *wujūd*.

Man's spiritual progress from the experience of existents to that of the Absolute Reality of *wujūd* can be compared to seeing objects around a room whose walls are covered with mirrors. Soon the observer looking at the walls realizes that the walls are mirrors and he sees nothing but the mirrors. Finally he sees the objects, yet no longer as independent objects but as reflections in the mirror. In the ascent towards the experience of *wujūd*, man first realizes that objects do not have a *wujūd* or reality of their own. Then he experiences *wujūd* in its Absoluteness and realizes that he and everything else in the universe are literally "no-thing" and have no reality of their own. Finally, he realizes that all things are "plunged in God," that the "transcendent unity of Being" means that *wujūd* is one yet manifests a world of multiplicity which does not violate its sacred unity.

The vast metaphysical synthesis of Islamic sages and philosophers has for its aim the opening of the mind to the awareness of that reality which can only be experienced by the whole of man's being and not by the mind alone. Yet, the doctrines in their diverse forms serve to prepare the mind for that intellection which is suprarational and to enable the mind to become integrated into the whole of man's being whose center is the heart. Only the person who is whole can experience that wholeness which belongs to the One, to *wujūd* in its Absoluteness.

These Islamic doctrines have also created a philosophical universe of discourse in which the inner dimension of things has never been forgotten, where the act of *wujūd* has been an ever present reality, preventing the reduction of the world to objects and things divorced from the inner dimension as has happened with post-medieval philosophy in the West leading to dire consequences for the human condition. The message of Islamic philosophy, as it concerns the study of *wujūd* and *māhiyyah*, is therefore of great significance for the contemporary world, which is suffocating in an environment of things and objects which have overwhelmed the human spirit. This philosophy is also of great significance for a world which lives intensely on the mental plane at the expense of other dimensions of human existence, for although this philosophy speaks to the mind it draws the mind once again to the heart. The heart is the center of the human being and seat of the intellect, where man is able to know experientially that Reality of *wujūd* which determines what we are, from which we issue, and to whose embrace we finally return. It is only in experiencing *wujūd*, not this or that *wujūd* but *wujūd* in its pure inviolability, in its absoluteness and infinity, that man is fully man and fulfills the purpose for which he was drawn from the bosom of *wujūd* to embark upon this short terrestrial journey, only to return finally to that One and Unique *wujūd* from which in reality nothing ever departs.

Tradition

13. *Scientia Sacra*

Scientia sacra is none other than that sacred knowledge which lies at the heart of every revelation and is the center of that circle which encompasses and defines tradition. The first question which presents itself is "How is the attainment of such a knowledge possible?" The answer of tradition is that the twin source of this knowledge is revelation and intellection or intellectual intuition, which involves the illumination of the heart and mind of man and the presence in him of knowledge of an immediate and direct nature which is tasted and experienced, the sapience which the Islamic tradition refers to as "presential knowledge" (*al-ʿilm al-ḥuḍūrī*). Man is able to know, and this knowledge corresponds to some aspect of reality. Ultimately, in fact, knowledge is knowledge of Absolute Reality and intelligence possesses the miraculous gift of being able to know that which is and all that partakes of being.

Scientia sacra is not the fruit of human intelligence speculating upon or reasoning about the content of an inspiration or a spiritual experience that itself is not of an intellectual character. Rather, what is received through inspiration is itself of an intellectual nature; it is sacred knowledge. The human intelligence which perceives this message and receives this truth does not impose upon it the intellectual nature or content of a spiritual experience of a sapiential character. The knowledge contained in such an experience issues from the source of this experience, which is the Intellect, the source of all sapience and the bestower of all principial knowledge, the Intellect which also modifies the human recipient that the Scholastics called the potential intellect. Here the medieval distinction between the active and passive or potential intellect can serve to elucidate the nature of this process of the illumination of the mind and to remove the error of seeing the sapiential and intellectual content of spiritual experience as being the result of the human mind meditating upon or reasoning about the content of such an experience, whereas spiritual experience on the highest level is itself of an intellectual and sapiential nature.

From another point of view, that of the Self which resides at the center of every self, the source of the *scientia sacra* revealed to man is the center and root of human intelligence itself, since ultimately "Knowledge of the Substance is the substance of knowledge," or knowledge of the Origin and the Source is the Origin and Source of knowledge. The truth descends upon the mind like an eagle landing upon a mountain top, or it gushes forth and inundates the mind like a deep well which has suddenly burst forth into a spring. In either case, the sapiential nature of what the human being receives through spiritual experience is not the result of man's mental faculty but issues from the nature of that experience itself. Man can know through intuition and revelation not because he is a thinking being who imposes the categories of his thought upon what he perceives, but because knowledge is being. The nature of reality is none other than consciousness, which, needless to say, cannot be limited to only its individual human mode.

Of course not everyone is capable of intellection or of having intellectual intuition, any more than everyone is capable of having faith in a particular religion. But the lack of possibility of intellection for everyone does not invalidate the reality of such a possibility, any more than does the fact that many people are not able to have faith invalidate the reality of a religion. In any case for those who have the possibility of intellectual intuition there is the means to attain a knowledge of a sacred character that lies at the heart of that objective revelation which constitutes religion and also at the center of man's being. This microcosmic revelation makes possible access to that *scientia sacra* which contains the knowledge of the Real and the means of distinguishing between the Real and the illusory.

What we have designated as *scientia sacra* is none other than metaphysics, if this term is understood correctly as the ultimate science of the Real. This term possesses certain unfortunate connotations because, first of all, the prefix *meta* does imply transcendence, but not immanence, and also it connotes a form of knowledge or science that comes after physics, whereas metaphysics is the primary and fundamental science or wisdom that comes before and contains the principles of all the sciences. Second, the habit of considering metaphysics in the West as a branch of philosophy, even in those philosophical schools which have a metaphysical dimension, has been instrumental in reducing the significance of metaphysics to just mental activity rather than seeing it as a sacred science concerned with the nature of Reality and wed to methods for the realization of this knowledge, a science which embraces the whole of man's being. In Oriental languages such terms as *prajnā*, *jñāna*, *maʿrifah*, or *ḥikmah* connote the ultimate science of the Real without their being reduced to a branch of another form of knowledge known as philosophy or its equivalent. And it is in this traditional sense of *jñāna* or *maʿrifah* that metaphysics, or the "science of the Real," can be considered as identical with *scientia sacra*.

If *scientia sacra* lies at the heart of each tradition and is not a purely human knowledge lying outside of the sacred precinct of the various traditions, then how can one speak of it without remaining bound within a single religious universe? The response to this question has led certain scholars and philosophers engaged in "comparative philosophy" in the context of East and West to speak of "meta-philosophy" and a meta-language which stands above and beyond the language of a particular tradition. From the traditional point of view, however, the language of metaphysics is inseparable from the content and meaning it expresses and bears the imprint of the message, this language having been developed by the metaphysicians and sages of various traditions over the ages. Each tradition possesses one or several "languages of discourse" suitable for metaphysical doctrines, and there is no need whatsoever to create a meta-language or invent a new vocabulary today to deal with such matters, since the English language is heir to the Western tradition and the several perfectly suitable metaphysical languages of the West such as those of Platonism, Thomism, and the school of Palamite theology. Moreover, contemporary traditional authors have already resuscitated the symbolic and intellectual aspects of modern languages, which have decayed in their symbolic and hierarchic aspects but which nevertheless contain metaphysical possibilities because of the very nature of human language. These authors have created a perfectly suitable language for the expression of *scientia sacra* drawing occasionally from such sacred languages as Sanskrit and Arabic for certain key concepts. In any case a meta-language to express a meta-philosophy in order to expound traditional metaphysics is totally unnecessary. The language needed has already been forged from existing European languages which, although reflecting the gradual degradation of thought from an intellectual point of view, have also preserved the possibility of revival precisely because of their inalienable link with the classical languages of the West and the traditional metaphysics expressed in them, and even in the earlier phases of the life of modern European languages.

If one were to ask what is metaphysics, the primary answer would be the science of the Real or, more specifically, the knowledge by means of which man is able to distinguish between the Real and the illusory and to know things in their essence or as they are, which means ultimately to know them *in divinis*. The knowledge of the Principle which is at once the absolute and infinite Reality is the heart of metaphysics, while the distinction between levels of universal and cosmic existence, including both the macrocosm and the microcosm, are like its limbs. Metaphysics concerns not only the Principle in Itself and in Its manifestations but also the principles of the various sciences of a cosmological order. At the heart of the traditional sciences of the cosmos, as well as traditional anthropology, psychology, and aesthetics, stands the *scientia sacra* which contains the principles of these sciences while being primarily concerned with the knowledge of the Principle; this is both sacred knowledge and knowledge of the sacred par excellence, since the Sacred as such is none other than the Principle.

The Principle is Reality in contrast to all that appears as real but which is not reality in the ultimate sense. The Principle is the Absolute compared to which all is relative. It is Infinite while all else is finite. The Principle is One and Unique while manifestation is multiplicity. It is the Supreme Substance compared to which all else is accident. It is the Essence to which all things are juxtaposed as form. It is at once Beyond-Being and Being while the order of multiplicity is comprised of existents. It alone *is* while all else becomes, for It alone is eternal in the ultimate sense, while all that is externalized partakes of change. It is the Origin but also the End, the alpha and the omega. It is Emptiness if the world is envisaged as fullness and Fullness if the relative is perceived in the light of its ontological poverty and essential nothingness. These are all manners of speaking of the Ultimate Reality which can be known but not by man as such. It can only be known through the sun of the Divine Self residing at the center of the human soul. But all these ways of describing or referring to the Principle possess meaning and are efficacious as points of reference and support for that knowledge of the Real that in its realized aspect always terminates in the Ineffable and in that silence which is the "reflection" or "shadow" of the non-manifested aspect of the Principle upon the plane of manifestation. From that unitary point of view, the Principle or the Source is seen as not only the Inward but also the Outward, not only the One but also the essential reality of the many which are but the reflection of the One. At the top of that mountain of unitive knowledge there resides but the One; discrimination between the Real and the unreal terminates in the awareness of the nondual nature of the Real, the awareness which is the heart of gnosis and which represents not human knowledge but God's knowledge of Himself, the consciousness which is the goal of the path of knowledge and the essence of *scientia sacra.*

The Ultimate Reality is at once Absolute and Infinite, since no finite reality can be absolute due to its exclusion of some domain of reality. This reality is also the Supreme Good or the Perfection which is inseparable from the Absolute. Reality, being at once Absolute, Infinite, and Supreme Goodness or Perfection, cannot but give rise to the world or multiplicity, which must be realized, for otherwise that Reality would exclude certain possibilities and not be infinite. The world flows from the infinitude and goodness of the Real, for to speak of goodness is to speak of manifestation, effusion, or creation and to speak of infinity is to speak of all possibilities including that of the negation of the Principle, in whose direction the cosmogonic process moves without ever realizing that negation completely, for that total negation would be nothingness pure and simple.

Goodness is also from another point of view the image of the Absolute in the direction of that effusion and manifestation which marks the descent from the Principle and constitutes the world. Herein lies the root of relativity but it is still on the plane of Divinity. It is relativity *in divinis* or what could be called, using the well-known Hindu concept, the Divine *māyā*. Relativity is a possibility of that Reality which is at once Absolute and Infinite; hence that Reality or the Absolute gives rise to that manifestation of the good which in descending hierarchy leads to the world. The world is ultimately good, as asserted by various orthodox traditions,[1] because it descends from the Divine Goodness. The instrument of this descent is the reflection of the Absolute upon the plane of that Divine Relativity, the reflection which is none other than the Supreme Logos, the source of all cosmic perfections, the "place" of the archetypes, the "Word" by which all things were made.

Since the world or manifestation or creation issues from that Reality which is at once Absolute, Infinite, and Perfection or Goodness, these Hypostases of the Real or the Divine must also be reflected in the manifested order. The quality of absoluteness is reflected in the very existence of things, that mysterious presence of each thing which distinguishes it from all other things and from nothingness. Infinitude is reflected in the world in diverse modes in space, which is indefinite extension, in time, which is potentially endless duration, in form, which displays unending diversity, in number, which is marked by endless multiplicity, and in matter, a substance which partakes potentially of endless forms and divisions. As for Goodness, it is reflected in the cosmos through quality itself, which is indispensable to existence however eclipsed it might become in certain forms in the world of multiplicity that are removed as far as possible from the luminous and essential pole of manifestation. Space which preserves, time which changes and transforms, form which reflects quality, number which signifies indefi-

[1] The point of view of Manichaeism, which sees the world as evil rather than good, is primarily initiatic and not metaphysical, that is, it begins not with the aim of understanding the nature of things but of providing a way for escaping from the prison of material existence. Buddhism possesses a similar practical perspective but, of course, with a different metaphysical background since it belongs to a different spiritual universe.

nite quantity, and matter which is characterized by limitless substantiality are the conditions of the existence of not only the physical world but the worlds above, reaching ultimately the Divine Empyrean and the Divine Hypostases of Absoluteness, Infinity, and Perfection themselves.

Moreover, each of the Divine Hypostases is reflected in a particular manner in the five conditions of existence. Absoluteness is reflected in space as center, in time as the present moment, in matter as the ether which is the principle of both matter and energy, in form as the sphere which is the most perfect of forms and generator of all other regular geometric forms, which are potentially contained in it, and in number as unity, which is the source and principle of all numbers. Infinitude is reflected in space as extension, which theoretically knows no bound, in time as duration, which logically has no end, in matter as the indefiniteness of material substantiality, in form as the unlimited possibility of diversity, and in number as the limitlessness of quantity. As for Perfection, it is reflected in space as the contents or objects in space reflecting Divine Qualities and also as pure existence which, as the Sufis say, is the "Breath of the Compassionate" (*nafas al-raḥmān*), in space and time likewise as shapes and events possessing quality, in form as beauty, and in number as that qualitative aspect of number always related to geometric forms which is usually associated with the idea of Pythagorean number. *Scientia sacra* sees these aspects of cosmic existence as reflections upon the plane or the multiple planes of manifestation of the Supreme Hypostases of Absoluteness, Infinitude, and Goodness which characterize the Real as such. It also sees each of these conditions of existence as reflecting directly an aspect of the Divinity: matter and energy the Divine Substance, form the Logos, number the Divine Unity which is inexhaustible, space the infinite extension of Divine Manifestation, and time the rhythms of the universal cycles of existence, which the Abrahamic traditions allude to in passing as far as their official, formal theologies are concerned and which Hinduism highlights, referring to them as days and nights in the life of Brahma.

Since metaphysics as developed in the Occident has almost always been related to ontology, it is important to pause a moment and discuss the relation of Being to the Principle or Ultimate Reality. If Being is envisaged as the principle of existence or of all that exists, then It cannot be identified with the Principle as such, because the Principle is not exhausted by its creating aspect. Being is the first determination of the Supreme Principle in the direction of manifestation, and ontology remains only a part of metaphysics and is incomplete as long as it envisages the Principle only as Being in the sense defined. But if Being is used to embrace and include the sense of Absoluteness and Infinity, then it can mean both the Supra-Being or Reality beyond Being and Being as its first determination, even if only the term *Being* is used. Such seems to be the case with *esse* as employed by certain of the Scholastics and also *wujūd* in some of the schools of Islamic philosophy and theosophy.

The distinction between Being and being, Being and existence, and existence and essence or quiddity, and the relation between quiddity or essence and existence in existents lie at the heart of medieval Islamic, Jewish, and Christian philosophy and have been discussed in numerous works of medieval thought. From the point of view of *scientia sacra* what caused this profound way of envisaging reality to become unintelligible and finally rejected in the West was the loss of intellectual intuition, which destroyed the sense of the mystery of existence and reduced the subject of philosophy from the study of the act of existence (*esto*) to the existent (*ens*), thereby gradually reducing reality to pure "it" divorced from the world of the Spirit and the majesty of Being, whose constant effusions uphold the world that appears to the senses as possessing a continuous "horizontal" existence divorced from the "vertical" Cause or Being per se. That Islamic philosophy did not end with that impasse which marks the study of ontology in Western philosophy is due to its insistence upon the study of Being and its act rather than existents and to the wedding of this philosophy, by Suhrawardī and those who were to follow him, to spiritual experience, which made the experience of Being not only a possibility, but also the source for all philosophical speculation concerning the concept and reality of being.

The Ultimate Reality which is both Supra-Being and Being is at once transcendent and immanent. It is beyond everything and at the very heart and center of man's soul. *Scientia sacra* can be expounded in the language of one as well as the other perspective. It can speak of God or the Godhead, Allah, the Tao, or even *nirvāṇa* as being beyond the world or forms or *samsāra*, while asserting ultimately that *nirvāṇa* is *samsāra*, and *samsāra*, *nirvāṇa*. But it can also speak of the Supreme Self, of *Ātman*, compared to which all objectivization is *māyā*. The Ultimate Reality can be seen as both the Supreme Object and the Innermost Subject, for God is both transcendent and immanent, but He can be experienced as immanent only after He has been experienced as transcendent. Only God as Being can allow man to experience the Godhead as Supra-Being. The unitive knowledge which sees the world not as a separative creation but as a manifestation that is united through symbols and the very ray of existence to the Source does not at all negate the majesty of transcendence. Without that majesty, the beauty of Divine Proximity cannot be beheld. Integral metaphysics is fully aware of the necessity, on their own level, of the theological formulations which insist upon the hiatus between God and man or the Creator and the world. The metaphysical knowledge of unity comprehends the theological one in both a figurative and literal sense, while the reverse is not true. That is why the attainment of that unitive knowledge is impregnated with the perfume of sanctity, which always strengthens the very foundations of the religion with which the formal theology in question is concerned, while the study of formal theology can never result in that *scientia sacra* which simply belongs to another dimension and which relies upon another aspect of the functioning of the Intellect upon the human plane.

Metaphysics does not distinguish only between the Real and the apparent, and Being and becoming, but also between grades of existence. The hierarchic nature of reality is a universal assertion of all traditions and is part and parcel of their religious practices as well as their doctrines, whether conceived in terms of various hosts and orders of angels as described in the famous *Celestial Hierarchies* of Dionysius, or levels of light and darkness as in certain schools of Islamic esoterism, or as various orders of gods and titans as in religions with a mythological structure such as Hinduism. Even in Buddhism, for which the Supreme Principle is seen as the Void or Emptiness rather than Fullness, the vast intermediate worlds are depicted with remarkable power and beauty in both Buddhist cosmological texts and Buddhist art. The emphasis upon the hierarchic structure of reality in traditional doctrines is so great that a famous Persian poem states that he who does not accept the hierarchy of existence is an infidel (*zindīq*). Here again *scientia sacra*, which is concerned with the nature of reality, is distinguished from theology as usually understood, which can remain satisfied with what concerns man directly and a simpler view of reality based on God and man without emphasis upon the hierarchy of existence, although even in theology many schools have not failed to take into consideration the existence if not always the full significance of the intermediate planes of reality.

14. Renaissance Humanism

Renaissance humanism, as understood in the sense of a new philosophy growing out of not only *studia humanitatis* but also influenced by other philosophic currents of the period, possesses certain basic characteristics that it is of the utmost importance for us to examine. The first characteristic of this humanism is that it conceives of man as an independent, earthly being, no longer integrated into the total cosmos of faith of medieval Christianity. To be sure, there were still men and women of faith, but the new man envisaged by humanism was no longer defined by his or her faith in God and the hereafter. This new conception of humanity is closely related to the rather rapid loss of the significance of angels and the angelic hierarchy, delineated by Dionysus, which had dominated the medieval worldview. Rather than being a half-angel, half-man cast on Earth, man now became completely terrestrial, at home in a newly discovered Earth and no longer an exile from the paradisal realm, which did not mean that he did not and does not continue to wreak havoc upon this newly discovered "home." Having banished the angels from the cosmos, the new man also became the only intelligent being on Earth, the only one possessing a "mind."

Worldliness became man's "natural" state, and the otherworldliness of the medieval Christian conception of man began to be looked upon with a sense of derision. Earthly man, rather than man before his fall from his Edenic perfection, became the normal man. It was to this idea of the fallen man taken as the norm that Montaigne, one of the Renaissance figures most responsible for forging the new image of humanity, referred when he asserted, "Every man bears the whole stamp of the human condition (*l'humaine condition*)."[1]

In forgetting the Heaven of the medieval period, man now discovered a new Earth with which he identified as "the world" and not as nature, over which he now felt the sense of greater domination than ever before. But to be "at home" in such a world he must have already become another man,

[1] Quoted in Giorgio Di Santillana, *The Age of Adventure* (New York: George Brazilier, 1957), p. 168. Montaigne does not of course mean the inner man, or what Islamic esotericism calls universal man (*al-insān al-kāmil*), but the "ordinary" nature of ordinary men.

no longer defined by his celestial archetype and Edenic perfection but by his individuality, reason, the senses, and corporeality. Man was redefined on the basis of a subjectivism that destroyed the objective archetypal reality of the human state and the symbolic and contemplative spirit, which was henceforth replaced by individualistic reason.

> The Renaissance thought that it had discovered man, whose pathetic convulsions it admired; from the point of view of laicism in all its forms, man as such had become to all intents and purposes good, and the earth too had become good and looked immensely rich and unexplored; instead of living only "by halves" one could at last live fully, be fully man and fully on earth; one was no longer a kind of half-angel, fallen and exiled; one had become a whole being, but by the downward path.[2]

The chief characteristic of this new man was both individualism and rationalism. The subjectivism and lack of objective metaphysical criteria characteristic of Renaissance humanism could not but lead to an individualism that affected even the mysticism of the period. Man's individuality became extolled at the expense of the universal to the extent that the new Renaissance man felt himself deeply different not only from members of other civilizations but even from men of earlier periods of Western history, when the individual order was defined in light of the universal. Even the heritage of antiquity was received on the basis of an individualistic interpretation that caused it to differ profoundly from the medieval understanding of the same heritage. The Plato of Hugo St. Victor is not the same Plato as one finds in the works of even a Pico, who issued from the Florentine Academy, the source for the dissemination of Platonic teachings in the Renaissance, and even more different from the Plato of a Galileo.

Closely allied with individualism is the rationalism that began to manifest itself to an ever greater degree in the Renaissance, leading finally to the complete separation of philosophy and revelation. Rationalism does not mean simply the use of reason, but the exclusive use of reason independent of both intellection and revelation and the consideration of reason as the highest and exclusive authority for the attainment of truth. This tendency

[2] Frithjof Schuon, *Light on the Ancient Worlds*, trans. Lord Northbourne (Bloomington, Ind.: World Wisdom Books, 1984), p. 31. It is of interest to note in this conjunction how Pico belittled the evil in man.

was to be seen not only in Renaissance Averroism, but also in certain aspects of humanistic studies themselves, leading to an even greater abandonment of intellection and the symbolic mode of thought in favor of a rationalism that could not but result in the development of the seventeenth-century rationalistic philosophy of Descartes and others.

As far as the conception of man is concerned, this rationalism came to identify man with a reason that was no longer wed to the intellect, the distinction between the two—that is, *intellectus* and *ratio*—in fact soon becoming obliterated. Man was now identified as a being possessing an independent individuality and a reason seeking to encompass reality without recourse to a principle beyond itself, leading of necessity to the infra-rational, which characterizes so much of modern and especially so-called post-modern thought. Henceforth European man gained a new conception of himself as a being endowed with reason, independent of Heaven and ready to conquer Earth, both its non-European humanity and the order of nature. The whole Enlightenment conception of reason and rational man is rooted in the profound transformation of the meaning of man during the Renaissance.

Renaissance rationalism was also accompanied by skepticism that, on the one hand, opposed the limited certitude reached through reason and, on the other, complemented the claim of rationalism in the exclusive use of human reason in the quest of knowledge. Skepticism was of course known not only in Greece and Rome but is particularly a Greco-Roman heritage. It can mean either that no knowledge is possible, as held by academic skeptics, or that there is not sufficient and adequate evidence to decide whether knowledge is possible or not. This latter view is associated with Pyrrhonism, whose foremost authority was Sextus Empiricus, who lived in the late second and early third centuries A.D. It is of much interest to note that while skepticism was known by St. Augustine and refuted by him, it disappeared from the Western intellectual tradition for a millennium after him, during which time reason was wed to the Christian revelation or the immanent Logos and had no need to examine the possibility of doubt presented by skeptical philosophies, and that it was resuscitated during the late Renaissance.

This event is of great significance for the understanding of later European thought and the origin of an important strand of the conception of man emanating from the Renaissance. In fact, the seventeenth-century French skeptic Pierre Bayle considered the introduction of skepticism during the Renaissance as the beginning of modern philosophy, and Descartes sought after a new ground for certitude because of the skepticism that had become prevalent. Thus, the Pyrrhonism associated with Sextus Empiricus became widespread with the publication of his complete Latin works in 1569. But even before that date Pyrrhonism had begun to be taken seriously. Already in 1510 Gian Francesco had sought to discredit all ancient philosophy in his *Examen Vanitatis Doctrinae Gentium* in which he mentions Pyrrhonism extensively and makes use of Sextus Empiricus to oppose other schools of philosophy. Even the famous French writer François Rabelais mentions Pyrrhonism in his novels *Gargantua* and *Pantagruel* where the philosopher Trouillogan is called "*pyrrhonien*." Likewise, Agrippa von Nettesheim wrote long diatribes against human knowledge that were read by Montaigne and helped revive ancient skepticism. Such figures as Petrus Ramus and his friend Omer Talon discussed both academic and Pyrrhonic skepticism, and even Giordano Bruno refers to the *pirroni* in his *La Cena de la Ceneri.*

The most important figure influenced by Sextus Empiricus, however, was Montaigne, who, while being instrumental in creating the Renaissance conception of man, also criticized prevalent theories through skepticism. His espousal of Pyrrhonism helped in fact to create what came to be known in the seventeenth century as *la crise pyrrhonienne*, and this left a profound effect upon the religious debates of his day. Renaissance skepticism not only affected later European thought, but it helped create a conception of man whose streak of doubt was not about his power to dominate the order of nature but to know ultimate principles and all that had defined man throughout human history.

In this second departure of Western man from the human family, the first being the Greece of the Sophists and Skeptics, once again the same distinguishing characteristics of rationalism and skepticism came into play. When a Spaniard stood next to a Native American, or a Portuguese next to a Chinese, or a Dutchman before a Javanese, or an Englishman or Frenchman before any African or Oriental in the Age of Exploration and expansion of European powers, among all the factors distinguishing one type of humanity from all others was the presence of this skeptical vein. It led to many scientific discoveries but also to the loss of sacred knowledge and in some cases the sense of the sacred itself. And it remains to this day a salient feature of that type of human being for whom the desecration of nature is meaningless because there is nothing sacred to start with.

Yet another characteristic of Renaissance humanism, again closely related to rationalism and skepticism despite appearances, is "naturalism," understood in the sense that man is part of nature, not in the neo-Confucian or Zen sense, but in that his own bodily pleasures are of importance.

This can be seen in Renaissance paintings that emphasize the discovery of nature; but outside those circles that continued to cultivate esoteric cosmologies, which still related nature to its metaphysical principles, this naturalism involved more the rediscovery of pleasure than of the spiritual significance of the body or nature, especially as far as the followers of the new humanism were concerned. This type of naturalism manifested itself by its opposition to medieval asceticism, as seen in Lorenzo Valla's *De Voluptate*, for which pleasure even became the goal of virtue and the sole goal of human existence. Valla denied the superiority of monastic life as claimed by medieval Christianity, and some of his arguments were echoed by others such as Coluccio Salutati. There was also a reappraisal of Epicurus, then considered by some as the master of human wisdom. Even Aristotle came to be extolled not because of his metaphysics but as a result of his appreciation of the importance of money.

There thus appeared this other important characteristic of modern man so prevalent to this day, that of being a prisoner of his senses, which he must seek constantly to satiate without limit, and that of the follower of a naturalism that is against the order of nature as a value in itself, a being devoted to the bodily gratification without the least interest in the significance of the body in the religious, metaphysical, and cosmological sense. Such a naturalism has not been necessarily opposed to the dualism that has dominated Western thought from Descartes to this day and has emphasized the importance of the gratification of the bodily senses without showing any concern for the body as an integral aspect of the human microcosm.

The new consciousness of man living amidst the world of nature was complemented by a new awareness of man's position in history. There developed at this time a historicism that represented the secularization of the Christian doctrine of the march of time and played an important role in creating a consciousness, within the new man, of his position in history considered as the secular flow of time rather than his position in the face of eternity. Traditional man, Christian or otherwise, always situates and orients himself vis-à-vis an Origin and a Center, both of which are Divine. The new humanism changed this matrix drastically by substituting historical time for eternity with profound consequences for the future; for it was this very inception of historicism that was to lead to the idea of indefinite material progress, evolution, social Darwinism, "the white man's burden," the negation of transhistorical realities, and many other developments that had and continue to have the most profound consequences for the relation between man and the order of nature.

Another basic element of the Renaissance conception of man and the subsequent humanism that has dominated the West since then is the new notion of freedom, which may in fact be considered as the main element of Renaissance and post-Renaissance humanism. This new understanding of freedom meant essentially independence from the sacred world of medieval Christianity and its cosmic order and not freedom from the limitations of the ego and the bonds of material existence as envisaged by seers and sages in East and West over the ages. Such figures as Giannozzo Manetti, Marsilio Ficino, and Giovanni Pico emphasized the ability of man to act independently of any other agent in the Universe. They exalted man's freedom to form and change the world as he willed, irrespective of any cosmic laws or even of the Divine Will, at least according to those who developed this idea later on the basis of the Renaissance humanistic notion of freedom. The glorification of man so emphasized in such treatises as Pico's *On the Dignity of Man* was directly based upon what such authors conceived to be the innate freedom of man from all constraints. Man now becomes the independent protagonist in the cosmic drama and he, rather than "Fortune," is now seen to control and direct the ship of human life. Even the emphasis upon the wonders of the human mind by such a figure as Pico is based on the freedom enjoyed by man.

Humanistic Renaissance authors also tended to associate freedom with reason. A case in point is *De libro arbitrio* of Lorenzo Valla, where freedom is judged from the point of view of reason and not religious dogma. Valla, in fact, insists that reason "is the best author" not to be contradicted by any other authority. He then goes on to criticize the sacred hierarchy of the Church and, despite accepting Christianity as pure truth, begins to submit it to the judgments of pure natural reason. There is thus created a link between the understanding of the notion of human freedom and rationalism, which dominated Western thought until the revolt against reason in nineteenth-century Western philosophy.

Even Renaissance Aristotelians—for example, Pietro Pomponazzi, who has been called the last Scholastic—were attracted to the new understanding of the notion of freedom. Pomponazzi emphasized the contrast between faith and reason and was interested in the freedom of man placed in the "field of tension" between the two. In fact, the whole spectrum of Renaissance philosophy extending from Pomponazzi to the Platonists of the Florentine Academy to Valla were interested in the question of the freedom of man related to his grandeur.

Pico, whose views concerning man became especially influential, went a step further in reversing the traditional rapport between being and acting.

According to traditional doctrines our actions depend upon our mode of being or, as the Scholastics stated it, *operari sequitur esse*. Pico reversed this relationship and claimed that "the being of man follows from his doing."[3] He thus stated philosophically the thesis of the primacy of action over contemplation and doing over being, which characterizes modern man and which has been of the greatest consequence for the destruction of the world of nature. The unlimited energy of a civilization turned totally outward to remold the natural world in complete "freedom" and without any inner constraints is at the heart of the relentless activity of modern man in the destruction of the natural environment vis-à-vis which he cannot simply "be" but toward which he must act aggressively to change and transform it.

In relation to this lack of a distinct *esse* that would be the source of human actions, Pico emphasizes the Protean nature of man. Proteus, a sea god of the Greeks, assumed all kinds of shapes and forms and was amoral. He thus became identified with restlessness and change and was attacked by Plato in the *Republic* (II.318D). Yet he came to be extolled by the Renaissance philosophers such as Pico, Giovanni Gelli, and Juan Luis Vives, who helped create that image of a restless creature with whom modern man identifies so closely. While Pico considers man as a chameleon imitating Heaven and Earth, Gelli in his *Circe* talks of Protean man "jumping up and down the Chain of Being at will."[4] As for Vives, he speaks in his *Fable about Man* of man miming all of Creation including multiform Proteus.

Perhaps the most famous description of this Protean character of man related to his complete freedom to act according to his will is the following passage of Pico from *On the Dignity of Man*:

> We have given to thee, Adam, no fixed seat, no form of thy very own, no gift peculiarly thine, that thou mayest feel as thine own, have as thine own, possess as thine own the seat, the form, the gifts which

[3] Ernst Cassirer, *The Individual and the Cosmos in Renaissance Philosophy* (New York: Harper and Row, 1964), p. 84. There is of course some truth in this statement in the sense that through our actions we weave our future "body of resurrection" and that our actions affect our mode of being; otherwise, spiritual practices would be meaningless. But it is not this understanding of the statement that Pico had in mind.

[4] Stevie Davies, *Renaissance Views of Man* (New York: Barnes & Noble, 1979), p. 10.

> thou shalt desire. A limited nature in other creatures is confined within the laws written down by Us. In conformity with thy free judgment, in whose hands I have placed thee, thou art confined by no bounds; and thou wilt fix limits of nature for thyself. I have placed thee at the center of the world, that from these thou mayest more conveniently look around and see whatsoever is in the world. . . . Thou, like a judge appointed for being honorable, art the molder and maker of thyself; thou mayest sculpt thyself into whatever shape thou dost prefer. Thou canst grow downward into the lower natures which are brutes. Thou canst again grow upward from thy soul's reason into the high natures which are divine.[5]

This celebrated passage echoes in many ways the traditional doctrine of man conceived as *al-insān al-kāmil* in Islam, who can occupy all levels of existence, and the last part is reminiscent in a certain sense of the famous Quranic passage "Surely We created man of the best stature, then We reduced him to the lowest of the low" (95:4-5). It also contains elements of the esoteric doctrines of man contained in Hermetic and Kabbalistic teachings, but all of this is interpreted in a Protean manner with results very different from what the traditions envisaged over the millennia.

The ideas of Pico found their immediate echo in Charles de Bouvelles (Carolus Bovillus), the French philosopher who was influenced by both the Florentine Platonists and Nicholas of Cusa. He was the author of *De sapiente*, written in 1509, which Ernst Cassirer has called "perhaps the most curious and in some respect the most characteristic creation of Renaissance philosophy."[6] While still influenced by traditional ideas of the relation between the microcosm and macrocosm, Bouvelles developed ideas that were much more in accord with modern philosophy than with the thought of his contemporaries and that have been compared to the idealism of Leibniz and Hegel. Bouvelles continued the theme of the Protean nature of man. Being journeys through *Esse*, *vivere*, *sentire*, and *intelligere* to arrive at Itself. Man possesses all these levels within himself, and through his reason the cycle of nature is completed and nature returns to herself. But upon returning, nature no longer has the form with which she started out.

[5] Pico della Mirandola, *On the Dignity of Man*, trans. Charles Wallis (Indianapolis: Bobbs-Merrill, 1965), pp. 4-5. See also Cassirer, *The Individual and the Cosmos*, pp. 85ff.

[6] Cassirer, *The Individual and the Cosmos*, p. 88.

> Once the first separation in man has been completed, once he has stepped out of the simplicity of his original state, he can never again return to this unbroken simplicity. He must go through the opposite in order to pass beyond it to find the true unity of his being—that unity which does not exclude difference but rather postulates and requires it.[7]

Man's freedom in fact issues from the contradictions in his being, from the fact that he does not possess a ready-made nature but a Protean one. Man must acquire his being through *virtus* and *ars* and must pass through the various levels of *Esse*, *vivere*, etc. In this process he can fall through the vice of inertia or *acedia* to the level of existence without consciousness, or rise to the highest level through self-consciousness, which implies also knowledge of the cosmos. According to Bouvelles,

> The man of nature, simple *homo*, must become the man of art, the *homo-homo*; but this difference is already overcome, inasmuch as it is recognized in its necessity. Above the first two forms arises now the last and highest; the trinity *homo-homo-homo*, in which the opposition of potency and act, of nature and freedom, of being and consciousness, is at once encompassed and resolved. Man no longer appears therein as a part of the universe but as its eye and mirror; and indeed, as a mirror that does not receive the images of things from outside but that rather forms and shapes them in itself.[8]

Man is the central point of the cosmos in whom all degrees of being converge, and he can journey through them since he is a Protean being capable of taking on all forms without a fixed place in the cosmos.

Bouvelles compared the wise man to Prometheus, for wisdom confers power upon its beholder and allows man to change his nature. Renaissance thought had in fact resurrected the ancient myth of Prometheus in seeking a pictorial and mythological expression for its idea of man. The new idea of Prometheus, far from being seen negatively as symbolizing man's rebellion against Heaven, came to be viewed in a positive light. The new man who proudly called himself Promethean saw himself as an independent agent free from both the theological and the natural order, which at that time included the astrological influence of the stars, from both *regnum gratiae*

[7] Ibid., p. 91.

[8] Ibid., p. 93.

and *regnum naturae*. There was thus born the prototype of modern man, whom we can call Promethean in contrast to the traditional or pontifical man who always remains aware of his role as bridge (*ponte*) between Heaven and Earth, in submission to Heaven and ruler of Earth in the name of Heaven and in harmony with cosmic laws. The conception of the order of nature as pure quantity perceptible to man's senses and object of man's reason and the development of a science founded upon the exercise of power over nature would not have been possible without the replacement in the West of pontifical man by the Promethean man so much extolled by Renaissance philosophers from Bouvelles to Bruno and celebrated so forcefully by a sculptor and painter such as Michelangelo, who depicts man in the Sistine Chapel as almost the equivalent of God.

Such a vision of man created an egoism and sense of *hubris* that is especially evident in the art of the period. The Renaissance praise of man was not, however, necessarily anti-Christian, as is seen in many Renaissance works such as Ficino's *De Christiana religione*, and sought even to be tolerant, although this tolerance never went beyond the borders of Christianity, as seen especially in the attitude during that period toward Judaism and Islam. Still, the aggrandizement of man not only brought about as response the skeptical reactions of a Montaigne but was also strongly opposed by both Calvin and Luther, who emphasized the wretchedness of the human condition. But even the Reformation emphasized individualism, as seen in the proliferation of Protestantism into so many branches. Moreover, after Luther, even in Germany greater emphasis came to be placed upon the freedom of human will, and the debates between the so-called Christian humanist Erasmus and Luther over free will and determinism influenced many future generations. Contrary views of man and his freedom dominated the scene and found their echo in Shakespeare and other major Western writers.

As far as the significance of the concept of man for the order of nature is concerned, however, what is most significant is the Prometheanism that came to dominate Western civilization to an ever greater degree despite the survival in certain circles of both the traditional Christian understanding of man and even the esoteric doctrines of the Kabbala and Hermeticism, which, although marginalized, did not disappear completely at that time. The main characteristics of Renaissance humanism can be in fact summarized in the new Promethean conception of man, with a reason made independent of revelation, a Protean being ready to rebel against Heaven and to master and dominate the Earth. Of course, the imprint of Christianity could not be obliterated from the soul of the new European man so quickly, but it was weakened enough for the new Promethean man to announce his declaration of independence from religion and revelation in many domains, of which the most significant for our present study was the order of nature.

* * *

In the matrix of the tapestry of the Renaissance, woven from so many often contradictory strands, from Hermeticism to Lutheranism, from Aristotelianism to the *studia humanitatis*, and from Platonism to experimental science, there grew the outline and form of that humanism which has characterized the modern world since that time and is only now being seriously challenged from below and to some extent from above. At the center of this humanism stood the Promethean vision of man, who now came to occupy the middle of the stage as an ontologically autonomous being. If certain esotericisms such as that of Islam had accepted the thesis that man is the measure of all things because they saw in man the full theophany (*tajallī*) of God's Names and Qualities, now man came to be the measure of all things as a purely earthly being. The consequence was the rise of an anthropomorphic perspective that has dominated all aspects of Western thought for the past half millennium.

Henceforth, man's reason, divorced from both revelation and intellection in the traditional sense of the term, came to be the sole criterion of verification of knowledge along with man's sensory perceptions. Only man's faculties determined knowledge even if faith in God still persisted to some extent. The presence of this faith, however, could not prevent the step-by-step desacralizing of knowledge that characterized European intellectual history from the Renaissance onward and that, beginning with knowledge of the order of nature, was finally to affect even theology itself. All modern modes of thought are in essence anthropomorphic in that they are based completely on purely human faculties. Even modern science, which paints a picture of the world to which human beings are for the most part alien, is purely anthropomorphic in that it is based completely on the human mind and the human senses even when it speaks of the most distant galaxies.

This new humanism was of course challenged by many forces over the centuries following the Renaissance, from religious opposition to the aggrandizement of man, to philosophies such as those of Hegel and Marx, which reduced man to simply an element in the human collectivity and society; to Darwinism, which reduced him to an accident in the process of the evolution of matter. During this century all types of reductionism, whether it be psychological in the behavioristic sense, or biological or social, have sought to destroy the centrality and independence of man declared by those Renaissance writers who first conceived of the idea of humanism in the sense described above. And yet the prevailing image of man, especially as it concerns the order of nature and the crisis that modern man has created vis-à-vis the environment, remains the Promethean image forged during the Renaissance, enhanced by the civilization and rationalism of the Age of Enlightenment and even strengthened in a certain sense by the anti-rationalistic forces of Romanticism that, despite its love of nature, sought nevertheless to aggrandize human genius, which is in a sense an invention of that age applied especially to the domain of the arts. One can hardly forget the Promethean image of man, at least its heroic aspect, when one hears Beethoven's *Eroica Symphony* or reads the poems of Shelley.

Irrespective of all the differences between various schools of thought in the West, the central image of man as the earthly god, conqueror of nature, and maker of his own destiny and the future of civilization continued. If a Ming Confucian scholar or a Seljuq Persian theologian were presented with the different images of man from Pico to Michelangelo to Montaigne to Descartes to Diderot and Voltaire and then on to the nineteenth-century philosophers and artists such as Hegel and Wagner, and even including Nietzsche with his idea of the *Übermensch*, they would be much more impressed with the similarities of these individuals than with their differences. They would see in all these modern versions of the Western concept of man a being very different from *jen* or *insān* in the Confucian and Islamic traditions, respectively. They would see a being who was no longer organically linked to either the cosmos or to God, to Heaven or Earth. They would immediately detect the radical difference between, on the one hand, the Islamic theocentrism—which is certainly close to the Christian perspective in many ways—and what has been called Confucian anthropocosmism, and, on the other, the anthropocentrism prevalent in the domineering culture of the West. They would even experience a closer sympathy with the Augustinian conception of man tainted by Original Sin, which they would reject, than with the humanistic idea of the innately "good" man so much discussed in the Enlightenment and thereafter, for despite all their differences, traditional views of humanity are all within the matrix of a theocentric universe, whereas humanism is of necessity grounded in anthropocentrism.

Or it might be said that all traditional views of man function in a Universe with a Center, and this includes the Shamanic and Chinese religions, which do not speak of Creation but nevertheless are dominated by a Divine Center so that their anthropocosmism is ultimately none other than a form of theocentrism. In contrast, the humanistic view envisages a man and a world that are ultimately without a center, for to place man at the center of things is to deny the reality of a center, the nature of the *anthrōpos* being too transient and nebulous to be able to act as a center unless the *anthrōpos* be envisaged in its theomorphic nature, which would bring us back to the traditional view of man. Consequently, the human collectivity characterized by a world having a Divine Center was now challenged by a new type of man who, conceiving himself as the center of things, reduced his world to a circle without a center with devastating consequences for the rest of humanity and the order of nature, for we know only too well that when the center disappears the circumference crumbles.

This new vision of Promethean man and the humanism characterizing it was to have the greatest effect upon the order of nature from a practical as well as theoretical point of view. In a sense, modern man, who is none other than the Promethean man described here, usurped the rights of both God and nature for himself. In all traditional civilizations a boundary was set upon human possibilities from above. Man had certain duties toward God and also certain duties toward His Creation even in the Abrahamic monotheisms, which have been so wrongly accused of late for the sins of post-medieval Western civilization.

In Islam, man is God's vicegerent on Earth (*khalīfat Allāh fi'l-arḍ*), and he has custodianship and rights over other creatures by virtue of this vicegerency and not simply as a result of being a purely earthly creature more clever and cunning than others. Renaissance humanism gave birth to a man who was no longer bound to a Divine Order or sacred hierarchy and who saw no limit upon his right to destroy nature. By stealing, á la Prometheus, the fire of a knowledge of the world that he came to divorce from all divine principles, this new man set out to conquer both other peoples and the world of nature.

Something of Christianity, of course, survived in modern man, but in most cases it was of little consequence as far as the destruction of nature was concerned. Equipped with a Faustian knowledge, secular in character, and based on power over the natural order, the new man began to create unprecedented havoc over the globe, for there was now no limit set by any spiritual laws upon his rights of dominion and no higher knowledge to set a limit upon his profane knowledge of the world. Other conquerors had come and gone, but none were equipped with such knowledge based upon domination, with a technology that knew no bounds in its destructive powers, nor with a self-image so divorced from that of a being in harmony with the cosmic ambience. Five hundred years of the devastating actions of Promethean man, opposed to both tradition and the world of nature, have borne consequences too evident to deny. It is not, therefore, an overstatement to speak of the tragic consequences of humanism understood not as a general appreciation of man but as placing earthly man at the center of the scheme of things and leading of necessity to an even greater secularization of man and ultimately to the subhuman. For to be truly human is to transcend the human. To be satisfied with the merely human is to fall ultimately below the human state.

15. God as Reality

The sensualist and empirical epistemology, which has dominated the horizon of Western man in the modern period, has succeeded in reducing reality to the world experienced by the external senses, hence limiting the meaning of reality and removing the concept of "reality" as a category pertaining to God. The consequence of this change in the very meaning of reality has been nothing less than catastrophic, reducing God and in fact all spiritual realms of being to the category of the abstract and finally to the unreal. At the base of the loss of the sense of the reality of God by modern man in his daily life lies the philosophic error of reducing the meaning of reality to the externally experienced world, of altering the meaning of "realist" in its early medieval sense to the connotation it has gained in various schools of philosophy since the rise of nominalism at the end of the Middle Ages. Cut off from the twin sources of metaphysical knowledge, namely revelation and intellection, and also deprived of that inner spiritual experience which makes possible the concrete realization of higher levels of being, modern man has been confined to such a truncated and limited aspect of reality that of necessity he has lost sight of God as Reality. Also, even if he continues to have faith in the Divinity, the conception of the Divinity as Reality does not at all accord with that empirically determined world view within which he lives and whose premises he accepts unwittingly or often unconsciously.

It is possible for man to gain knowledge of God and to come to know Him as Reality because of the very nature of human intelligence, which was made to know the Absolute as such. But to gain this knowledge, it is necessary to have access to the twin sources of metaphysical knowledge and certitude, namely revelation and intellection. Moreover, the second is accessible to man in his present state only by virtue of the first, while the fruit of wisdom which it bears lies at the heart of revelation and also resides at the center of man's own being. Reaching the inner man or the heart, which is the seat of the intellect, with the aid of the grace issuing from revelation, and reaching the heart of revelation by means of the penetrating rays of this sanctified intellect enable man to gain an adequate metaphysical knowledge of God as Ultimate Reality and, in the light of this knowledge, an awareness of relativity as relativity or more precisely as veil.

It can be said that not only does modern man not possess an adequate doctrine of God as Reality in its absolute sense, but also that because of this lack of knowledge he is deprived of an adequate understanding of relativity as veil. To conceive the Absolute in relative terms is also to absolutize the relative in some sense. To remove from God the attribute of reality is also to fail to see the world as only partial reality, as a veil which at once hides and manifests, the veil which, as *al-ḥijāb* in Islam or *māyā* in Hinduism, plays such a basic role in Oriental metaphysics.

Moreover, it is necessary to mention that whereas an adequate metaphysical doctrine pertaining to God as Reality can be found in traditional Christian metaphysics as seen in the works of such masters as Erigena, St. Bonaventure, and St. Thomas, the doctrine of the veil is more implicit and less clearly stated even in traditional schools in the West than it is in either Islam or Hinduism, although there are certainly allusions to it in the works of such sages as Meister Eckhart. The reformulation of an adequate metaphysical doctrine concerning the nature of God in a contemporary language requires, therefore, not only a doctrine concerning God as Ultimate Reality or the absolutely Real, but also the doctrine of cosmic illusion, the veil, or that creative power which at once manifests the Divine Principle as relativity and veils the Principle through that very manifestation which is none other than the veil—so that a Sufi could address God as "O Thou who hidest Thyself by that which is none other than Thee."

God as Ultimate Reality is not only the Supreme Person but also the source of all that is, hence at once Supra-Being and Being, God as Person and the Godhead or Infinite Essence, of which Being is the first determination. Both He or She and It, and yet beyond all pronominal categories, God as Ultimate Reality is the Essence which is the origin of all forms, the Substance compared to which all else is accident, the One who alone is and who stands even above the category of being as usually understood.

God as Reality is at once absolute, infinite, and good or perfect. In Himself He is the Absolute which partakes of no relativity in Itself or in Its Essence. The Divine Essence cannot but be absolute and one. All other considerations must belong to the order of relativity, to a level below that of the Essence. To assert that God is one is to assert His absoluteness and to envisage Him in Himself, as such. The Divine Order partakes of relativity in the sense that there is a Divine Relativity or Multiplicity which is included in the Divine Order, but this relativity does not reach the abode of the Divine Essence. God in His Essence cannot but be one, cannot but be the Absolute. To speak of God as Reality is to speak of God as the Absolute.

God as Reality is also infinite, *the* Infinite, as this term is to be understood metaphysically and not mathematically. Ultimate Reality contains the source of all cosmic possibilities and in fact all possibilities as such, even the metacosmic. God is infinite not only in the sense that no limit can be set upon Him, but also in the sense that, as Ultimate Reality, He contains all possibilities. Metaphysically, He is the All-Possibility. When the Bible states that with God all things are possible or the Quran asserts that God has power over all things, these scriptural statements must not be understood only in the usual theological sense of alluding to God's infinite power. They also refer to God's nature as the All-Possibility and confirm in other language the Quranic verse, "In His hands is to be found the dominion (*malakūt*) of all things" (26:83), that is, the essential reality of all things is to be found in the Divine Nature. It is useful to recall here that the words possibility, puissance, and potentiality are from the same root. To say that God is the All-Powerful, the All-Potent, is also to say that He is the All-Possibility.

The understanding of the Divine Infinity is so essential to an adequate doctrine of the nature of God that its neglect has been the main cause for the philosophical objections to the religious idea of God as goodness and perfection, the source of all that is good and at the same time Creator of an imperfect world. No problem has been as troublesome to Western man's understanding of God as presented in the mainstream of Christian theology and philosophy as the famous problem of theodicy, that is, the question of the creation of a world in which there is evil by a Creator who is good. The lack of a complete metaphysical doctrine in the modern West has brought about the eclipse of the doctrine of Divine Infinity and the grades of manifestation or levels of being, with the help of which it is possible to understand perfectly well why a world in which there is evil has its origin in God who is pure goodness.

Here it is necessary to add that there would in fact be no agnostics around if only it were possible to teach metaphysics to everyone. One cannot expect every person to comprehend metaphysics, any more than one can expect everyone to understand physics or mathematics. But strangely enough, whereas modern man accepts the discoveries of physics on faith and is willing to undergo the necessary training to master the subject if he wishes to understand physics himself, unlike traditional man he does not extend this faith to the fruits of metaphysical knowledge. Without being willing to undergo the necessary discipline and training, which in traditional metaphysics, and in contrast to modern science, includes also moral and spiritual considerations, modern man expects to understand metaphysics immediately and without any intellectual or spiritual preparation. If he fails to comprehend the subject, then he rejects the very possibility of that knowledge which alone can solve the antinomies and apparent contradictions of the problem of theodicy and evil. In fact many people in the modern world do not even accept the revealed truths on the basis of faith, as was the case of traditional man, who usually possessed a greater awareness of his own limitations than does his modern counterpart.

In any case, the doctrine of the Divine Infinity makes it possible to understand why there is a world which is limited and imperfect. The Divine contains all possibilities, including the possibility of its own negation, without which it would not be infinite. But this possibility implies a projection toward nothingness which, however, is never reached. This projection constitutes the world, or rather the many worlds standing below their Divine Origin. Since only God is good, this projection means, of necessity, separation from the source of goodness and hence the appearance of evil, which is a kind of "crystallization of nothingness," real on its own level of existence but an illusion before God, who alone is Reality as such. The root of the world resides in the infinity of the Divine Nature.

* * *

Such a doctrine of the Divine requires not only an adequate knowledge of the Principle as absolute but also an adequate grasp of the meaning of relativity, of the levels and hierarchy of existence, of the relatively real and even of the "relatively absolute," an elliptical term which, far from being contradictory, contains an indispensable key to the understanding of the science of God. To use the two mutually exclusive categories of Creator and created, as is done theologically, is to fall into certain dichotomies which can only be bridged over by an act of faith, in the absence of which there is usually skepticism concerning the very tenets of revealed religion. To begin with the world considered as reality, as is done by most modern philosophy, is to reach an even more dangerous impasse. This of necessity leads to nihilism and skepticism by reducing God to an abstraction, to the "unreal," and philosophy itself to the discussion of more or less secondary questions or to providing clever answers to ill-posed problems.

To avoid such impasses, it is essential to revive the doctrine of the veil already alluded to above and to rediscover the traditional teaching about the gradations of reality or of being. To understand God as Reality, it is necessary to understand that there are levels of reality and that reality is not only an empirically definable psychophysical continuum "out there." The world is real to the extent that it reveals God who alone is Real. But the world is also unreal to the extent that it hides and veils God as Reality.

Only the saint who sees God everywhere can claim that what is seen and experienced "everywhere" is real.

Moreover, a particular object cannot be said to be real or unreal in only one sense of these terms, but it partakes of levels of reality, or one might say unreality, from its being an opaque object, an "it" or "fact" as understood in modern science, which is its face as *māyā* in the sense of illusion, to its being a transparent symbol, a theophany, a reflection of the Divine Presence and a witness to the Divine *māyā* which is none other than the Divine Creativity. To understand God as Reality is also to grasp the world as unreality, not nothingness pure and simple, but as relative reality. It is to be saved from that central error of false attribution which issues from our ignorance and which causes us to attribute reality to the illusory and, as a consequence, the character of illusion to that which is Reality as such and which ultimately is alone Real.

To reinstate the doctrine of God as Reality is, needless to say, impossible without a change in the way we envisage the question and possibility of knowledge. As long as the prevalent empiricism or its complementary rationalism continue to reign or are replaced by that irrationalism which erupted in nineteenth-century Europe from below, there is no possibility to grasp the validity of that traditional wisdom, or that *sophia perennis*, which has always seen God as Reality and the world as a dream from which the sage awakens through realization and remembrance and the ordinary man through death. To grasp this doctrine, the traditional sapiential perspective based on the possibility of principial knowledge from the twin source of the intellect and revelation must be reinstated along with the metaphysics which is the fruit of this way of knowing.

In light of this fact, the role of traditional wisdom or what the Quran calls *al-ḥikmah* in the contemporary discussion on the nature of God becomes clear. This wisdom resides at the heart of all traditions and can be discovered in those traditions which have preserved their sapiential dimension to this day. It can be found in one of its purest forms in the Vedanta, and one can see an alternative formulation of it in Buddhism. It can likewise be found in the Kabbala and in traditional Christian metaphysics as found in the works of Christian sages such as Eckhart and Erigena. It is also expressed with great clarity in traditional Islamic metaphysics. Furthermore, Islam is a religion which is based completely on the doctrine of the oneness of God, and is a religion in which God is seen as both Reality and Truth, the Arabic term *al-Ḥaqīqah* meaning both. In fact the word *al-Ḥaqq* (The Truth), which is related to *Ḥaqīqah*, is a Name of God. Therefore, Islamic wisdom can play an important role in enabling modern man to rediscover that plenary doctrine of the nature of God as Reality, a doctrine whose loss has led to the unprecedented skepticism and relativism which characterize the modern world. Islam is able to help in the achievement of this goal not only because of the nature of the Quranic revelation, based as it is in an uncompromising manner upon the doctrine of Divine Unity, but also because it has preserved intact to this day its sapiential tradition. This tradition guards the absoluteness of God and His transcendence in its formal teachings meant for everyone. But it also allows those who possess the qualifications necessary to attain wisdom to gain full access to the metaphysical doctrine of God as at once absolute, infinite, and perfect good, and makes it possible for those who have realized this wisdom to hear in the song of the bird and smell in the perfume of the rose the sound and breath of the Beloved, and to contemplate in the very veil of creaturely existence the Face of God. According to Islam's own teachings, this doctrine is not unique to Islam but lies at the heart of all revelations. But as the last echo of the primordial Word upon the stage of human history during this present cycle of terrestrial existence, Islam still reverberates in a particularly vivid manner to that eternal melody of Divine Oneness, recalling man to his perennial vocation as witness on earth to that Reality which is at once absoluteness, infinitude, and boundless goodness and mercy.

16. Time and Eternity

Man lives in the world of change and becoming wherein he experiences time, which marks his earthly life and which finally conquers him as it leads him ineluctably to his death. Yet he is in turn able to conquer time because he has issued forth from the Eternal Order. Man has an innate awareness of Eternity, whose idea is deeply imprinted upon his mind, and its experience still echoes in the depth of his soul, where something remains of the lost paradise which he inhabited before joining the caravan of terrestrial life. The traditional universe is dominated by the two basic realities of Origin and Center, both of which belong to the realm of the Eternal. Man lives a life removed from the Origin on a circumference distanced from the Center. And it is precisely this removal and distancing which constitute for him the experience of time. He is, therefore, a being suspended between time and Eternity, neither a purely temporal creature nor a being of the Eternal Realm, at least in his ordinary earthly state. That is why all religions focus their teachings upon the question of the relation between time and Eternity, as do all traditional philosophies. To understand the nature of man is to become aware of his existential situation as a being belonging to the Eternal Order but living in time, which itself cannot but be related to Eternity since all orders of reality are of necessity interrelated.

The question thus revolves around the meaning of Eternity and of time, whose understanding has been so central to both the metaphysical and religious concerns of humanity over the ages. The comments which follow seek to elucidate but a few strands in the vast tapestry of traditional doctrines concerning time and Eternity and to contrast them when necessary with certain prevalent modern concepts which have succeeded in veiling the traditional teachings in those sectors of the contemporary world which are called modern and now increasingly post-modern.

The notion of Eternity evokes at once the idea of changelessness, immutability, and perfection. It is related to the Divine Order, to the Divine Principle itself as well as the world of the Spirit residing in the Divine Proximity, hence the usage of the term "eternal life." It is known by man through the tenets of revelation as well as through intellection and can be experienced even in this life through spiritual realization and the "eye of the heart" or the frontal eye of Śiva, whose gaze is ever fixed upon the Eternal Order. In any case there is in principle no need for the world of becoming in order for man to know the Eternal, except that as the subject of this knowledge man is himself situated in the world of becoming. Even there, however, he is able to know and experience Eternity directly as a being who belongs ultimately to the Eternal Order, though not simply as a creature who is the product of the world of change and becoming, for only the like can know the like.

As for time, man has an immediate awareness of it and lives in this world as if he knew perfectly well what time is. But a further analysis of the meaning of time reveals it to be the most elusive of the parameters of cosmic existence, unlike space, form, matter, and number, which are easier both to define and to measure. That is why philosophers have often found time to be one of the most difficult of problems to treat and why, especially since the rise of modern science and its adoption of the purely quantitative notion of time, those concerned with the traditional understanding of the subject have had to emphasize the distinction between time and duration, qualitative and quantitative time, or even levels of meaning of time itself. Paradoxically, while time seems to be so much easier to grasp and experience than Eternity, it is not possible to know or measure it as it is usually understood without the world of becoming which surrounds man. While there is a direct nexus between man and Eternity independent of this world, the relation of man to time always involves this world, for there is no time without becoming.

In order to experience time in the ordinary sense of the word, there is need of the manifested or created order in its changing aspect, hence the world of becoming. There is also need of the polarity between the subject and the object. It is human subjectivity with its particular hierarchic structure which is able to know time and duration and, because it is the human subject, it is able to experience time while being aware of its termination for the particular subject who is experiencing time, hence the awareness of death. The yearning for transcendence which characterizes normal man means that he is not only able to experience time but also to have an awareness of its limitation and termination and of his own existence as an immortal being beyond time. To understand time in itself and in relation to Eternity, it is therefore necessary to turn to the ontological status of the world of becoming and the universal hierarchy of existence which makes it possible to understand the meaning of time and also its relation to Eternity, of which it is the "moving image."

The Divine Principle is at once the Absolute, the Infinite, and the Supreme Good, which cannot but manifest Itself as the myriad of worlds that become ever farther removed from It as a result of their separation from their ontological origin. The Divine Infinitude, by virtue of its infinity, must contain the possibility of manifestation or creation, a possibility which must of necessity be realized, as it is in the nature of the Good to give of itself and to radiate. This radiation, however, implies projection, hence separation from the Divine Principle, which remains unaffected by Its manifestations, as *Ātman* remains unaffected by the cosmic veils of *māyā*, to use the language of Hinduism. The very infinitude of the Divine Principle implies the necessity of the existence of the world or many worlds, hence ontologically speaking the world of becoming as distinct from Being.

Metaphysically, one can distinguish between the Supreme Principle or Beyond-Being, Its self-determination or Being, and cosmic existence, which can be identified, except for its summit, with the world of becoming. Beyond-Being and Being of course do not become or change, although the phases of what Hinduism calls the days and night of Brahma contain the principle of the cosmic cycles and hence the rhythms according to which the world of becoming is manifested. In the highest sense, the quality of Eternity belongs to Beyond-Being and Being, although that which participates in the world of the Spirit, which lies at the center of the cosmos and in the proximity of the Divine Reality Itself, can also be said to be eternal, hence the eternal life of the blessed spoken of in various religious traditions as distinct from the perpetual or unending state which characterizes the infernal states.

As for the world of becoming, it is already removed from Eternity by the very fact that it is becoming. The origin of time resides in this very separation of the world of becoming from its ontological principle and origin. To become is to change or to move, as this verb is understood in traditional natural philosophy such as that of Aristotle. Moreover, in the same way that becoming has its roots in Being and the cosmos derives its existence from Being, without which it would be literally nothing, time, which characterizes the state of becoming, must be related to and have its root in the Eternal Order; hence the famous Platonic saying that time is the moving image of Eternity. This metaphysical assertion summarizes the relation of time to Eternity. It asserts first of all that Eternity has an "image," that is, the Eternal Principle manifests Itself. Secondly, since this manifestation is in the mode of becoming and in fact constitutes the world of becoming, it is a moving image. And time is none other than this moving image. If there were to be no moving image there would be no time, and if there were no Eternity or the Eternal Reality which is at once the Absolute, the Infinite, and the Perfect Good, there would be no moving image.

The very fact that the Absolute alone is absolute while the world is contingent necessitates the distinction between Eternity and time. Those who deny the Eternal Order are also those who fail to distinguish between the Absolute and the contingent and hence bestow upon the world the quality of absoluteness which belongs to the Divine Principle alone. Moreover, Eternity characterizes the Divine Infinitude and also the transcendent aspect of the Divine Principle with its quality of majesty and rigor, while the Divine Omnipresence which complements Eternity is related to Immanence with its quality of beauty and mercy. One is the principle of time and the other of space, one of change, transformation, death, and rebirth and the other of preservation and permanence, which in the world of becoming must of course be understood in a relative manner.

Moreover, the very principle of manifestation implies hierarchy. In the same way that there are vast universes of light or angelic realities separating Being from the material part of the cosmos in which man resides, Eternity is separated from time as ordinarily understood by intermediate stages and levels. That is why various traditions speak of *aeons*, *zurvān*, *dahr*, etc., which belong to intermediate ontological levels between the Supreme Principle or the Eternal as such and the world of time.

In the Islamic tradition for example, a distinction is made between *sarmad* (Eternity or the purely changeless), *dahr* (the relation of the changeless to that which changes), and *zamān* (time, which concerns the relation between the changing and the changing). It is furthermore said that *dahr* is the principle or spirit (*rūḥ*) of *zamān* while *sarmad* is the principle or spirit of *dahr*.

Traditional doctrines also distinguish between the ordinary experience of time and the experience of other modalities of time belonging to higher levels of reality and consciousness, without those modalities being simply the consequence of individual subjective experience lacking correspondence with an objective realm. The more a person rises in the hierarchy of existence and levels of consciousness from the world of outward experience toward the Divine Empyrean which is the Eternal, the more he experiences higher modes of what one could still call "time," which are penetrated to an ever greater degree by Eternity, until he leaves the domain of becoming altogether. It is not accidental that the Quran asserts, "A day with Thy Lord is as a thousand years" (22:47), that in Hinduism a single day in the life of Brahma corresponds to a vast number of years according to man's earthly reckoning, and that the Psalmist sings, "From everlasting to everlasting, Thou art God. . . . A thousand years in Thy sight are but as yesterday" (Psalm 90.2, 4).

Turning to the experience of the phenomenal world itself, it can be said that the content of this world is constituted of matter (whose dynamic dimension is energy), form (as this term has been understood traditionally), and number. As for the container of this content, it is constituted of time and space. If there were to be no phenomenal world, there would be no becoming and hence no time or space as these terms are usually understood. In man's experience of the world, however, it seems that time and space stand there as objective realities within which material objects possessing form function and move. Both of these views have been reflected in traditional schools of philosophy, although it is only since Descartes that the purely quantitative conception of time and space, as defined mathematically by the x,y,z Cartesian coordinates to which t (time) is added, has come to replace the earlier teachings in which time was never reduced to pure quantity. For the nexus between the phenomenal world and higher levels of existence was never forgotten and the parameters of cosmic existence were never reduced to mathematical abstractions of a purely quantitative nature.

As a matter of fact, all the parameters mentioned above have their principle in higher levels of being. There is a matter of the intermediate psychic and higher celestial worlds as there are forms belonging to these worlds. There are symbolic meanings to numbers, and higher worlds have their own "space" as well as their own "time" as already mentioned. That is why in certain traditions such as Hinduism which combine the metaphysical and the mythical, the functions of the gods and various divinities acting in different worlds above the terrestrial are related to the cosmic significance of the principles of those realities which appear to man on earth as matter, form, number, space, and time.

Coming back to time as experienced in the phenomenal world, it must be added that this existential condition has an objective and a subjective mode. There is what one can call "objective time" and what can be called "subjective time," to which certain authors have given other names. Also the basic distinction between the Principle and its manifestation is reflected also on the level of phenomenal existence in what is usually called "abstract" and "concrete," the former being beyond human experience and notional and the second the subject of possible human experience. There is therefore an *abstract* time and a *concrete* time.

As far as concrete time is concerned, it is the most immediate and most easily understood type of time. It is the time which we associate with changing phenomena within the sea of becoming in which we are immersed. In the same way that a person thrown in the sea experiences immediately the wetness of water, being immersed in the sea of becoming enables us to experience immediately the changing character of phenomena which constitute concrete time. As for abstract time, it is the duration which is measurable as a result of this change. This is the time to which Aristotle referred when he said that time is the measure of motion. Without motion, which in Aristotelian physics means change, there would be no time in the sense of abstract time, which most human beings divide into hours and minutes with little awareness of its relation to Eternity and impervious to the fact that with the passage of every one of those very hours and minutes, man draws a step closer to the meeting with that Reality which is none other than the Eternal.

As far as objective time is concerned, it consists of the spiroidal flow of cosmic becoming and is comprised of four basic phases. These phases can be seen first of all in the doctrine of the four cosmic cycles developed more elaborately in Hinduism than in any other tradition. They are also to be seen in the time which surrounds man directly in his life such as the four seasons, the four periods of the day, and the four stages of human life consisting of childhood, youth, maturity, and old age. Objective time is cyclic rather than linear, being related to the universal cycles of manifestation which then determine cycles on lower levels of existence. Objective time is measured by the movement of the earth around its axis or the heavens around the earth, depending on which reference point is used for the measurement of motion, and then the motion of the heavens, all of which are circular, or almost circular. Moreover, these motions correspond to cosmic rhythms which are cyclic or more exactly spiroidal in the sense that a cycle never returns exactly to the same point as before, for there cannot be an exact repetition in manifestation. That is why what is called the "myth of eternal return," although a powerful way of speaking of cosmic cycles, is not cosmologically exact, since there is never an exact return to the previous point of origin of a cycle in the same way that the new spring season is never exactly the previous spring but nevertheless it is a return to spring.

In any case the traditional understanding of objective time based upon cycles is totally different from the linear conception of the flow of time which has developed in the West especially in modern times. The secularization of the Christian conception of the march of historical time, marked by the three central events of the fall of Adam, the first coming of Christ, and his second coming, has led to a quantitative and linear conception of history that is totally alien to the cyclic conception seen in Hinduism, the ancient Greek religion, and even Islam if one takes into consideration the meaning of the cycles of prophecy (*dā'irat al-nubuwwah*) which mark Islamic sacred history. To reduce objective time, whether it be cosmic or historical, to a quantitatively conceived linear time, to which is usually added the idea of indefinite progress in eighteenth and nineteenth century European thought, is to lose sight of the nature of time as the moving image of Eternity. It is to bestow a kind of absoluteness on time itself by forgetting its relation to the cosmic cycles of manifestation which reach, in an ever-ascending order, the Supreme Principle of all manifestation or the Eternal as such.

While speaking of linear time, which came to the fore in Western philosophy and science as a result of a complex set of factors related to the secularization of the Christian doctrine of the incarnation as well as certain other philosophical and scientific ideas, it is important to distinguish between qualitative and quantitative objective time. Mainstream modern Western thought, especially its more scientific vein, not only rejects the idea of Eternity and other categories of time mentioned above, but it also reduces time to pure quantity, emptying it of all qualitative aspects. It either speaks of an empty quantitative time stretching for "billions of years" within which cosmic events take place, or it relates time to matter and energy as in the theory of relativity but once again in a purely quantitative manner. That is why in modern science and all philosophies derived from it, there is a uniformitarianism which governs the history of the cosmos and its laws. Such a perspective cannot conceive of the crystallization of higher forms of being in the spatiotemporal complex at certain moments of cosmic history and not at others. Hence its need to posit the logically absurd theory of evolution as practically a dogma not allowed to be even questioned by serious scientists. Nor can such a perspective even imagine the possibility of the integration of the physical part of the cosmos into higher orders of reality at other moments of cosmic history corresponding to what various religions have described as eschatological events of various orders leading finally to the Apocatastasis, *al-qiyāmat al-kubrā*, or *mahāpralaya*.

Then there is subjective time, which is experienced directly by the consciousness of the human subject without any external measurement. Nor is in fact any quantitative measurement of this "inner time" possible. The individual subject can experience subjective time in many ways, in a state of contraction or expansion, in pain or in joy, in separation from God or in His proximity. The very duration of this experienced time differs according to these inner conditions. When the soul is in a state of spiritual deprivation or suffering, subjective time expands and an hour measured objectively is experienced as a much longer time. On the contrary, when the soul is in a state of spiritual contemplation or ecstasy, a contraction of time itself takes place. Many hours appear as if they were a moment. In this case, because of the rise of the experiencing subject in the levels of being, subjective time approaches Eternity or that "eternal present" which is the direct reflection of Eternity in time, the moment when according to Dante, "every *where* and every *when* is focused" (*Paradiso*, 29.12).

Subjective time is also experienced as past, present, and future. The past is experienced precisely as the past of a particular subject experiencing time, as are the present and the future. This tripartite division of time, although illusory from the point of view of the "Eternal Now" which alone is ultimately real, is nevertheless of metaphysical and spiritual significance. The past represents not only what has already disappeared from life and is therefore no longer accessible, but also the Origin from which man hails and hence the Divine Alpha. The future is not only indefinite moments of earthly life in which the imagination continues its dream of worldly forgetfulness, but also the direction toward paradise for which the soul prepares itself through its actions on earth and for which it has deep nostalgia as its homeland of origin. For as the poet Ḥāfiẓ has said,

> I was an angel and the exalted paradise was my abode,
> It was Adam who brought me to this flourishing ruined convent.

Finally there is the present, which not only corresponds to the point through which man can assert his passionate impulses, immersing himself in immediate gratification of the senses and impervious to his origin and his end as an immortal being, but also constitutes the only moment which connects man to the Eternal. It is in the present moment that man can assert his faith, can perform correct action, and above all can remember and recollect (the *dhikr* of Sufism) who he is and what is Reality. The present moment is the only gateway in this life to the abode of Eternity because this moment stands already outside of time and "is" in principle already in the Eternal Realm. The present moment is already beyond time, like the moment of death when serial time comes to an end. That is why in the Catholic rosary the faithful pray to the Virgin Mary for mercy "now" and at the moment of death.

* * *

One can carry out endless discourse about time and Eternity while the flow of time itself draws human life ever closer to the moment of truth when subjective time as experienced on earth comes to an end. But that discourse itself will not lead to the Eternal, which is the goal of human life. What is needed is to seize the present moment, to live in it and to pierce, with the help of the "eye of the heart," the cosmic veils of *māyā* and hence to know and experience that reality which is Eternity. All the traditional doctrines which speak of the present moment as the "point whereto all times are present"[1] do so in order to guide the soul to seize the present moment as the unique point of contact with the eternal Reality rather than to daydream about a past over which man can no longer wield any power or a future which has not yet come and in which again man cannot act. Man can be, know, and act only now. Even the poems of the Persian sage Khayyām, long considered as a hedonist in the West, refer in reality to the metaphysical and initiatic significance of the Eternal Now. When Khayyām sings,

> Ah, fill the Cup:—what boots it to repeat
> How Time is slipping underneath our Feet:
> Unborn, Tomorrow, and dead yesterday,
> Why fret about them if To-day be sweet!,[2]

he is not encouraging hedonism and Epicurean pleasure-seeking, which is the opposite of the attitude of the sage, but rather wishes to underline the significance of the present moment, of today, of the only moment when we can *be* and become what we are in reality in the Eternal Order. That is why the Sufi is called the son of the moment (*ibn al-waqt*), for he lives in the Eternal Moment, already dead to the illusory life of forgetfulness. He who lives in the present is in fact already dead in the traditional sense, in which the spiritual man is referred to as a walking dead man and in which the Prophet of Islam advised his followers to die before dying. To die to the corrosive flow of a time spent in the forgetfulness of God is to live already in Eternity while being still outwardly alive in this world. It is in fact to possess real life compared to which the life of the world is a petrified imitation, a death parading as life.

But while man possesses potentially this most precious treasure of the present moment, it is difficult for him to make it actually his own by virtue of living in it rather than in the past or the future. The fallen nature of the

[1] Dante, *Paradiso*, 27.17.

[2] Quoted by W.N. Perry, *A Treasury of Traditional Wisdom* (New York, 1986), p. 840.

humanity of this present phase in the cosmic cycle is such that the mind is too dispersed and the imagination too entangled in worldly forms to enable the vast majority of men to simply live in the eternal present by their own will. There is need of help from the Eternal Itself to make this attachment to the Eternal possible. Hence, the necessity of revelation and sacred forms which, issuing from the Eternal, enable man to live in the Eternal Now.

At the heart of these sacred and revealed forms and teachings which constitute religion stands prayer, which links man who lives in time to God and the Eternal Order. Through prayer man transcends the accidentality of time and space and regains his direct contact with the Eternal. The temporal and the Eternal are miraculously united in prayer as in the realization of the Truth through sapiential knowledge. The subject who prays to the Eternal, and the subject who knows that only the Supreme Reality is I, has already journeyed beyond the realm of temporality to reside in the Eternal Order. He has ceased to become and, having passed through the solar gate, can only be said to be. For him time has ceased to manifest itself as the moving image of Eternity. It has become a constellation of eternal moments or rather a single moment of the Eternal Now whose reverberations through the levels of cosmic manifestation make it appear as many moments.

The sacred itself is the manifestation of the Eternal in the temporal order, as are miracles. That is why the means which make possible the realization of the Eternal for a humanity living in historic time are contained in sacred tradition. Through sacred rites, objects and forms in time are brought back to the bosom of Eternity. Time itself is sacralized through celebrations of rites and recollection of theophanic realities. A distinction is thereby made between secular time, which is the time associated with what has come to be known as ordinary life, and sacred time, which redeems life by inundating the soul in the river of the eternal spring of the Spirit.

Likewise, miracles mark an irruption of the Eternal Order in the temporal. And since the Eternal Order is real, this irruption takes place no matter how much the downward flow of time, which characterizes cosmic and historical cycles, makes the temporal world appear to be independent of the Eternal. In the occurrence of miracles, not only are the ordinary laws of physical existence penetrated by laws belonging to higher orders of reality, but the ordinary rapport between time and Eternity is drastically changed. The particular time-span in which the miracle takes place partakes of the Eternal, and hence the trace of such a "time" imprints itself in a permanent manner upon the souls of the individuals who have experienced the miraculous event. This is true for miracles of a limited nature surrounding a particular saint or sage as well as the major miracles surrounding the life of the founder of a new religion or an *avatār*. In the latter case, the perfume of the Eternal subsisted permanently for a whole human collectivity, who therefore celebrate such events annually or in other cyclic periods of times on occasions which transcend history and bring the life of the humanity concerned back again and again to that moment when Heaven and earth touched each other and when the Eternal transformed a particular span of cosmic and historical time.

17. Pontifical and Promethean Man

The concept of man as the pontiff, *pontifex*, or bridge between Heaven and earth, which is the traditional view of the *anthrōpos*, lies at the antipode of the modern conception of man, which envisages him as the Promethean earthly creature who has rebelled against Heaven and tried to appropriate the role of the Divinity for himself. Pontifical man, who, in the sense used here, is none other than traditional man, lives in a world which has both an Origin and a Center. He lives in full awareness of the Origin which contains his own perfection and whose primordial purity and wholeness he seeks to emulate, recapture, and transmit. He also lives on a circle of whose Center he is always aware and which he seeks to reach in his life, thought, and actions. Pontifical man is the reflection of the Center on the periphery and the echo of the Origin in later cycles of time and generations of history. He is the vicegerent of God (*khalīfat Allāh*) on earth, to use the Islamic term, responsible to God for his actions, and the custodian and protector of the earth of which he is given dominion on the condition that he remain faithful to himself as the central terrestrial figure created in the "form of God," a theomorphic being living in this world but created for eternity. Pontifical man is aware of his role as intermediary between Heaven and earth and his entelechy as lying beyond the terrestrial domain over which he is allowed to rule provided he remains aware of the transient nature of his own journey on earth. Such a man lives in awareness of a spiritual reality which transcends him and yet which is none other than his own inner nature against which he cannot rebel, save by paying the price of separation from all that he is and all that he should wish to be. For such a man, life is impregnated with meaning and the universe peopled with creatures whom he can address as thou. He is aware that precisely because he is human there is both grandeur and danger connected with all that he does and thinks. His actions have an effect upon his own being beyond the limited spatiotemporal conditions in which such actions take place. He knows that somehow the bark which is to take him to the shore beyond after the fleeting journey that comprises his earthly life is constructed by what he does and how he lives while he is in the human state.

To be sure, the image of man as depicted in various traditions has not been identical. Some have emphasized the human state more than others and they have envisaged eschatological realities differently. But there is no doubt that all traditions are based on the central and dominant images of the Origin and the Center and see the final end of man in the state or reality which is other than this terrestrial life with which forgetful or fallen man identifies himself once he is cut off from revelation or religion that constantly hearkens back to the Origin and the Center.

Promethean man, on the contrary, is a creature of this world. He feels at home on earth, earth not considered as the virgin nature which is itself an echo of paradise, but as the artificial world created by Promethean man himself in order to make it possible for him to forget God and his own inner reality. Such a man envisages life as a big marketplace in which he is free to roam around and choose objects at will. Having lost the sense of the sacred, he is drowned in transience and impermanence and becomes a slave of his own lower nature, surrender to which he considers to be freedom. He follows passively the downward flow of the cycle of human history and in doing so takes pride by claiming that he has created his own destiny. But still being man, he has a nostalgia for the Sacred and the Eternal and thus turns to a thousand and one ways to satisfy this need, ways ranging from psychological novels to drug-induced mysticism.

He also becomes stifled by the prison of his own creation, wary of the destruction he has wrought upon the natural environment and the vilification of the urban setting in which he is forced to live. He seeks for solutions everywhere, even in teachings by which pontifical man, or traditional man, has lived over the ages. But these sources are not able to help him, for he approaches even these truths as Promethean man. This recently born creature, who has succeeded in wreaking havoc upon the earth and practically upsetting the ecological balance of the natural order itself in only some five centuries, is little aware that to overcome the impasse into which modern man has thrown himself as a result of attempting to forget what it really means to be man he must rediscover himself. He must come to understand the nature of man as that pontifical and central creature on this earth who stands as witness to an origin from which he descends and a center to which he ultimately returns. The traditional doctrine of man and not the measurement of skulls and footprints is the key for the understanding of that *anthrōpos* who, despite the rebellion of Promethean man against Heaven from the period of the Renaissance and its aftermath, is still the inner man of every man, the reality which no human being can deny wherever and whenever he lives, the imprint of a theomorphic nature which no historical change and transformation can erase completely from the face of that creature called man.

* * *

As far as the traditional doctrine of man is concerned, it is based in one way or another on the concept of primordial man as the source of perfection, the total and complete reflection of the Divinity and the archetypal reality containing the possibilities of cosmic existence itself. Man is the model of the universe because he is himself the reflection of those possibilities in the principial domain which manifest themselves as the world. Man is more than merely man so that this way of envisaging his rapport with respect to the cosmos is far from being anthropomorphic in the usual sense of this term. The world is not seen as the reflection of man qua man but of man as being himself the total and plenary reflection of all those Divine Qualities whose reflections, in scattered and segmented fashion, comprise the manifested order.

In traditions with a strongly mythical character this inward relationship between man and the cosmos is depicted in the myth of the sacrifice of the primordial man. For example, in the Iranian religions the sacrifice of the primordial man is associated with the creation of the world and its various orders and realms, different parts of the "body" of the primordial man being associated with different orders of creatures such as animals, plants, and minerals. Sometimes, however, a more particular relationship is emphasized as in those Zoroastrian sources where Gayōmart, who is the first man, is associated with the generation of the minerals, for as the *Greater Bundahišn* says, "When Gayōmart was assailed with sickness, he fell on his left side. From his head lead came forth, from his blood zinc, from his marrow silver, from his feet iron, from his bones brass, from his fat crystal, from his arms steel, and from his soul as it departed, gold."[1] In Hinduism there is the famous passage in the *Ṛg-Veda* (X, 90) according to which, from the sacrifice of Puruṣa or primordial man, the world and the human race consisting of the four castes are brought into being, the *brahmins* from his mouth, the *rājanyas* or *kṣatriyas* from his arms, the *vaiśyas* from his belly, and the *śūdras* from his feet— his sacrifice, or *yajña*, being the model of all sacrifice. Primordial man is the archetype of creation as he is its purpose and entelechy. That is why according to a *ḥadīth*, God addresses the Prophet of Islam, whose inner reality is the primordial man par excellence in the Islamic tradition, in these terms, "If thou wert not, I would not have created the world." This perspective envisages the human reality in its divine and cosmic dimensions in exact opposition to philosophical

[1] Quoted in R. C. Zaehner, *The Teachings of the Magi* (London, 1956), p. 75; see also M. Molé, *Le Problème zoroastrien et la tradition mazdéenne* (Paris, 1963).

anthropomorphism. Man does not see God and the world in his image but realizes that he is himself in his inner reality that image which reflects the Divine Qualities and by which cosmic reality is created, the possibilities being contained in the Logos "by which all things were made."

The metaphysical doctrine of man in the fullness of his being, in what he is but not necessarily in what he appears to be, is expounded in various languages in the different traditions with diverse degrees of emphasis which are far from being negligible. Some traditions are based more upon the divinized human receptacle while others reject this perspective in favor of the Divinity in Itself. Some depict man in his state of fall from his primordial perfection and address their message to this fallen creature, whereas others, while being fully aware that the humanity they are addressing is not the society of perfect men living in paradise, address that primordial nature which still survives in man despite the layers of "forgetfulness" and imperfection which separate man from himself.

That primordial and plenary nature of man which Islam calls the "Universal or Perfect Man" (*al-insān al-kāmil*) and to which the sapiential doctrines of Graeco-Alexandrian antiquity also allude in nearly the same terms, except for the Abrahamic and specifically Islamic aspects of the doctrines absent from the Neoplatonic and Hermetic sources, reveals human reality to possess three fundamental aspects. The Universal Man, whose reality is realized only by the prophets and great seers, since only they are human in the full sense of the word, is first of all the archetypal reality of the universe; second, the instrument or means whereby revelation descends into the world; and third, the perfect model for the spiritual life and the ultimate dispenser of esoteric knowledge. By virtue of the reality of the Universal Man, terrestrial man is able to gain access to revelation and tradition, hence to the sacred. Finally, through this reality, which is none other than man's own reality actualized, man is able to follow that path of perfection which will finally allow him to gain knowledge of the sacred and to become fully himself. The saying of the Delphic oracle, "Know thyself," or that of the Prophet of Islam, "He who knoweth himself knoweth his Lord," is true not because man as an earthly creature is the measure of all things but because man is himself the reflection of that archetypal reality which is the measure of all things. That is why in traditional sciences of man the knowledge of the cosmos and the metacosmic reality are usually not expounded in terms of the reality of terrestrial man. Rather, the knowledge of man is expounded through and in reference to the macrocosm and metacosm, since they reflect in a blinding fashion and in an objective mode what man is if only he were to become what he really is. The traditional doctrine of Primordial or Universal Man with all its variations—Adam Kadmon, jen, Puruṣa, *al-insān al-kāmil*, and the like—embraces at once the metaphysical, cosmogonic, revelatory, and initiatic functions of that reality which constitutes the totality of the human state and which places before man both the grandeur of what he can be and the pettiness and wretchedness of what he is in most cases, in comparison with the ideal which he carries always within himself. Terrestrial man is nothing more than the externalization, coagulation, and often inversion and perversion of this idea and ideal of the Universal Man cast in the direction of the periphery. He is a being caught in the field of the centrifugal forces which characterize terrestrial existence as such, but is also constantly attracted by the Center where the inner man is always present.

It is also by virtue of carrying this reality within himself and bearing the characteristics of a theomorphic being, because he is such a being in his essential reality, that man remains an axial creature in this world. Even his denial of the sacred has a cosmic significance, his purely empirical and earthly science going to the extent of imposing the danger of destroying the harmony of the terrestrial environment itself. Man cannot live as a purely earthly creature totally at home in this world without destroying the natural environment, precisely because he is not such a creature. The pontifical function of man remains inseparable from his reality, from what he is. That is why traditional teachings envisage the happiness of man in his remaining aware and living according to his pontifical nature as the bridge between Heaven and earth. His religious laws and rites have a cosmic function and he is made aware that it is impossible for him to evade his responsibility as a creature who lives on the earth but is not only earthly, as a being strung between Heaven and earth, of both a spiritual and material mold, created to reflect the light of the Divine Empyrean within the world and to preserve harmony in the world through the dispensation of that light and the practice of that form of life which is in accordance with his inner reality as revealed by tradition. Man's responsibility to society, the cosmos, and God issues ultimately from himself, not his self as ego but the inner man who is the mirror and reflection of the Supreme Self, the Ultimate Reality which can be envisaged as either pure Subject or pure Object since It transcends in Itself all dualities, being neither subject nor object.

The situation of man as bridge between Heaven and earth is reflected in all of his being and his faculties. Man is himself a supernaturally natural being. When he walks on the earth, on the one hand he appears as a creature of the earth; on the other, it is as if he were a celestial being who has descended upon the earthly realm. Likewise, his memory, speech, and imagination partake at once of several orders of reality. Most of all his intelligence is a supernaturally natural faculty, a sacrament partaking of all that the term supernatural signifies in Christianity, yet functioning quasi-naturally within him with the help of revelation and its unifying grace. That is why, while even in this world, man is able to move to the other shore of existence, to take his stance in the world of the sacred and to see nature herself as impregnated with grace. He is able to remove that sharp boundary which has been drawn between the natural and the supernatural in most schools of official Christian theology but which is not emphasized in the same manner in other traditions and is also overcome in the sapiential aspects of the Christian tradition itself.

Metaphysically speaking then, man has his archetype in that primordial, perfect, and universal being or man who is the mirror of the Divine Qualities and Names and the prototype of creation. But each human being also possesses his own archetype and has a reality *in divinis* as a possibility unto himself, one which is unique since that person reflects the archetype of the human species as such in the same way that every point on the circumference of a circle reflects the center and is yet distinct from other points. The reality of man as a species as well as of each human being has its root in the principial domain. Therefore man as such, as well as each human being, comes into the world through an "elaboration" and process which separates him from the Divine, and he departs from the world through paths, which in joy or sorrow, depending on his life on earth, finally lead him back to the Divine.

* * *

It is remarkable that, while traditional teachings are aware that other creatures preceded man on earth, they believe that man precedes them in the principial order and that his appearance on earth is the result of a descent, not an ascent. Man precipitates on earth from the subtle state, appearing out of the cloud or on a chariot as described in various traditional accounts, this "cloud" symbolizing the intermediary condition between the subtle and the physical. He appears on earth already as a central and total being, reflecting the Absolute not only in his spiritual and mental faculties but even in his body. If Promethean man finally lost sight completely of the higher levels of existence and was forced to take recourse in some kind of mysterious temporal process called evolution which would bring him out of the primordial soup of molecules envisaged by modern science, pontifical man has always seen himself as the descent of a reality which has been elaborated through many worlds to arrive on earth in a completed form as the central and theomorphic being that he is. From the point of view of man's being conscious of not only earthly, horizontal causes but also Heaven and the vertical dimension of existence and chains of causes, the monkey is not what he had once been and is no longer, but what he could never be precisely because of what he always is and has been. Pontifical man has always been man, and the traditional perspective which is his views the presence of the monkey as a cosmic sign, a creature whose significance is to display what the central human state excludes by its very centrality. To study the state of the monkey metaphysically and not just biologically is to grasp what man is not and could have never been.

Traditional sciences of man have spoken at length about the inner structure and faculties of man as well as the significance of his body and its powers. One discovers in such sources the repeated assertion that man has access to multiple levels of existence and consciousness within himself and a hierarchy of faculties and even "substances" which in any case cannot be reduced to the two entities of body and soul or mind and body, reflecting the dualism so prevalent in post-Cartesian Western thought. This dualism neglects the essential unity of the human microcosm precisely because duality implies opposition and, in contrast to trinity, is not a reflection of Unity. On the first level of understanding the human microcosm, therefore, one must take into consideration the tripartite nature of the human being consisting of spirit, soul, and body—the classical *pneuma*, *psyché*, and *hylé* or *spiritus*, *anima*, and *corpus* of Western traditions both Graeco-Alexandrian and Christian—at least as far as Christian Hermeticism is concerned. The soul is the principle of the body, but in the "normal" human being is itself subservient to the spirit and reaches its salvation and beatitude through the wedding to the spirit of which so many alchemical texts speak.

This tripartite division, however, is a simplification of a more complex situation. Actually man contains within himself many levels of existence and layers. Such traditions as Tantrism and certain schools of Sufism as well as Western Hermeticism speak not of body as opposed to soul and spirit but of several bodies of man of which the physical body is only the most outward and externalized envelope. Man possesses subtle as well as spiritual bodies in conformity with the different worlds through which he journeys. There is, moreover, an inversion between various levels of existence so that man's soul (used here in the general sense of all that is immaterial in his being), molded in this world by his actions, becomes externalized in the intermediate world as his "body." It is in reference to this principle that the Imams of Shi'ism, referring to the posthumous states of man and especially the "perfect man" represented by the Imams, have declared, "*Arwāḥunā ajsādunā wa ajsādunā arwāḥunā*" (Our spirits are our bodies and our bodies are our spirits). The sojourn of man through the levels of existence and forms, which the popular interpretation of Indian religions identifies with a return to the same level of reality and the esoteric dimension of the Abrahamic traditions with multiple levels of reality, corresponds to his journey within himself and through all the layers of his own being.

Man possesses an incorruptible ethereal body as well as a radiant spiritual body corresponding to the other "earths" of the higher states of being. In the same way that to speak of body and soul corresponds to the perspective of heaven or several heavens and earth, to envisage the several bodies of man corresponds to seeing the higher levels of reality as each possessing its own heaven and earth. After all, through the grace of the Amida Buddha man is born in the "Pure Land" and not "pure heaven," but here the symbolism of land includes the paradisal and heavenly. It is the celestial earth to which also Islamic esoterism often refers and which played such an important role in Zoroastrianism, where the earth itself was conceived as having been originally an angel.

The various "bodies" of the inner man have been envisaged in very different terms in different traditions but everywhere they are related to the realization of sacred knowledge and the attainment of virtue. The beauty of man's physical body is God-given and not for him to determine. But the type of "body" attained either in the posthumous state or through initiatic practices and ways of realization depends upon how man spends that precious gift which is human life, for once this life comes to an end, the door that is open toward the Infinite closes. Only man can pass through the door while enjoying possibilities of the human state. It makes literally all the difference in the world whether man *does* pass through that door while he has the possibility or not.

In any case, as far as the positive and not negative and infernal possibilities are concerned, the various bodies of the Buddhas and Bodhisattvas mentioned in northern schools of Buddhism and so central to Buddhist eschatology and techniques of meditation, the Hindu *chakras* as centers of the subtle bodies and energies, the *ōkhēma symphyēs* ("psychic vehicle") of Proclus or the *laṭā'if* or subtle bodies of Sufism, all refer to the immense reality unto which the human microcosm opens if only man were to cease to live on the surface of his being. Certain schools also speak of the man of light and the whole anatomy and physiology of the inner man, which is not the subject of study of modern biology but which, nevertheless, affects the human body, the physical body itself reflecting the Absolute on its own level and possessing a positive nature of great import for the understanding of the total nature of man.

The human body is not the seat of concupiscence but only its instrument. Although asceticism is a necessary element of every authentic spiritual path, for there is something in the soul that must die before it can reach perfection, the body itself is the temple of God. It is the sacred precinct in which the Divine Presence or the Divine Light manifests itself as asserted not only in the Oriental religions but also in Hesychasm within Orthodox Christianity where the keeping of the mind within the body and the Divine Name within the center of the body, which is the heart, plays a crucial role. This perspective is also to be found in Christian Hermeticism but has not been greatly emphasized in Western Christian theology.

The human body consists of three basic elements: the head, the body, and the heart. The heart, which is the invisible center of both the subtle and the physical body, is the seat of intelligence and the point which relates the terrestrial human state to the higher states of being. In the heart, knowledge and being meet and are one. The head and the body are like projections of the heart: the head, whose activity is associated with the mind, is the projection of the intelligence of the heart and the body the projection of being. This separation already marks the segmentation and externalization of man. But the compartmentalization is not complete. There is an element of being in the mind and of intelligence in the body which become forgotten to the extent that man becomes engrossed in the illusion of the Promethean mode of existence and forgets his theomorphic nature. That is why modern man, who is Promethean man to the extent that such a perversion of his own reality is possible, is the type of man most forgetful of the tranquility and peace of mind which reflects being and of the intelligence of the body. That is also why those contemporary men in quest of the sacred and the rediscovery of pontifical man seek, on the one hand, techniques of meditation which would allow the agitated mind to simply be and to overcome that excessive cerebral activity which characterizes modern man and, on the other hand, to rediscover the wisdom and intelligence of the body through yoga, Oriental forms of medicine, natural foods, and the like. Both attempts are in reality the quest for the heart, which, in the spiritual person aware of his vocation as man, "penetrates" into both the head and the body, integrating them into the center, bestowing a contemplative perfume on mental activity and an intellectual and spiritual presence on the body, which is reflected in its gestures and motions.

In the prophet, the *avatār*, and the great saint, both the face and the body directly manifest and display the presence of the heart through an inwardness which attracts toward the center and a radiance and emanation of grace which inebriates and unifies. For those not blessed by the vision of such beings, the sacred art of those traditions based on the iconography of the human form of the founder or outstanding spiritual figures of the tradition is at least a substitute for and reminder of what a work of art man himself is. To behold a Japanese or Tibetan Buddha image, with eyes drawn inward toward the heart and the body radiating the presence of the Spirit that resides in the heart, is to grasp in a concrete fashion what the principial and ideal relation of the heart is to both the head and the body, which preserve their own intelligible symbolism and even their own wisdom, whether a particular "mind" cut off from its own roots is aware of it or not.

The central and "absolute" nature of the human body is also to be seen in man's vertical position, which directly reflects his role as the axis connecting heaven and earth. The clear distinction of his head protruding toward heaven reflects his quest for transcendence. The chest reflects glory and nobility, of a more rigorous nature in the male and generous in the female, and the sexual parts hierogenesis, divine activity whose terrestrial result is the procreation of another man or woman who miraculously enough is again not merely a biological being, although outwardly brought into the world through biological means. From the perspective of *scientia sacra* the human body itself is proof that man has sprung from a celestial origin and that he was born for a goal beyond the confines of his animality. The definition of man as a central being is reflected not only in his mind, speech, and other internal faculties but also in his body, which stands at the center of the circle of terrestrial existence and possesses a beauty and significance which is of a purely spiritual nature. The very body of man and woman reveals the destiny of the human being as a creature born for immortality, as a being whose perfection resides in ascending the vertical dimension of existence, having already reached the center of the horizontal dimension. Having reached the point of intersection of the cross, it is for man to ascend its vertical axis, which is the only way for him to transcend himself and to remain fully human, for to be human is to go beyond oneself. As Saint Augustine has said, to remain human, man must become superhuman.

Man also possesses numerous internal faculties, including a memory much more prodigious than those who are the product of modern education can envisage and one which plays a very positive role in both the intellectual and artistic activity of traditional man. He possesses an imagination which, far from being mere fantasy, has the power to create forms corresponding to cosmic realities and to play a central role in religious and even intellectual life, far more than can be conceived by the modern world, whose impoverished view of reality excludes the whole domain of what might be called the imaginal, to distinguish it from the imaginary. Man also possesses that miraculous gift of speech through which he is able to exteriorize the knowledge of both the heart and the mind. His speech is the direct reflection and consequence of his theomorphic nature and the Logos which shines at the center of his being. It is through his speech that he is able to formulate the Word of God and it is also through his speech in the form of prayer and finally the quintessential prayer of the heart, which is inner speech and silent invocation, that he himself becomes prayer. Man realizes his full pontifical nature in that theophanic prayer of Universal Man in which the whole creation, both Heaven and earth, participate.

From the point of view of his powers and faculties man can be said to possess essentially three powers or poles which determine his life, these being intelligence, sentiment, and will. As a theomorphic being he possesses or can possess that absolute and unconditioned intelligence which can know the truth as such; sentiments which are capable of going beyond the limited conditions of man and of reaching out for the ultimate through love, suffering, sacrifice, and also fear; and a will which is free to choose and which reflects the Divine Freedom.

Because of man's separation from his original perfection and all the ambivalence that the human condition involves as a result of what Christianity calls the fall, none of these powers function necessarily and automatically according to man's theomorphic nature. The fall of man upon the earth, like the descent of a symbol from a higher plane of reality, means both reflection and inversion, which in the case of man leads to perversion. Intelligence can become reduced to mental play; sentiments can deteriorate to little more than gravitation around that illusory coagulation which we usually call "ourselves" but which is only the ego in its negative sense as comprising the knots of the soul; and the will can be debased to nothing other than the urge to do that which removes man from the source of his own being, from his own real self. But these powers, when governed by tradition and imbued with the power of the light and grace which emanates from revelation, begin to reveal, like man's body, dimensions of his theomorphic nature. The body, however, remains more innocent and true to the form in which God created it, whereas the perversion of man and his deviation from his Divine Prototype is manifested directly in this intermediate realm with which man identifies himself, namely, the realm of the will and the sentiments and even the mental reflection of the intelligence, if not the intelligence itself. In the normal situation, which is that of pontifical man, the goal of all three human powers or faculties, that is, intelligence, the sentiments, and will, is God. Moreover, in the sapiential perspective both the sentiments and the will are related to intelligence and impregnated by it, for how can one love without knowing what one loves and how can one will something without some knowledge at least of what one wills?

The understanding of the reality of man as *anthrōpos* can be achieved more fully by also casting an eye upon the segmentations and divisions of various kinds which characterize mankind as such. The original *anthrōpos* was, according to traditional teachings, an androgynic figure, although some traditions speak of both a male and a female being whose union is then seen as the perfection identified with the androgynic state. In either case, the wholeness and perfection inherent in the human state and the bliss which is associated with sexual union belong in reality to the androgynic state before the sexes were separated. But the dualities which characterize the created order and which manifest themselves on all levels of existence below the principial, such as yin-yang, *puruṣa-prakṛti*, activity and passivity, form and matter, could not but appear upon the plane of that androgynic reality and give birth to the male and the female, which do not, however, correspond to pure yin and pure yang. Since they are creatures they must contain both principles within themselves with one of the elements of the duality predominating in each case. The male and the female in their complementarity recreate the unity of the androgynic being and in fact sexual union is an earthly reflection of that paradisal ecstasy which belonged to the androgynic *anthrōpos*. But that androgynic reality is also reflected in both man and woman in themselves, hence both the sense of complementarity and rivalry which characterizes the relation between the sexes. In any case the distinction between the male and female is not only biological. It is not even only psychological or spiritual. It has its roots in the Divine Nature Itself, man reflecting more the Absoluteness of the Divine and the woman Its Infinitude. If the face of God towards the world is envisaged in masculine terms, His inner Infinitude is symbolized by the feminine as are His Mercy and Wisdom. Human sexuality, far from being a terrestrial accident, reflects principles which are ultimately of a metacosmic significance. It is not without reason that sexuality is the only means open for human beings not endowed with the gift of spiritual vision to experience "the Infinite" through the senses, albeit for a few fleeting moments, and that sexuality leaves such a profound mark upon the soul of men and women and affects them in a manner far more enduring than other physical acts. To understand the nature of the male-female distinction in the human race and to appreciate the positive qualities which each sex displays is to gain greater insight into the nature of that androgynic being whose reality both the male and female carry at the center of their being.

Man is not only divided according to sex but also temperament, of which both sexes partake. The four temperaments of traditional Galenic medicine, which have their counterparts in other schools of traditional medicine, concern not only the physical body but also the psychic substance and in fact all the faculties which comprise what we call the soul. They affect not only the sentiments but also the will and even the modes of operation of intelligence, which in themselves remain above the temperamental modifications. The same could be said of the three *guṇas* of Hindu cosmology, those fundamental tendencies in the primary substance of the universe, or *prakṛti*, which concern not only the physical realm but also human types. One can say that human beings are differentiated through the dual principles of yin-yang; the three *guṇas*, which are *sattva*, the ascending, *rajas*, the expansive, and *tamas*, the descending tendencies; and the temperaments, which have a close correlation with the four natures, elements, and humors as expounded in various cosmological schemes.

Human types can also be divided astrologically, here astrology being understood in its cosmological and symbolic rather than its predictive sense. Astrological classifications, which are in fact related to traditional medical and physical typologies, concern the cosmic correspondences of the various aspects of the human soul and unveil the refraction of the archetype of man in the cosmic mirror in such a way as to bring out the diversity of this refraction with reference to the qualities associated with the zodiacal signs and the planets. Traditional astrology, in a sense, concerns man on the angelic level of his being but also unveils, if understood in its symbolic significance, a typology of man which reveals yet another facet of the differentiation of the human species. The correspondence between various parts of the body, as well as man's mental powers, and astrological signs, and the intricate rapport created between the motion of the heavens, various "aspects" and relations between planets, and human activity are also a means of portraying the inward link that binds man as the microcosm to the cosmos.

Mankind is also divided into castes and races, both of which must be understood in their essential reality and without the pejorative connotations which have become associated with them in the modern world. The division of humanity into castes does not necessarily mean immutable social stratification, for there have been strictly traditional societies, such as the Islamic, where caste has not existed as a social institution in the same way it was found in ancient Persia or in India. The traditional science of man sees the concept of caste as a key for the understanding of human types. There are those who are contemplative by nature and drawn to the quest of knowledge, who have a sacerdotal nature and in normal times usually fulfill the priestly and intellectual functions in their society. There are those who are warriors and leaders of men, who possess the courage to fight for the truth and to protect the world in which they live, who are ready to sacrifice themselves in battle as the person with a sacerdotal nature sacrifices himself in prayer to the Divinity. Members of this second caste have a knightly function and in normal times would be the political leaders and warriors. Then there are those given to trade, to making an honest living and working hard to sustain and support themselves and those around them. They have a mercantile nature and in traditional societies comprise those who carry out the business and economic functions of normal society. Finally, there are those whose virtue is to follow and to be led, to work according to the dictates of those who lead them. These castes, which Hinduism identifies as the *brahmin*, *kṣatriya*, *vaiśya*, and *śūdra*, are not necessarily identified with birth in all societies. In any case, as far as the study of human types is concerned, they are to be found everywhere in all times and climes wherever men and women live and die. They represent fundamental human types complementing the tripartite Neoplatonic division of human beings into the pneumatics, psychics, and "hylics" (the *hylikoi* of the Neoplatonists). To understand the deeper significance of caste is to gain an insight into a profound aspect of human nature in whatever environment man might function and live.

Finally, it is obvious that human beings are divided into racial and ethnic types. There are four races, the yellow, the red, the black, and the white, which like the four castes act as the pillars of the human collectivity, four symbolizing stability and being associated with the earth itself with its four cardinal directions and the four elements of which the physical world is composed. Each race is an aspect of that androgynic reality and possesses its own positive features. In fact, no one race can exhaust the reality of the human state, including human beauty, which each race, both its male and female members, reflect in a different fashion. The very plenitude of the Divine Principle and richness of the reality of the Universal Man, who is the theater for the theophany of all the Divine Names and Qualities, requires this multiplicity of races and ethnic groups, which in their unbelievable variety manifest the different aspects of their prototype and which together give some idea of the grandeur and beauty of that first creation of

God which was the human reality as such, that primordial reflection of the face of the Beloved in the mirror of nothingness.

The division of mankind into male and female, the various temperamental types, astrological divisions of human beings, different natures according to caste, various racial types, and many other factors along with the interpenetration of these modes of perceiving the human state, reveal something of the immense complexity of that creature called man. But as analysis leads in turn to synthesis, this bewildering array of types all return to that primordial reality of the *anthrōpos* which each human being reflects in himself or herself. To be human is to be human wherever and whenever one may live. There is therefore a profound unity of traditional mankind which only the traditional science of man can comprehend without reducing this unity to a uniformity and a gross quantitative equality that characterizes so much of the modern concern for man and the study of the human state.

Through all these differences of types, tradition detects the presence of that pontifical man born to know the Absolute and to live according to the will of Heaven. But tradition is also fully aware of the ambivalence of the human state, of the fact that men do not live on the level of what they are in principle, but below themselves, and of the imperfection of all that participates in what is characteristically human. This trait includes even those direct manifestations of the Absolute in the relative which comprise religion with revelation at its heart. Man is such a being that he can become prophet and spokesman for the Word of God, not to speak of the possibility of the divinized man, which certain traditions like Islam, based on the Absolute itself, reject. But even in these cases there is a human margin and within each religion there exists an element of pure, unqualified Truth and a margin which already belongs to the region where the Truth penetrates into the human substance. Moreover, revelation is always given in the language of the people to whom God addresses Himself. As the Quran says, "And We never sent a messenger save with the language of his people that he might make [the message] clear for them" (14:4). Hence the multiplicity of religions in a world with multiple "humanities." The human state therefore gives a certain particularity to various revelations of the Truth while the heart of these revelations remains above all form. In fact, man himself is able to penetrate into that formless Essence through his intelligence sanctified by that revelation and even come to know that the formless Truth is modified by the form of the recipient according to the Divine Wisdom and Will, God having Himself created that recipient which receives His revelation in different climes and settings.

How strange it appears that agnostic humanism, which remains content with the vessel without realizing the origin of the divine elixir that the human vessel contains, should be only a half-way house to that which is inhuman! Pontifical man has lived on the earth for millennia and continues to survive here and there despite the onslaught of modernism. But the life of Promethean man has been indeed short-lived. The kind of humanism associated with the Promethean revolt of the Renaissance has led in only a few centuries to the veritably infrahuman, which threatens not only the human quality of life but the very existence of man on earth. The reason for such a phenomenon, which seems so unexpected from the perspective of Promethean man, is quite obvious from the traditional point of view. It lies in the fact that to speak of the human is to speak, at the same time, of the Divine. Although scholars occasionally discuss what they call Chinese or Islamic humanism, there has in fact never been a humanism in any traditional civilization similar to the one associated with the European Renaissance and what followed upon its wake. Traditional civilizations have spoken of man and of course created cultures and disciplines called the humanities of the highest order, but the man they have spoken of has never ceased to be that pontifical man who stands on the axis joining Heaven and earth and who bears the imprint of the Divine upon his very being.

It is this basic nature of man which makes a secular and agnostic humanism impossible. It is not metaphysically possible to kill the gods and seek to efface the imprint of the Divinity upon man without destroying man himself; the bitter experience of the modern world stands as overwhelming evidence to this truth. The face which God has turned toward the cosmos and man (the *wajh Allāh* of the Quran) is none other than the face of man toward the Divinity and in fact the human face itself. One cannot "efface" the "face of God" without "effacing" man himself and reducing him to a faceless entity lost in an anthill. The cry of Nietzsche that "God is dead" could not but mean that "man is dead," as the history of the twentieth century has succeeded in demonstrating in so many ways. But in reality the response to Nietzsche was not the death of man as such but of the Promethean man who had thought he could live on a circle without a center. The other man, the pontifical man, although forgotten in the modern world, continues to live even within those human beings who pride themselves in having outgrown the models and modes of thought of their ancestors; he continues to live and will never die.

That man who remains man and continues to survive here and there even during this period of eclipse of spirituality and the desacralization of life is the being who remains aware of his destiny, which is transcendence, and the function of his intelligence, which is knowledge of the Absolute. He is fully aware of the preciousness of human life, which alone permits a creature living in this world to journey beyond the cosmos, and is always conscious of the great responsibility which such an opportunity entails. He knows that the grandeur of man does not lie in his cunning cleverness or titanic creations but resides most of all in the incredible power to empty himself of himself, to cease to exist in the initiatic sense, to participate in that state of spiritual poverty and emptiness which permits him to experience Ultimate Reality. As the Persian poet Saʿdī says,

> Man reaches a stage where he sees nothing but God—
> See how exalted is the station of manhood![2]

Pontifical man stands at the perigee of an arc half of which represents the trajectory through which he has descended from the Source and his own archetype *in divinis* and the other half the arc of ascent which he must follow to return to that Source. The whole constitution of man reveals this role of the traveler who becomes what he "is" and is what he becomes. Man is fully man only when he realizes who he is and in doing so fulfills not only his own destiny and reaches his entelechy but also illuminates the world about him. Journeying from the earth to his celestial abode, which he has left inwardly, man becomes the channel of grace for the earth, and the bridge which joins it to Heaven. Realization of the truth by pontifical man is not only the goal and end of the human state but also the means whereby Heaven and earth are reunited in marriage, and that Unity which is the Source of the cosmos and the harmony pervading it, is reestablished. To be fully man is to rediscover that primordial Unity from which all the heavens and earths originate and yet from which nothing ever *really* departs.

[2] *Kulliyyāt-i Shaykh Saʿdī*, edited A. Qarīb (Tehran: Jāwīdān, n.d.), p. 577.

18. The Cosmos as Theophany

Although the goal of sacred knowledge is the knowledge of the Sacred as such, that is, of that Reality which lies beyond all cosmic manifestation, there is always that stage of the gathering of the scattered leaves of the book of the universe, to paraphrase Dante, before journeying beyond it. The cosmos plays a positive role in certain types of spirituality, and any integral tradition must account for it and include it in its total perspective, which is not to say that the adept of every kind of spiritual path need study the pages of the cosmic book. But precisely because the cosmos *is* a book containing a primordial revelation of utmost significance and man a being whose essential, constitutive elements are reflected upon the cosmic mirror and who possesses a profound inner nexus with the cosmic ambience around him, sacred knowledge must also include a knowledge of the cosmos that is not simply an empirical knowledge of nature nor even just a sensibility toward the beauties of nature, no matter how noble this sensibility, of the kind expressed by so many English Romantic poets, might be.

In the traditional world there is a science of the cosmos—in fact many sciences of the cosmos or cosmological sciences which study various natural and cosmic domains ranging from the stars to minerals, but from the point of view of metaphysical principles. All traditional cosmology is in fact the fruit of the applications of metaphysical principles to different domains of cosmic reality by an intelligence which is itself still wed to the Intellect and has not completely surrendered to sensorial impressions. Such sciences also deal with the natural world and have produced knowledge of that world which is "scientific" according to the current understanding of this term, but not only scientific. Even in these instances, however, the aim of such traditional sciences has been to produce not a knowledge of a particular order of reality in a closed system and cut off from other orders of reality and domains of knowledge, but a knowledge which relates the domain in question to higher orders of reality as that knowledge itself is related to higher orders of knowledge. There is such a thing as traditional science distinct from modern science dealing with the same realms and domains of nature which are treated in the sciences today. Yet these traditional sciences, although of much importance in understanding the rise of modern science, which in many cases employed their outward content without comprehending or accepting their world view, have a significance wholly other than the modern sciences of nature.

The traditional sciences of the cosmos make use of the language of symbolism. They claim to expound a *science* and not a sentiment or a poetic image of the domain which is their concern, but a science which is expounded in the language of symbolism based on the analogy between various levels of existence. In fact, although there are numerous cosmological sciences, sometimes even several dealing with the same realm within a single tradition, one can speak of a *cosmologia perennis* which they reflect in various languages of form and symbol, a *cosmologia perennis* which, in one sense, is the application and, in another, the complement of the *sophia perennis* which is concerned essentially with metaphysics.

There is also another type of the "study" of the cosmos in the traditional context which complements the first. That is the contemplation of certain natural forms as reflecting Divine Qualities and the vision of the cosmos *in divinis*. This perspective is based on the power of forms to be occasions for recollection in the Platonic sense and the *essential* and of course not *substantial* identity of natural forms with their paradisal origin. Spiritual realization based on the sapiential perspective implies also this "metaphysical transparency of natural forms and objects" as a necessary dimension and aspect of "seeing God everywhere."[1] In reality the traditional cosmological sciences lend themselves to being such a support for contemplation besides making available a veritable science of various realms of the cosmos. What is in fact traditional cosmology but a way of allowing man to contemplate the cosmos itself as an icon! Therefore, both types of knowledge of the cosmos, as viewed from the perspective of sacred knowledge and through eyes which are not cut off from the sanctifying rays of the "eye of the heart," reveal the cosmos as theophany. To behold the cosmos with the eye of the intellect is to see it not as a pattern of externalized and brute facts, but as a theater wherein are reflected aspects of the Divine Qualities, as a myriad mirrors reflecting the face of the Beloved, as the theophany of that Reality which resides at the Center of the being of man himself. To see the cosmos as theophany is to see the reflection of one-Self in the cosmos and its forms.

In traditions based upon a sacred scripture the cosmos also reveals its meaning as a vast book whose pages are replete with the words of the Author and possess multiple levels of meaning like the revealed book of the religion in question. This perspective is to be found in Judaism and

[1] See Schuon, "Seeing God Everywhere," in his *Gnosis, Divine Wisdom* (London: John Murray, 1957), pp. 106-21.

Islam where the eternal Torah and the Quran as the *Umm al-kitāb* are seen as prototypes of both the revealed book and that other grand book of virgin nature which reflects God's primordial revelation. In Christianity also, where there is greater emphasis upon the Son as Logos than on the book, the vision of the universe as the book of God is not only present but has been repeated through the ages, especially in the utterance of those who have belonged to the sapiential perspective. In fact, this view, so majestically depicted by Dante, did not disappear until the inner meaning of revelation itself became inaccessible. Exegesis turned to the interpretation of the outward, literal meaning of the sacred text while cosmic symbols were becoming facts and, instead of revealing the cosmos as theophany, were limiting the reality of the world to the categories of mass and motion. The veiling of pontifical man and his transformation to the Promethean could not but result in the cosmic book becoming illegible and sacred Scripture reduced to only its outward meaning.

In Islam the correspondence between man, the cosmos, and the sacred book is central to the whole religion. The sacred book of Islam is the written or composed Quran (*al-Qur'ān al-tadwīnī*) as well as the cosmic Quran (*al-Qur'ān al-takwīnī*). Its verses are called *āyāt*, which means also signs or symbols, to which the Quran itself refers in the verse, "We shall show them Our signs upon the horizons (*āfāq*) and within themselves (*anfus*), until it be manifest unto them that it is the truth" (41:53). The *āyāt* are the Divine Words and Letters which comprise at once the elements of the Divine Book, the macrocosmic world, and the inner being of man. The *āyāt* manifest themselves in the Holy Book, the horizons (*āfāq*) or the heavens and earth, and the soul of man (*anfus*). To the extent that the *āyāt* of the sacred book reveal their inner meaning, while man's outer faculties and intelligence become wed once again to the inner faculties and the heart and man realizes his own being as a sign of God, the cosmos manifests itself as theophany and the phenomena of nature become transformed into the *āyāt* mentioned by the Quran, the *āyāt* which are none other than the *vestigia Dei* which an Albertus Magnus or John Ray sought to discover in their study of natural forms. Likewise, the theophanic aspect of virgin nature aids in man's discovery of his own inner being. Nature is herself a divine revelation with its own metaphysics and mode of prayer, but only a contemplative already endowed with sacred knowledge can read the gnostic message written in the most subtle manner upon the cliffs of high mountains, the leaves of the trees, the faces of animals, and the stars of the sky.

In certain other traditions of a primordial character where the revelation itself is directly related to natural forms, as in the tradition of the American Indians, especially those of the Plains, and in Shintoism, the animals and plants are not only symbols of various Divine Qualities but also direct manifestations of the Divine Principle in such a way that they play a direct role in the cultic aspect of the religion in question. Moreover, in such traditions there exists a knowledge of nature which is direct and intimate yet inward. The Indian not only sees the bear or the eagle as divine presences but has a knowledge of what one might call the eagle-ness of the eagle and the bear-ness of the bear as if he saw in these beings their Platonic archetypes. The revelation of God in such cases embraces both men and nature in such a way that would be inconceivable for the exteriorized reason of postmedieval man, who externalized his alienation from his own inner reality by increasing his sense of aggression and hatred against nature, an aggression made somewhat easier by the excessively rigid distinction made in Western Christianity between the supernatural and the natural. In any case, the animal masks of certain archaic traditions or the waterfalls of Taoist paintings depicting the descent of the One into the plane of multiplicity are neither animism in its pejorative sense nor a naive projection of the human psyche upon creatures of the external world. They are epiphanies of the Sacred based on the most profound knowledge of the very essence of the natural forms involved. They represent a knowledge of the cosmos which is not by any means negated or abrogated by what physics may discover about the dynamics of a waterfall or anatomy about the animal in question. One wonders who knows more about the coyote, the zoologist who is able to study its external habit and dissect its cadaver or the Indian medicine man who identifies himself with the "spirit" of the coyote?

Not only do the traditional sciences of the cosmos study the forms of nature with respect to their essential archetypes and do contemplatives within these traditions view the phenomena of virgin nature as theophanies, but also the astounding harmony of the natural world is seen as a direct result and consequence of that sacrifice of the primordial man described in different metaphysical or mythical languages in various traditions. The unbelievable harmony which pervades the world, linking the life cycles of fishes on the bottom of tropical oceans to land creatures roaming northern tundras in an incredible pattern, has been all but neglected by Western science until very recent times. But it forms an important element of that traditional science of nature which, whether in terms of the Pythagorean theory of harmony related to the World Soul or in other terms, remains always aware of that harmony between animals, plants, and minerals, between the creatures of various climes and also between the physical, subtle, and spiritual realms of beings which make the life of the cosmos possible. This harmony, whose grand contour has been only partly revealed by some recent ecological studies, is like the harmony of the parts of the human body as well as of the body, soul, and spirit of pontifical or traditional man and, in fact, is profoundly related to this concretely experienced harmony of man, because this latter type of harmony, like that of the cosmos, is derived from the perfect harmony of the being of the Universal Man, who is the prototype of both man and the cosmos. If the cosmos is a crystallization of the sounds of music and musical harmony a key for the understanding of the structure of the cosmos from planetary motion to quantum energy levels, it is because harmony dwelt in the very being of that archetypal reality through which all things were made. If God is a geometer who provides the measure by which all things are made, He is also the musician who has provided the harmony by which all things live and function and which is exhibited in a blinding and miraculous fashion in the cosmos.

The cosmos has of course its own laws and rhythms. Modern science speaks of laws of nature and even in modern physics, although this concept has been modified, the idea of statistical laws dominating over aggregates remains while the laws of macrophysics continue to be studied as the proper subject of science. Through a long history related to the rise of the idea of natural law as opposed to revealed law in the Christian tradition, whose own laws were in fact general spiritual and moral injunctions rather than a detailed codified law as in Judaism and Islam, a cleavage was created in the mind of Western man between laws of nature and spiritual principles. While the integral Christian tradition was alive in the Middle Ages, the cleavage was overcome by sapiential and even theological teachings such as those of Erigena and Saint Thomas which related natural laws themselves to God's Wisdom and Power. Nevertheless there was no Divine Law in the sense of the Islamic *Sharīʿah* within Christianity itself, which could be seen in its cosmic aspect to include the laws according to which other beings in the cosmos function. The cleavage was never totally overcome, so that with the advent of the revolt against the medieval synthesis during the Renaissance, the "laws of nature" and the "laws of God" as found in religion began to part ways to the extent that viewing the laws whose functioning is to be observed everywhere in the cosmos as Divine Law soon became outmoded and relegated to the pejorative category of "anthropomorphism." Moreover, since Christianity emphasizes the importance of the unparalleled event of the birth of Christ and his miraculous life, the evidence of religion seemed to many a European mind to rely upon the miracle which breaks the regularity of the laws observed in nature, whereas that regularity itself is no less evidence of the primacy of the Logos and the Wisdom of God reflected in His creation. The fact that the sun does rise every morning is, from the sapiential point of view, as much a cause for wonder as if it were to rise in the West tomorrow.

It is of interest to note how Islam views this same subject of law. The Quranic revelation brought not only a set of ethical practices and a spiritual path for its followers but also a Divine Law, the *Sharīʿah*, by which all Muslims must live as the means of surrendering their will to God's will. By extension the *Sharīʿah* is seen by Muslims as embracing all orders of creation and corresponding to what is understood in Western intellectual history as "laws of nature." Many an Islamic source has spoken of the Divine Law of this or that animal. Interestingly enough, the Greek word for cosmic law, *nomos*, which reached Muslims through translations of Greek texts, especially the *Laws* of Plato, became Arabized as *nāmūs*—the *Laws* of Plato itself being called *Kitāb al-nawāmīs.* Through such figures as al-Fārābī in his *Ārāʾ ahl al-madīnat al-fāḍilah* (*The Views of the Inhabitants of the Virtuous State*), it entered into the mainstream of Islamic thought and its meaning became practically synonymous with the *Sharīʿah.* To this day Muslim philosophers and theologians, as well as simple preachers in the pulpit, speak of the *nāwāmīs al-anbiyāʾ*, the Divine Laws brought by the prophets, and *nāmūs al-khilqah*, the Divine Law which governs creation. There is no difference of nature between them. God has promulgated a law for each species of being and order of creatures which for man becomes religious law or the *Sharīʿah* as understood in its ordinary sense. The only difference is that other creatures have not been given the gift of free will and therefore cannot rebel against the laws which God has meant for them, against their "nature," while man, being the theomorphic creature that he is, participates also in the Divine Freedom and can revolt against God's laws and himself. From a metaphysical point of view the rebellion of man against Heaven is itself proof of man's being made "in the image of God," to use the traditional formulation.

In this crucial question as in so many others, the Islamic perspective joins that of other Oriental traditions, where no sharp distinction is made between the laws governing man and those governing the cosmos. The Tao is the origin of all things, the law governing each order of existence and every individual being within that order. Each being has its own Tao. Likewise *dharma* is not limited to man; all creatures have their own *dharma.* From the point of view of *scientia sacra* all laws are reflections of the Divine Principle. For man to discover any "law of nature" is to gain some knowledge of the ontological reality of the domain with which he is concerned. Moreover, the discovery of such laws is always through man's own intelligence and the use of logic, which reflects an aspect of his own ontological reality. Therefore, in an ultimate sense, the study of the "laws of nature" is inseparable from the study of the reality of that Universal Man or macrocosmic reality whose reflection comprises the cosmos. It is a study of man himself. To study the laws of the cosmos, like studying its harmony or the beauty of its forms, is a way of self-discovery, provided the subject carrying out such a study does not live in a truncated order of reality in which the study of the external world serves only to fragment further man's soul and alienate him from himself, creating, paradoxically enough, a world in which man himself no longer has a place.

What pertains to cosmic laws also holds true for causes, which are reduced to the purely material in modern science, as if the material order of reality could be totally divorced from other cosmic and metacosmic orders. The traditional sciences take into consideration not only the material or immediate causes of things but also the nonmaterial and ultimate ones. Even the four Aristotelian causes, the formal, material, efficient, and final, are systematized approximations of all the causes involved in bringing about any effect, for these causes include not only what is outwardly understood by the formal, efficient, and final causes but all that such causes mean metaphysically. The formal cause includes the origin of a particular form in the archetypal world, the efficient cause the grades of being which finally result in the existentiation of a particular existent, and the final cause a hierarchy of beings belonging to higher orders of reality that terminates with the Ultimate Cause, which is the Real as such. It is in fact in this perspective that many later metaphysical rather than only rationalistic commentators of Aristotle viewed the significance of the Aristotelian four causes.

In any case, the causes which are responsible for various effects in the natural world are not limited to the natural world but embrace all orders of being. Moreover, these causes operate within man himself and between man and his cosmic environment. Each being in fact is related by a set of causes to the milieu in which it exists, the two being inseparable. Man is bound to his world not only by the set of physical causes which bind him to that world but also by metaphysical ones. The net of causality is much vaster than that cast by those sciences which would limit the cosmos to only its material aspect and man to a complex combination of the same material factors caught in the mesh of that external environment which penetrates within him and determines his behavior and manner of being. Modern behaviorism is in many ways a parody of the Hindu doctrine of *karma*, which expresses the central importance of causality in the domain of manifestation without either limiting it to only the psycho-physical realm or denying the possibility of deliverance, or *mokṣa*, from all chains of cause and effect, even those belonging to higher levels of existence. To behold the cosmos as theophany is not to deny either the laws or the chain of cause and effect which pervade the cosmos, but to view the cosmos and the forms it displays with such diversity and regularity as reflections of Divine Qualities and ontological categories rather than a veil which would hide the splendor of the face of the Beloved.

To achieve such a goal and see the cosmos as theophany and not veil, it is necessary to return again and again to the truth that reality is hierarchic, that the cosmos is not exhausted by its physical aspect alone. All traditional cosmologies are based in one way or another on this axial truth. Their goal is to present in an intelligible fashion the hierarchy of existence as reflected in the cosmos. The "great chain of being" of the Western tradition, which survived in the West until it became horizontalized and converted from a ladder to Heaven to an evolutionary stream moving toward God knows where, was a synthesis of this idea, which has its equivalents in Islam, India, and elsewhere, even if not as thoroughly elaborated in all traditions. The cosmologies which appeal to the immediate experience of the cosmos by terrestrial man have no other aim but to convey this metaphysical and central truth concerning the multiple states of existence in a vivid and concrete fashion. Cosmologies based on Ptolemaic astronomy or other astronomical schemes based on the way the cosmos presents itself to man are not in any way invalidated by the rejection of this geocentric scheme for the heliocentric one, because they make use of the immediate experience of the natural world as symbol rather than fact, a symbol whose meaning, like that of any other symbol, cannot be grasped through logical or mathematical analysis.

If one understands what symbols mean, one cannot claim that medieval cosmologies are false as a result of the fact that, if we were standing on the sun, we would observe the earth moving around it. The fact remains that we are not standing on the sun and if the cosmos, from the vantage point of the earth where we were born, does possess a symbolic significance, surely it would be based on how it *appears* to us as we stand on earth. To think otherwise would be to destroy the symbolic significance of the cosmos. It would be like wanting to understand the meaning of a *maṇḍala* by looking at it under a microscope. In doing so one would discover a great deal about the texture of the material upon which the *maṇḍala* has been drawn but nothing about the symbolic significance of the *maṇḍala*, which was drawn with the assumption that it would be looked upon with the normal human eye. Of course, in the case of the cosmos the other ways of envisaging and studying it, as long as they conform to some aspect of cosmic reality, also possess their own profound symbolism—such as, for example, the heliocentric system, which was in fact known long before Copernicus, or the vast dark intergalactic spaces—but the destruction of the immediate symbolism of the cosmos as it presents itself to man living on earth cannot but be catastrophic.

To look upon the vast vault of the heavens as if one lived on the sun creates a disequilibrium which cannot but result in the destruction of that very earth that modern man abstracted himself from in order to look upon the solar system from the vantage point of the sun in the absolute space of classical physics. This disequilibrium would not necessarily have resulted had the type of man who rejected the earth-centered view of the cosmos been the solar figure, the image of the supernal Apollo, the Pythagorean sage, who in fact knew of the heliocentric astronomy without this knowledge causing a disruption in his world view. But paradoxically enough, this being who abstracted himself from the earth to look upon the cosmos from the sun, through that most direct symbol of the Divine Intellect, was the Promethean man who had rebelled against Heaven. The consequences could, therefore, not be anything but tragic.

The destruction of the outward symbol of traditional cosmologies destroyed for Western man the reality of the hierarchic structure of the universe which these cosmologies symbolized and which remains independent of any particular type of symbolism used to depict it. This structure could be and in fact has been expressed by other means, ranging from traditional music, which reflects the structure of the cosmos, to mathematical patterns of various kinds, to metaphysical expositions not directly bound to a particular astronomical symbolism. The exposition of the hierarchic levels of reality as the "five Divine Presences" (*al-ḥaḍarāt al-ilāhiyyat al-khams*) by the Sufis, such as Ibn ʿArabī, is a perfect example of this latter kind. Ibn ʿArabī speaks of each principal order of reality as a *haḍrah* or "Divine Presence" because, metaphysically speaking, being or reality is none other than presence (*ḥaḍrah*) or consciousness (*shuhūd*). These presences include the Divine Ipseity Itself (*hāhūt*), the Divine Names and Qualities (*lāhūt*), the archangelic world (*jabarūt*), the subtle and psychic world (*malakūt*), and the physical world (*mulk*). Each higher world contains the principles of that which lies below it and lacks nothing of the lower level of reality.

That is why in God one is separate from nothing. Although these presences possess further inner divisions within themselves, they represent in a simple fashion the major levels of cosmic existence and metacosmic reality without there being the need to have recourse to a particular astronomical symbolism. This does not mean, however, that certain other later cosmologists did not point to correlations between these presences and various levels of the hierarchic cosmological schemes that still possessed meaning for those who beheld them.

In Islam we encounter numerous cosmological schemes associated with the Peripatetics, Illuminationists, Isma'ilis, alchemical authors like Jābir ibn Ḥayyān, Pythagoreans, various schools of Sufism, and of course the cosmologies based upon the language and text of the Quran and related to its inner meaning, which served as source of inspiration and principle for the other cosmologies drawn from diverse sources. But throughout all of these cosmological schemes, there remains the constant theme of the hierarchic universe manifested by the Divine Principle and related intimately to the inner being of man. The same theme is found at the center of those sometimes bewildering cosmologies found in India, in Kabbalistic and Hermetic texts, in the oral traditions of the American Indians, in what survives of ancient Sumerian and Babylonian religions, among the Egyptians, and practically everywhere else. The diversity of symbolism is great but the presence of the vision of the cosmos as a hierarchic reality bound to the Origin and related to man not only outwardly but also inwardly persists as elements of what we referred to earlier as *cosmologia perennis*. This vision is that of pontifical man and therefore has had to be present wherever and whenever pontifical man, who is none other than traditional man, has lived and functioned.

Likewise, these traditional cosmologies as perceived within the sapiential perspective have been concerned with providing a map of the cosmos as well as depicting it as an icon to be contemplated and as symbol of metaphysical truth. The cosmos is not only the theater wherein are reflected the Divine Names and Qualities. It is also a crypt through which man must journey to reach the Reality beyond cosmic manifestation. In fact man cannot contemplate the cosmos as theophany until he has journeyed through and beyond it. That is why the traditional cosmologies are also concerned with providing man with a map which would orient him within the cosmos and finally enable him to escape beyond the cosmos through that miraculous act of deliverance with which so many myths have been concerned. From this point of view the cosmos appears as a labyrinth through which man must journey in a perilous adventure where literally all that he is and all that he has is at stake, a journey for which all traditions require both the map of traditional knowledge and the spiritual guide who has himself journeyed before through this labyrinth. It is only by actually experiencing the perilous journey through the cosmic labyrinth that man is able to gain a vision of that cathedral of celestial beauty which is the Divine Presence in its metacosmic splendor.

Having journeyed through and beyond the cosmos, man, who is then "twice born" and a "dead man walking" in the sense of being spiritually resurrected here and now, is able finally to contemplate the cosmos and its forms as theophany. He is able to see the forms of nature *in divinis* and to experience the Ultimate Reality not as transcendent and beyond but as here and now. It is here that the cosmos unveils its inner beauty ceasing to be only externalized fact or phenomenon but becoming immediate symbol, the reflection of the noumenon, the reflection which is not separated but essentially none other than the reality reflected. The cosmos becomes, to use the language of Sufism, so many mirrors in which the various aspects of the Divine Names and Qualities and ultimately the One are reflected. The Arabic word *tajallī* means nothing but this reflection of the Divine in the mirror of the cosmos which, metaphysically speaking, is the mirror of nothingness. Objects appear not only as abstract symbols but as concrete presence. For the sage a particular tree is not only a symbol of the grade of being that he has come to know through his intelligence and the science of symbolism, which his intelligence has enabled him to grasp, it is also a tree of paradise conveying a presence and grace of a paradisal nature.

This immediate experience, however, is not only not separate from the science of symbols, sacred geometry, and the significance of certain sacred forms, but it also provides that immediate intuition which only increases the grasp of such sciences and makes possible their application to concrete situations. Zen gardens are based on the science of sacred geometry and the metaphysical significance of certain forms, but they cannot be created by just anyone who might have a manual on the symbolism of space or rock formations. The great gardens are expressions of realized knowledge leading to the awareness of natural forms as "presence of the Void," which in turn has made possible the application of this knowledge to specific situations resulting in some of the greatest creations of sacred art. The same rapport can be found *mutatis mutandis* elsewhere in traditions which do not emphasize as much as Zen knowledge of natural forms as immediate experience but where complete teachings in the cosmological sciences are available. Everywhere the knowledge of cosmic symbols goes hand in hand with that direct experience of a spiritual presence which results from spiritual realization, although there are always individual cases where a person may be given the gift of experiencing some aspect of the cosmos or a particular natural form as theophany without a knowledge of the science of symbolism; or, as is more common in the modern world, a person may have the aptitude to understand the meaning of symbols, which is itself a precious gift from Heaven, but lack spiritual realization and therefore lack the possibility of ever experiencing the cosmos as theophany. In the sapiential perspective, in any case, the two types of appreciation of cosmic realities usually go hand in hand, and certainly, in the case of the masters of gnosis, complement each other.

Of special significance among cosmological symbols which are related to the contemplation of the cosmos as theophany and the experience of the presence of the sacred in the natural order are those connected with space. Space and time along with form, matter or substance, and number determine the condition of human existence and in fact of all existence in this world. Tradition therefore deals with all of them and transforms all of them in order to create that sacred world in which traditional man breathes. The symbolism of number is revealed through its qualitative aspect as viewed in the Pythagorean tradition, and certain theosophers in the West have even spoken of an "arithmosophy" to be contrasted with arithmetic. Form and matter are sacralized through their symbolic rapport and their relation to the archetypal realities reflected by forms on the one hand and the descent or congelation of existence, which on the physical plane appears as matter or substance, on the other.[2] The nature of time is understood in its relation to eternity and the rhythms and cycles which reflect higher orders of reality. Finally space, which is central as the "container" of all that comprises terrestrial existence, is viewed not as the abstract, purely quantitative extension of classical physics but as a qualitative reality which is studied through sacred geometry.

Qualitative space is modified by the presence of the sacred itself. Its directions are not the same; its properties are not uniform. While in its empty vastness it symbolizes the Divine All-Possibility and also the Divine Immutability, it is the progenitor of all the geometric forms which are so many projections of the geometric point and so many reflections of the One, each regular geometric form symbolizing a Divine Quality. If Plato specified that only geometers could enter into the temple of Divine Knowl-

[2] We are not using matter here in its Aristotelian but in its everyday sense as the "stuff" or "substance" of which things are made.

edge, it was because, as Proclus was to assert in his commentary upon the *Elements* of Euclid, geometry is an ancillary to metaphysics. The orientation of cultic acts, the construction of traditional architecture, and many of the traditional sciences cannot be understood without grasping the significance of the traditional conception of qualified space. What is the experience of space for the Muslim who turns to a particular point on earth, wherever he might be, and then is blessed one day to enter into the *Kaʿbah* itself beyond the polarization created upon the whole earth by this primordial temple built to celebrate the presence of the One? Why are the remarkable Neolithic structures of Great Britain round and why do the Indians believe that the circle brings strength? Most remarkable of all is the immediate experience of a wholly other kind of space within a sacred precinct. How did the architects of the medieval cathedrals create a sacred space which is the source of profound experience even for those Christians who no longer follow their religion fully? In all these and numerous other instances what is involved is the application of a traditional science of space which makes possible the actualization of a sacred presence and also the contemplation of an element of the cosmic reality as theophany. It is through this science of qualified space that traditional science and art meet and that cosmological science and experience of the sacred become wed in those places of worship, rites, sites of pilgrimage, and many other elements which are related to the very heart of tradition.

This science is closely associated with what has been called "sacred geography" or even "geosophy," that symbolic science of location and space concerned with the qualitative aspects of points on earth and the association of different terrestrial sites with traditional functions, ranging from the location of sanctuaries, burial sites, and places of worship to places for the erection of gardens, planting of trees, and the like in that special form of sacred art associated with the Japanese garden and the traditional art of the Persian garden with all its variations, ranging from Spanish gardens to the Mogul ones of India. The science of sacred geography ranges from, on the one hand, popular and often folkloric practices of geomancy in China to the most profound sensitivity to the grace of the Divine Presence which manifests itself in certain natural forms and locations on the other.

This science is thus closely allied to that particular kind of sapience which is wed to the metaphysics of nature and that spiritual type among human beings who is sensitive to the *barakah* or grace that flows in the arteries of the universe. Such a person is drawn by this *barakah* into the empyrean of spiritual ecstasy like an eagle that flies without moving its wings upon an air current which carries it upward toward the illimitable expanses of the heavenly vault. For such a person nature is the supreme work of sacred art; in traditions based upon such a perspective, like Islam or the American Indian tradition, virgin nature as created by God *is* the sanctuary par excellence. The mosque of the Muslim is the earth itself as long as it has not been defiled by man, and the building called the mosque only extends the ambience of this primordial mosque which is virgin nature into the artificial urban environment created by man. Likewise, for the American Indian, that wilderness of enchanting beauty which was the American continent before the advent of the white man was the cathedral in which he worshiped and wherein he observed the greatest works of art of the Supreme Artisan, of *Wakan-Tanka.* This perspective, moreover, is not limited to only certain traditions but is to be found in one way or another within all integral traditions. This sensitivity to the *barakah* of nature and the contemplation of the cosmos as theophany cannot but be present wherever pontifical man lives and breathes, for nature is a reflection of that paradisal state that man still carries within the depth of his own being.

Such a vision has, needless to say, become blurred and is denied in the world of Promethean man whose eminently successful science of nature has blinded human beings to possibilities of other sciences and other means of beholding and understanding nature. Moreover, this negation and denial has occurred despite the fact that the cosmos has not completely followed man in his rapid fall. It might be said that, although both nature and man have fallen from that state of perfection characterized as the paradisal state, what still remains of virgin nature is closer to that prototype than the type of Promethean man who increases his domination upon the earth every day. That is why what does remain of virgin nature is so precious not only ecologically but also spiritually. It is the only reminder left on earth of the normal condition of existence and a permanent testament to the absurdity of all those modern pretensions which reveal their true nature only when seen in the light of the truth. Excluding revealed truth, nothing in the orbit of human experience unveils the real nature of the modern world and the premises upon which it is based more than the cosmos, ranging from the starry heavens to the plants at the bottom of the seas. That is why Promethean man has such an aggressive hatred for virgin nature; why also the love of nature is the first sign among many contemporaries of their loss of infatuation with that model of man who began his plunder of the earth some five centuries ago.

19. Traditional Art

Tradition speaks to man not only through human words but also through other forms of art. Its message is written not only upon pages of books and within the grand phenomena of nature but also upon the face of those works of traditional and especially sacred art which, like the words of sacred scripture and the forms of nature, are ultimately a revelation from that Reality which is the source of both tradition and the cosmos. Traditional art is inseparable from sacred knowledge because it is based upon a science of the cosmic that is of a sacred and inward character and in turn is the vehicle for the transmission of a knowledge that is of a sacred nature. Traditional art is at once based upon and is a channel for both knowledge and grace or that *scientia sacra* which is both knowledge and of a sacred character. Sacred art, which lies at the heart of traditional art, has a sacramental function and is, like religion itself, at once truth and presence, and this quality is transmitted even to those aspects of traditional art which are not strictly speaking sacred art, that is, not directly concerned with the liturgical, ritual, cultic, and esoteric elements of the tradition in question but which nevertheless are created according to traditional norms and principles.

To understand how traditional art is related to knowledge of the sacred and sacred knowledge, it is necessary first of all to clarify what is meant by traditional art. Since we have already identified religion with that which binds man to God and which lies at the heart of tradition, it might be thought that traditional art is simply religious art. This is not at all the case, however, especially since in the West from the Renaissance onward, traditional art has ceased to exist while religious art continues. Religious art is considered religious because of the subject or function with which it is concerned and not because of its style, manner of execution, symbolism, and non-individual origin. Traditional art, however, is traditional not because of it subject matter but because of its conformity to cosmic laws of forms, to the laws of symbolism, to the formal genius of the particular spiritual universe in which it has been created, its hieratic style, its conformity to the nature of the material used, and, finally, its conformity to the truth within the particular domain of reality with which it is concerned. A naturalistic painting of Christ is religious art but not at all traditional art, whereas a medieval sword, book cover, or even stable is traditional art but not directly religious art although, because of the nature of tradition, indirectly even pots and pans produced in a traditional civilization are related to the religion that lies at the heart of that tradition.

Traditional art is concerned with the truths contained in the tradition of which it is the artistic and formal expression. Its origin therefore is not purely human. Moreover, this art must conform to the symbolism inherent in the object with which it is concerned as well as the symbolism directly related to the revelation whose inner dimension this art manifests. Such an art is aware of the essential nature of things rather than their accidental aspects. It is in conformity with the harmony which pervades the cosmos and the hierarchy of existence, which lies above the material plane with which art deals and yet penetrates into this plane. Such an art is based on the real and not the illusory, so that it remains conformable to the nature of the object with which it is concerned rather than imposing a subjective and illusory veil upon it.

Traditional art, moreover, is functional in the most profound sense of this term, namely, that it is made for a particular use, whether it be the worshiping of God in a liturgical act or the eating of a meal. It is, therefore, utilitarian but not with the limited meaning of utility identified with purely earthly man in mind. Its utility concerns pontifical man for whom beauty is as essential a dimension of life and need as the house that shelters man during the winter cold. There is no place here for such an idea as "art for art's sake," and traditional civilizations have never had museums nor ever produced a work of art just for itself. Traditional art might be said to be based on the idea of art for man's sake, which, in the traditional context where man is God's vicegerent on earth, the axial being on this plane of reality, means ultimately art for God's sake, for to make something for man as a theomorphic being is to make it for God. In traditional art there is a blending of beauty and utility which makes of every object of traditional art, provided it belongs to a thriving traditional civilization not in the stage of decay, something at once useful and beautiful.

It is through its art that tradition forges and forms an ambience in which its truths are reflected everywhere, in which men breathe and live in a universe of meaning in conformity with the reality of the tradition in question. That is why, in nearly every case of which we have a historical record, the tradition has created and formalized its sacred art before elaborating its theologies and philosophies. Saint Augustine appears long after the sarcophagus art of the catacombs which marks the beginning of Christian art, as Buddhist architecture and sculpture came long before Nagārjuna. Even in Islam, which developed its theological and philosophical schools rapidly, even the early Mu'tazilites, not to speak of the Ash'arites or al-Kindī and the earliest Islamic philosophers, follow upon the wake of the construction of the first Islamic mosques, which were already distinctly Islamic in character. In order to breathe and function in a world, religion must remold that world not only mentally but also formally; and since most human beings are much more receptive to material forms than to ideas, and material forms leave the deepest effect upon the human soul even beyond the mental plane, it is the traditional art which is first created by the tradition in question. This is especially true of sacred art, which exists already at the beginning of the tradition, for it is related to those liturgical and cultic practices which emanate directly from the revelation. Therefore, the first icon is painted by Saint Luke through the inspiration of the angel, the traditional chanting of the Vedas is "revealed" with the Vedas, the Quranic psalmody originates with the Prophet himself, etc. The role of traditional art in the forging of a particular mentality and the creation of an atmosphere in which contemplation of the most profound metaphysical truths is made possible are fundamental to the understanding of both the character of traditional art and the sapiential dimension of tradition itself.

From this point of view art is seen as a veil that hides but also reveals God. There are always within every tradition those who have belittled the significance of forms of art in that they have gone beyond them, but this has always been in a world in which these forms have existed, not where they have been cast aside and destroyed. Those who have eschewed forms of art have been certain types of contemplatives who have realized the supraformal realities, those who, to use the language of Sufism, having broken the shell and eaten the nut inside, cast the shell aside. But obviously one cannot throw away a shell that one does not even possess. To go beyond forms is one thing and to fall below them another. To pierce beyond the phenomenal surface to the noumenal reality, hence to see God through forms and not forms as veils of the Divine, is one thing, and to reject forms of traditional art in the name of an imagined abstract reality above formalism is quite another. Sacred knowledge, in contrast to desacralized mental activity, is concerned with the supraformal Essence but is perfectly aware of the vital significance of forms in the attainment of the knowledge of that Essence. This knowledge, even when speaking of the Supreme Reality above all forms, does so in a chant which is in conformity with the laws of cosmic harmony and in a language which, whether prose or poetry, is itself an art form. That is why the possessor of such a knowledge in its realized aspect is the first person to confirm the significance of forms of traditional art and the relation of this art to the truth and the sacred; for art reflects the truth to the extent that it is sacred, and it emanates the presence of the sacred to the extent that it is true.

It is of course pontifical or traditional man who is the maker of traditional art; therefore, his theomorphic nature is directly related to this art and its significance. Being a theomorphic creature, man is himself a work of art. The human soul when purified and dressed in the garment of spiritual virtues is itself the highest kind of beauty in this world, reflecting directly the Divine Beauty. Even the human body in both its male and female forms is a perfect work of art, reflecting something of the essentiality of the human state. Moreover, there is no more striking reflection of Divine Beauty on earth than a human face in which physical and spiritual beauty are combined. Now man is a work of art because God is the Supreme Artist. That is why He is called *al-muṣawwir* in Islam, that is, He who creates forms, why Śiva brought the arts down from Heaven, why in the medieval craft initiations, as in Freemasonry, God is called the Grand Architect of the Universe. But God is not only the Grand Architect or Geometer; He is also the Poet, the Painter, the Musician. This is the reason for man's ability to build, write poetry, paint, or compose music, although not all forms of art have been necessarily cultivated in all traditions—the types of art developed depending upon the spiritual and also ethnic genius of a traditional world and humanity.

Being "created in the image of God" and therefore a supreme work of art, man is also an artist who, in imitating the creative powers of his Maker, realizes his own theomorphic nature. The spiritual man, aware of his vocation, is not only the musician who plucks the lyre to create music. He is himself the lyre upon which the Divine Artist plays, creating the music which reverberates throughout the cosmos, for as Rūmī says, "We are like the lyre which Thou plucketh."[1] If Promethean man creates art not in imitation but in competition with God, hence the naturalism in Promethean art which tries to imitate the outward form of nature, pontifical man creates art in full consciousness of his imitating God's creativity not through competition but with submission to the Divine Model which tradition provides for him. He therefore imitates nature not in its external forms but in its manner of operation, as asserted so categorically by Saint Thomas.[2] If in knowing God man fulfills his essential nature as *homo sapiens*, in creating

[1] *Mathnawī*, Book 1, verse 598.

[2] St. Thomas insists that the artist must not imitate nature but must be accomplished in "imitating nature in her manner of operation" (*Summa Theologica*, Q. 117, a. I).

art he also fulfills another aspect of that nature as *homo faber.* In creating art in conformity with cosmic laws and in imitation of realities of the archetypal world, man realizes himself, his theomorphic nature as a work of art made by the hands of God; and likewise in creating an art based on his revolt against Heaven, he separates himself even further from his own Divine Origin. The role of art in the fall of Promethean man in the modern world has been central in that this art has been both an index of the new stages of the inner fall of man from his sacred norm and a major element in the actualization of this fall, for man comes to identify himself with what he makes.

It is not at all accidental that the breakup of the unity of the Christian tradition in the West coincided with the rise of the Reformation. Nor is it accidental that the philosophical and scientific revolts against the medieval Christian world view were contemporary with the nearly complete destruction of traditional Christian art and its replacement by a Promethean and humanistic art which soon decayed into that unintelligible nightmare of baroque and rococo religious art that drove many an intelligent believer out of the church. The same phenomenon can be observed in ancient Greece and the modern Orient. When the sapiential dimension of the Greek tradition began to decay, Greek art became humanistic and this-worldly—the art which is already criticized by Plato, who held the sacerdotal, traditional art of ancient Egypt in such high esteem. Likewise, in the modern East, intellectual decline has everywhere been accompanied by artistic decline. Conversely, wherever one does observe major artistic creations of a traditional character, there must be a living intellectual and sapiential tradition present even if nothing is known of it externally. Even if at least until very recently the West knew nothing of the intellectual life of Safavid Persia, one could be sure that the creation of even one dome like that of the Shaykh Luṭfallāh mosque or the Shah mosque, which are among the greatest masterpieces of traditional art and architecture, would be itself proof that such an intellectual life existed at that time. A living orthodox tradition with its sapiential dimension intact is essential and necessary for the production of major works of traditional art, especially sacred art, because of that inner nexus which exists between traditional art and sacred knowledge.

Traditional art is brought into being through such a knowledge and is able to convey and transmit this knowledge. It is the vehicle of an intellectual intuition and a sapiential message which transcends both the individual artist and the collective psyche of the world to which he belongs. On the contrary, humanistic art is able to convey only individualistic inspirations or at best something of the collective psyche to which the individual artist belongs but never an intellectual message, the sapience which is our concern. It can never become the fountain of either knowledge or grace because of its divorce from those cosmic laws and the spiritual presence which characterize traditional art.

Knowledge is transmitted by traditional art through its symbolism, its correspondence with cosmic laws, its techniques, and even the means whereby it is taught through the traditional craft guilds, which in various traditional civilizations have combined technical training in the crafts with spiritual instruction. The presence of the medieval European guilds, the Islamic guilds (*aṣnāf* and *futuwwāt*), some of which survive to this day, the training of potters by Zen masters, or of metallurgists in initiatic circles in certain primitive societies, all indicate the close nexus that has existed between the teaching of the techniques of the traditional arts or crafts, which are the same as the arts in a traditional world, and the transmission of knowledge of a cosmological and sometimes metaphysical order.

But in addition to these processes for the transmission of knowledge related to the actual act of creating a work or of explaining the symbolism involved, there is an innate rapport between artistic creation in the traditional sense and sapience. This rapport is based on the nature of man himself as the reflection of the Divine Norm, and also on the inversion which exists between the principial and the manifested order. Man and the world in which he lives both reflect the archetypal world directly and inversely according to the well-known principle of inverse analogy. In the principial order God creates by externalizing. His "artistic" activity is the fashioning of His own "image" or "form." On the human plane this relation is reversed in that man's "artistic" activity in the traditional sense involves not the fashioning of an image in the cosmogonic sense but a return to his own essence in conformity with the nature of the state of being in which he lives. Therefore, the "art" of God implies an externalization and the art of man an internalization. God fashions what God makes and man is fashioned by what man makes;[3] and since this process implies a return

[3] "There is here a metaphysical inversion of relation that we have already pointed out: for God, His creature reflects an exteriorized aspect of Himself; for the artist, on the contrary, the work is a reflection of an inner reality of which he himself is only an outward aspect; God creates His own image, while man, so to speak, fashions his own essence, at least symbolically. On the principial plane, the inner manifests itself in the outer, but on the manifested plane, the outer fashions the

to man's own essence, it is inalienably related to spiritual realization and the attainment of knowledge. In a sense, Promethean art is based on the neglect of this principle of inverse analogy. It seeks to create the image of Promethean man outwardly, as if man were God. Hence, the very "creative process" becomes not a means of interiorization and recollection but a further separation from the Source, leading step by step to the mutilation of the image of man as *imago Dei*, to the world of subrealism—rather than surrealism—and to purely individualistic subjectivism. This subjectivism is as far removed from the theomorphic image of man as possible; the art it creates cannot in any way act as a vehicle for the transmission of knowledge or grace, although certain cosmic qualities occasionally manifest themselves even in the nontraditional forms of art, since these qualities are like the rays of the sun which finally shine through some crack or opening no matter how much one tries to shut one's living space from the illumination of the light of that Sun which is both light and heat, knowledge, love, and grace.

To understand the meaning of traditional art in its relation to knowledge, it is essential to grasp fully the significance of the meaning of form as used in the traditional context (as *forma*, *morphē*, *nāma*, *ṣūrah*, etc.). In modern thought dominated by a quantitative science, the significance of form as that which contains the reality of an object has been nearly lost. It is therefore necessary to recall the traditional meaning of form and remember the attempts made by not only traditional authors but also certain contemporary philosophers and scholars to bring out the ontological significance of form. According to the profound doctrine of Aristotelian hylomorphism, which serves so well for the exposition of the metaphysics of art because it originated most likely as an intellectual intuition related to traditional art, an object is composed of form and matter in such a way that the form corresponds to that which is actual and matter to what is potential in the object in question. Form is that by which an object is what it is. Form is not accidental to the object but determines its very reality. It is in fact the essence of the object, which the more metaphysical Neoplatonic commentators of Aristotle interpreted as the image or reflection of the essence rather than the essence itself, the essence belonging to the archetypal

inner, and a sufficient reason for all traditional art, no matter of what kind, is the fact that in a certain sense the work is greater than the artist himself, and brings back the latter, through the mystery of artistic creation, to the proximity of his own Divine Essence" (Frithjof Schuon, *The Transcendent Unity of Religions* [London: Faber & Faber, 1953], pp. 72-73).

world. In any case, form is not accidental but essential to an object whether it be natural or man-made. It has an ontological reality and participates in the total economy of the cosmos according to strict laws. There is a science of forms, a science of a qualitative and not quantitative nature, which is nevertheless an exact science, or objective knowledge, exactitude not being the prerogative of the quantitative sciences alone.

From the point of view of hylomorphism, form *is* the reality of an object on the material level of existence. But it is also, as the reflection of an archetypal reality, the gate which opens inwardly and "upwardly" unto the formless Essence. From another point of view, one can say that each object possesses a form and a content which this form "contains" and conveys. As far as sacred art is concerned, this content is always the sacred or a sacred presence placed in particular forms by revelation, which sanctifies certain symbols, forms, and images to enable them to become "containers" of this sacred presence and transforms them into vehicles for the journey across the stream of becoming. Moreover, thanks to those sacred forms which man is able to transcend from within, man is able to penetrate into the inner dimension of his own being and, by virtue of that process, to gain a vision of the inner dimension of all forms. The three grand revelations of the Real, or theophanies, namely, the cosmos or macrocosm, man or the microcosm, and religion, are all comprised of forms which lead to the formless, but only the third enables man to penetrate to the world beyond forms, to gain a vision of forms of both the outer world and his own soul, not as veil but as theophany. Only the sacred forms invested with the transforming power of the sacred through revelation and the Logos which is its instrument can enable man to see God everywhere.

Since man lives in the world of forms, this direct manifestation of the Logos which is revelation or religion in its origin cannot but make use of forms within which man is located. It cannot but sanctify certain forms in order to allow man to journey beyond them. To reach the formless man has need of forms. The miracle of the sacred form lies in fact in its power to aid man to transcend form itself. Traditional art is present not only to remind man of the truths of religion which it reflects in man's fundamental activity of making, as religious ethics or religious law does for man's doing, but also to serve as a support for the contemplation of the Beyond which alone gives ultimate significance to both man's making and man's doing. To denigrate forms as understood in traditional metaphysics is to misunderstand, by token of the same error, the significance of the formless Essence.

At the root of this error that mistakes form for limitation and considers "thought" or "idea" in its mental sense as being more important than form is the abuse of the terms abstract and concrete in modern thought. Modern man, having lost the vision of the Platonic "ideas," confuses the concrete reality of what *scientia sacra* considers as idea with mental concept and then relegates the concrete to the material level. As a result, the physical and the material are automatically associated with the concrete, while ideas, thoughts, and all that is universal, including even the Divinity, are associated with the abstract. Metaphysically, the rapport is just the reverse. God is the concrete Reality par excellence compared to Whom everything else is an abstraction; and on a lower level the archetypal world is concrete and the world below it abstract. The same relation continues until one reaches the world of physical existence in which form is, relatively speaking, concrete and matter the most abstract entity of all.

The identification of material objects with the concrete and mental concepts with the abstract has had the effect of not only destroying the significance of form vis-à-vis matter on the physical plane itself but also obliterating the significance of the bodily and the corporeal as a source of knowledge. This tendency seems to be the reverse of the process of exteriorization and materialization of knowledge, but it is in reality the other side of the same coin. The same civilization that has produced the most materialistic type of thought has also shown the least amount of interest in the "wisdom of the body," in physical forms as a source of knowledge, and in the non-cerebral aspects of the human microcosm as a whole. As mentioned already, those within the modern world who have sought to regain knowledge of a sacred order have been also those who have protested most vehemently against this over-cerebral interpretation of human experience and who have sought to rediscover the "wisdom of the body," even if this has led in many cases to all kinds of excesses. One does not have to possess extraordinary perspicacity to realize that there is much more intelligence and in fact "food for thought" in the drumbeats of a traditional tribe in Africa than in many a book of modern philosophy. Nor is there any reason why a Chinese landscape painting should not bear a more direct and succinct metaphysical message than not only a philosophical treatise which is anti-metaphysical but even one which favors metaphysics, but in which, as a result of a weakness of logic or presentation, the truth of metaphysical ideas is barely discernible.

The consequence of this inversion of the rapport between the abstract and the concrete has in any case been a major impediment in the appreciation of the significance of forms in both the traditional arts and sciences and in the understanding of the possibility of forms of art as vehicles for knowledge of the highest order. This mentality has also prevented many people from appreciating the traditional doctrines of art and the nonhuman and celestial origin of the forms with which traditional art is concerned.

According to the principles of traditional art, the source of the forms which are dealt with by the artist is ultimately divine. As Plato, who along with Plotinus has provided some of the most profound teachings on traditional art in the West, asserts, art is the imitation of paradigms which, whether visible or invisible, reflect ultimately the world of ideas. At the heart of tradition lies the doctrine that art is the *mimēsis* of *paradeigma*, the invisible model or exemplar. But to produce a work of art which possesses beauty and perfection the artist must gaze at the invisible for, as Plato says, "The work of the creator, whenever he looks to the unchangeable and fashions the form and nature of his work after an unchangeable pattern, must necessarily be made fair and perfect, but when he looks to the created order only, and uses a created pattern, it is not fair or perfect."[4]

Likewise in India, the origin of the form later externalized by the artist in stone or bronze, on wood or paper, has always been considered to be of a supra-individual origin belonging to the level of reality which Platonism identified with the world of ideas. The appropriate art form is considered to be accessible only through contemplation and inner purification. It is only through them that the artist is able to gain that angelic vision which is the source of all traditional art, for at the beginning of the tradition the first works of sacred art, including both the plastic and the sonoral, were made by the angels or *deva*s themselves. In the well-known *Śukranītisāra* of Śukrāćarya, for example, it is stated, "One should make use of the visual-formulae proper to the angels whose images are to be made. It is for the successful accomplishment of this practice (*yoga*) of visual-formulation that the lineaments of images are prescribed. The human-imager should be expert in this visual-contemplation, since thus, and in no other way, and verily not by direct observation, [can the end be achieved]."[5]

The same type of teachings can be found in all traditions which have produced a sacred art. If the origin of the forms used by this art were not "celestial," how could an Indian statue convey the very principle of life from within? How could we look at an icon and experience ourselves being looked upon by the gaze of eternity? How could a Chinese or Japanese butterfly capture the very essence of the state of being a butterfly? How could

[4] *Timaeus* 28A, B, trans. Jowett.

[5] Quoted in Coomaraswamy, *The Transformation of Nature in Art* (New York: Dover, 1934), p. 113.

Islamic ornamentation reveal on the physical plane the splendor of the mathematical world considered not as abstraction but as concrete archetypal reality? How could one stand at the portal of the Chartres Cathedral and experience standing in the center of the cosmic order if the makers of that cathedral had not had a vision of that center from whose perspective they built the cathedral? Anyone who grasps the significance of traditional art will understand that the origin of the forms with which this art deals is nothing other than that immutable world of the essences or ideas which are also the source of our thoughts and knowledge. That is why the loss of sacred knowledge or gnosis and the ability to think anagogically—not only analogically—goes hand in hand with the destruction of traditional art and its hieratic formal style.

The origin of forms in traditional art can perhaps be better understood if the production of works of art is compared to the constitution of natural objects. According to the Peripatetic philosophies of the medieval period, whether Islamic, Judaic, or Christian, and following Aristotle and his Neoplatonic commentators, objects are composed of form and matter which in the sublunar region undergo constant change. Hence this world is called that of generation and corruption. Whenever a new object comes into being the old form "returns" to the Tenth Intellect, which is called the "Giver of forms" (*wāhib al-ṣuwar* in Arabic), and a new form is cast by this Intellect upon the matter in question. Therefore, the origin of forms in the natural world is the Intellect. Now, the form of art must be conceived in the same way as far as traditional art is concerned. The source of these forms is the Intellect which illuminates the mind of the artist or the original artist who is emulated by members of a particular school; the artist in turn imposes the form upon the matter in question, matter here being not the philosophical *hylé* but the material in question, whether it be stone, wood, or anything else which is being fashioned. In this way the artist imitates the operation of nature rather than her external forms.

Moreover, the form which is wed with matter and the form which is the "idea" in the mind of the artist are from the same origin and of the same nature except on different levels of existence. The Greek *eidos* expresses this doctrine of correspondence perfectly since it means at once form and idea whose origin is ultimately the Logos.

Traditional art, therefore, is concerned with both knowledge and the sacred. It is concerned with the sacred inasmuch as it is from the domain of the sacred that issue both the tradition itself and the forms and styles which define the formal homogeneity of a particular traditional world.

It is also concerned with knowledge inasmuch as man must know the manner of operation of nature before being able to imitate it. The traditional artist, whether he possesses direct knowledge of those cosmic laws and principles which determine that "manner of operation" or has simply an indirect knowledge which he has received through transmission, needs such a knowledge of a purely intellectual nature which only tradition can provide. Traditional art is essentially a science just as traditional science is an art. The *ars sine scientia nihil* of Saint Thomas holds true for all traditions and the *scientia* in question here is none other than the *scientia sacra* and its cosmological applications.

20. The Wisdom of the Body

It is only in our physical body that we experience directly the order of nature from within, and it is obviously through the body that we are able to encounter the world of nature about us. Our body is at once an extension of the world of nature and part of our "self," which we are able to know directly and of which we have an immediate consciousness, in contrast to what surrounds us and what we distinguish from "us" or that which we grasp immediately and intuitively as our "self" in our ordinary consciousness. We identify ourselves with our body and yet distinguish ourselves from it; and while we know our body and experience it directly, we do not *really* know it, at least not all of us. Furthermore, there are those whose consciousness of the body is developed in such a way that they gain a new relation with it and even exercise certain controls over the body that are literally extraordinary, because most people do not possess such powers nor seek such a state of consciousness.

Religions have spoken of the body as a barrier to spiritual advancement and at the same time as a sacred precinct. But in all cases religion has been traditionally most acutely interested in the physical body, whereas in the modern world the secularization of the understanding of the order of nature has become increasingly reflected in modern men and women's understanding of their own bodies, resulting in an ever greater conflict with the religious view, a conflict that has now exploded upon the public stage in the West with the progressive penetration of modern technologies into the very processes of life. It is now a major public issue to decide where family planning stops and murder begins and even wherein lies the sanctity of life that modern civilization insists upon on the one hand—at least as far as human life is concerned—and destroys with such impunity on the other.

The great drama concerning the origin of human life and the enormous questions posed by bioengineering and related problems of bioethics all point to the truth that the religious understanding of the order of nature, as far as the human body is concerned, is now faced with a final challenge by the scientistic and secularist view. With the acquiescence, to a large extent, of Western religion, this view succeeded in secularizing the cosmos and extending its mechanistic view—or for that matter its agnostic, vitalistic view—of the order of nature to an ever greater degree to the human body. Consequently, the human body has come to be seen by many as no more than a part of that purely quantitative order of nature governed by the laws of physics and chemistry to which many seek to reduce biology itself. For that very reason the recovery of the religious view of nature must turn to the central issue of the body where the spiritual, psychic, and physical elements combine in a unity, the whole of which is of necessity of significance to religion. That is also why the greatest resistance has been shown even in the modern West to the exclusive claims of a materialistic understanding of the body and a purely materialistic medicine. Both the environmental crisis and the rediscovery of the significance of nature by religious thinkers have therefore been accompanied during the past few decades with a remarkable rise of interest in the physical body and its religious significance. And it is here that the greatest struggle is now taking place in the West between the claims of diametrically opposed views concerning the meaning of life and death and the significance of the human body.

Let it be said at the outset that in all traditional religions the human body is considered sacred. This is true not only of the primal religions or a religion such as Hinduism but also of the Abrahamic ones, despite the eclipse of this aspect of religion in many of the mainstream circles of Western Christianity during the past few centuries and its relegation to occultist circles associated with such figures as Mme. Blavatsky and Alice Bailey. In the Bible it is stated "Our bodies are the temple of the Holy Spirit which is in us" (I Cor. 6:19). And in the Quran God says, "I breathe into him [Adam] My Spirit" (28:72). The body is thus the locus of the presence of the Spirit, and by virtue of that presence it is as sacred as a temple.

The body has also been compared to a city belonging to God and is therefore His domain; although given to us and made obedient to our will, the body is ultimately responsible to God. Furthermore, we are also responsible to God for its preservation and well-being. In any case, the sacredness of the human body, with its correspondences to the macrocosm and even its metacosmic significance, symbolically speaking, is so evident in the various religions of the world that it hardly needs to be debated or demonstrated. It is sufficient to view the sacred architecture of places as different as Luxor and Chartres, all related to the body of what the Sufis call the Universal Man, to realize the universality of the doctrine of the sacredness of the body of the prophet and *avatār* and by extension of all human beings, a doctrine that still survives to a large extent in many parts of the world.

It was this central truth of religion that was challenged in the West starting in the Renaissance, as reflected in the drawings of the physical body by Leonardo da Vinci, which already reveal an almost mechanical conception of various organs and parts. From the interest in the anatomy of a dead cadaver identified as "the body" at that time, it was a short step to the mechanical view of the body and even the conception of the body as a machine, proposed by Descartes and especially Julien de La Mettrie and accepted by many philosophers and physicians, if not the public at large. From that period to this day there has been a continuous destruction of the mystery of the human body and its transformation from an inner space, private, and belonging to God, to a public space from which all sense of mystery is removed.[1] The consequence has been the creation of a medicine at once marvelous in its achievements and horrendous in its failures and in the final dehumanization of the human patient, which has now become such a major moral issue and which along with the excessive commercialization and "technologization" of medicine has drawn many people, even in the West, to alternative forms of medicine based on the holistic view of the human being that embraces body, soul, as well as spirit.

The change in the conception of the body resulting in the image that has now become prevalent was a gradual one. Even a century ago people in the West had a different understanding of their bodies than they do now, as reflected in part in their views about sexuality. The change inaugurated by Descartes and William Harvey about the human body did not begin to have a broader impact until the end of the eighteenth and beginning of the nineteenth centuries. The idea of the body as "constant" biological reality is a recent one triggered by a clinical view that saw the patient's body as though it were dead. The reality of the soul was cast aside, and the relation between it or the self and the body, if not totally denied, was made much less central from what one finds in traditional schools of medicine. Henceforth the body became a concrete object as one would find in a chemistry or physics laboratory and no longer a living psycho-biological entity. The human body became a public and social entity parallel with the new defini-

[1] It needs to be mentioned that religion did not give up the body as rapidly as it gave up the cosmos to a science of matter and motion. Opposition to dissection, based on the idea of the sacredness of the human body, continued as did faith healing, prayer as a means of healing, and emphasis upon the role played by a healthy soul in the health of the body. One need only recall that Christian Science belongs to nineteenth-century New England and that even today religious views of the health and sickness of the body, either in opposition or complementary to mainstream medical views, are very much alive in both America and Europe. If anything, they are on the rise.

tion of man as *homo aeconomicus* shorn of his mystery, and the body lost its sacred character and "magic" with which followers of all religions had associated it. Today, as asserted by Barbara Duden, the process has reached its limit, at least in the mainstream scientific understanding of the body, which has now lost all its mystery and become "public space."[2]

It is in the light of this historical process, whose details we cannot examine here, that the present crisis in the understanding of the significance of the body must be considered. Today, there is the general tendency in the West to seek to rediscover the significance of the body both religiously and otherwise. This tendency ranges from the glorification of sports and athletics beyond all proportions and the desacralization of sexuality, peddled ever more commercially, to the reintroduction of spiritual techniques dealing with the body in Christian monasticism and the attempt to rediscover the sacred character of sexuality. It ranges from the emphasis upon bodily movements, loud sounds, bright colors, etc., that characterize so much of popular culture today, a culture that has rebelled through emphasis upon bodily reality against the excessively cerebral civilization of the modern world and its dualism of mind and body, to reappraising the relation between body and soul in various forms of holistic medicine.

In the West two opposing forces seem to be interacting and confronting each other, sometimes in an explosive manner, in the realm concerned with the meaning of the human body. On the one hand there is the movement toward the rediscovery of the sacred nature of the body within mainstream churches as well as in so-called New-Age religions. This is seen in the much greater interest shown today in the study of the subtle (that is, non-material) body in earlier Western sources; in non-Western traditions dealing with the body as demonstrated in the spread of Haṭha Yoga; in alternative schools of medicine such as acupuncture and Ayurvedic medicine, which are holistic in nature; and many other kinds of treatments of the body based on the concept of the wholeness of the body, in natural foods, in what is now called "body theology" and even in faith healing and prayer to cure illnesses.

On the other hand there is an ever greater scientific penetration into the workings of the body considered as a complicated machine and even

[2] Barbara Duden, *The Woman Beneath the Skin: A Doctor's Patients in Eighteenth-Century Germany*, trans. Thomas Dunlap (Cambridge, Mass.: Harvard University Press, 1991), pp. 1-4; idem, *Disembodying Women: Perspectives on Pregnancy and the Unborn*, trans. Lee Hoinacki (Cambridge, Mass.: Harvard University Press, 1993).

on the basis of a scientific understanding of the physical world no longer in vogue among many contemporary physicists. The result is a crisis of major proportions with ethical, economic, and social repercussions that are evident for everyone to see, although few have turned to the central issue, which is the diversity of views held as to what constitutes the human body.

It is true that the Christian view of the human body, as far as its sanctity is concerned, despite being attacked, has never been completely abandoned in the West. Still, it is an enigma for someone studying the West from the outside to understand how a religion based upon the Incarnation, upon the penetration of the Logos into the very body of Christ, and which believes in the resurrection of the body as a central element of its teaching, should allow so easily to have the physical body be taken out of its domain of intellectual concern and to concentrate for so long on theologies that no longer take the spiritual significance of the body seriously. Nor is it easy to understand how mainstream Western Christianity, in contrast to other religions and even Orthodox Christianity, lost for the most part its spiritual techniques involving the body as well as the mind. In any case, as part of the effort to rediscover the religious order of nature, and in fact at the heart of this effort, stands the necessity to realize anew that the body is the temple of God; not only in a metaphorical sense, but also in a symbolic and therefore real sense, the human body is the theater for the manifestation of God's Wisdom, the microcosm possessing a cosmic significance and a reality having a role in spiritual realization. It is also essential to realize the significance of the corporeal body in recovering the traditional and hence normal rapport of man with the world of nature.[3]

* * *

[3] The profound link between our conception of our body and the world has been realized by several contemporary thinkers concerned with "the theology of the body." For example, the theologian James B. Nelson writes, "Descartes, whose philosophy so profoundly influenced the body understandings of modern medicine, taught us that the body is essentially a machine. . . . One of the invidious results of this social construction of body meanings is our disconnection from nature. If my body is essentially a complex machine, I am also strongly inclined to view the earth's body mechanistically. I see neither its organic wholeness nor my deep connection to it. I feel essentially 'other than' the earth" (Nelson, *Body Theology* [Louisville, Ky.: Westminster, John Knox, 1992], p. 49).

According to the religious understanding of the body, it is, to use the language of theism, the House of God wherein resides the Spirit and in fact, as Islam states, God's Spirit. It is therefore sacred and participates mysteriously in the Divine Presence associated with the Spirit. It is also the depository of His Wisdom revealing even on a purely phenomenal and quantitative level the incredible intelligence that makes its functioning possible. The body, in fact, has its own intelligence and speaks its own "mind," reflecting a wisdom before which the response of any human intelligence not dulled by pseudo-knowledge or veiled by pride and the passions can only be wonder and awe at the Wisdom of the Creator. It needs a much greater leap of faith to believe that such a wonder as the body could be the result of simple chance and so-called evolutionary processes than belief in God as its creator or the Tao or *Dharma* as principles that in a nonpersonal way determine the laws of the cosmos and make possible the incredible workings of the body.

The human body also corresponds to the cosmos, not only in the sense of sharing with it the same constituent elements, but in containing in miniature form the whole cosmos. It is by virtue of this correspondence between us as living bodies, soul, and spirit and the cosmos as a whole, which is also alive—having its own "soul" and dominated by the Spirit—that we are able to know the cosmos. We also occupy a special and central position in it because of our being the cosmic totality in miniature form, a replica of the Universe, so that in the deepest sense the body of the cosmos is *our* body. Our intimate contact with the forms of nature around us as well as attraction to the beauty of the stars issues not from simple sentimentality but from an inner *sympatheia*, which relates us to all things, a union of essences or "inner breath," to which Rūmī refers as *hamdamī* and which joins us, in our mind and body bi-unity, to the world about us and finally to the entire cosmos. This link is, however, much greater than simply the presence of iron in our blood and in rocks. It involves the Spirit, which inbreathes our body, and the cosmos and the Divine Archetype, which our bodies reflect, the same supernal realities that are also reflected in the mineral realm but delimited according to the particular level of existence associated with that kingdom, the same holding true also for the plant and animal worlds.

The body is at once a separate reality from the soul and in unity with it. As already mentioned, the total human microcosm is in fact comprised of *spiritus*, *anima*, and *corpus*, as asserted by the Western tradition, and not only the mind and body of the prevailing dualism of modern thought. Moreover, the body is an integral part of our being, not only in this world but also in our ultimate destiny. Herein lies the significance of the doctrine of the Resurrection of the body emphasized especially in Christianity and Islam. The material body conceived by modern science as consisting of molecules and atoms is not only a physical and independent reality. Rather, the body is the result of a descent from above and is reintegrated ultimately into its principle.

Being the locus for the manifestation of the Spirit, the body is also a most important instrument for spiritual practice. The rapport between "mind" and body in fact depends on our spiritual state of awareness and is not constant among all human beings. The body can be experienced as the "crystallization" of the spirit, as in spiritual alchemy where the goal is the spiritualization of the body and corporealization of the spirit. It is the inner rapport between body and spirit and the transformation brought about in the former by the latter that underlies the vast spectrum of phenomena dealing with the incorruptibility of the bodies of saints, as noted by both Christianity and Islam, the special characteristics of the body of the *jivān-mukti* in Hinduism, the attraction of the bodily remains of saints for the faithful, the illumination of the countenance of saintly people, the presence of halos that appear also in the iconography of the sacred art of many religions, and even faith healing and many other phenomena too diverse to describe here.

The human body, seen from the point of view of traditional religions, is not the result of accidents or evolutionary changes brought about by chance. Rather, it is a divine creation reflecting certain archetypal realities through its symbolism. Man's erect position, his gait, the separation of the head from the shoulders, the breast, the genital parts representing divine procreativity and, of course, the face all symbolize divine realities. Moreover, the male and female bodies each reflect an aspect of a whole and a divine prototype that causes each sex to view the other as a pole of "divine attraction" and find in bodily union a source of liberation, albeit momentarily, from the confines of our everyday, worldly consciousness. It is enough to understand the symbolism of the human body to comprehend its spiritual origin, why it participates in the Resurrection, and why it constitutes an integral part of our reality as beings living in time but destined for immortality. It also becomes easy to comprehend why in such religions as Christianity, Hinduism, and Buddhism the body of the God-man or *avatār* in human form plays such a central role not only in everyday religious rites and in sacred art but also esoterically and why it is able to reflect not only cosmic but also metacosmic realities.

Although many traditional schools of thought speak of the hierarchy of spirit, soul, and body within man, there is also a hierarchy of the body itself. Not only are we endowed with a physical body, but also a subtle body, an imaginal body, and even "bodies" on higher planes reaching the Divine Order itself in which it is possible to speak of the Divine Body.[4] We possess *bodies* situated in a hierarchic fashion and corresponding to the various levels of the cosmic and metacosmic hierarchy. Through these "bodies" we are connected to all the cosmic realms as, of course, our own existence is stretched into realms beyond the physical body, realms in which we participate not only with our intelligence, mind, and imagination (understood in the traditional sense of *imaginatio* and not as fantasy) but also with our "bodies." And it is these "bodies" that participate along with their lowest projection on the physical plane in our ultimate reintegration *in divinis.*

Finally, the rediscovery of the wisdom of the body and its assertion as authentic knowledge is the key to the reestablishment of the correct rapport with the world of nature and the rediscovery of its sacred quality. As long as we consider the body as a mere machine, it is not possible to take seriously the religious understanding of the order of nature nor to live in harmony with it. To rediscover the body as the theater of Divine Presence and manifestation of Divine Wisdom as well as an aspect of reality that is at once an intimate part of our being and a part of the natural order is to reestablish a bridge between ourselves and the world of nature beyond the merely physical and utilitarian. To rediscover the body as the abode of the Spirit, worthy of Resurrection before the Lord, and intimate companion in the soul's journey in this world, sacred in itself and in the life which permeates it, is to rediscover at the same time the sacredness of nature. It is to reestablish our link with the plants and animals, with the streams, mountains, and the stars. It is to experience the presence of the Spirit in the physical dimension of our existence as well as in the world of nature to which we are linked both physically and spiritually, through our bodies as well as our souls and the Spirit which is reflected in both our bodies as the temples of God and the world of nature as the theater of theophanies and mirror of Divine Creativity.

[4] This is not only true of Buddhism, which speaks of the *Dharmakāya*, but even Islam where a figure such as Mullā Ṣadrā, while confirming the transcendence of the Divine Essence, states why the Quran speaks of the "Eyes" or "Hands" of God and that these refer to the concept of the body in the highest sense of the term in the Divine Order Itself. If the supreme principle of the body had not existed in that Order, God would not have spoken of certain of His Attributes in terms referring to various parts of the body. Mullā Ṣadrā, of course, insisted upon the doctrine of transcendence or *tanzīh* while also emphasizing *tashbīh* or symbolic comparison without which the various parts of the body referred to in the Quran would not possess any meaning. Moreover, Mullā Ṣadrā refuted completely the views of those early sects that identified parts of the body literally with God, thereby attributing anthropomorphic traits to Him against orthodox Islamic teachings. This aspect of Mullā Ṣadrā's teachings is to be found especially in his *Sharḥ uṣūl al-kāfī.*

21. In the Beginning was Consciousness

One alone is the Dawn beaming over all this.
It is the One that severally becomes all this.
Ṛg-Veda VIII, 58:2

The nameless [Tao] is the beginning of Heaven and Earth,
The named [Tao] is the mother of ten thousand things.
Tao Te Ching, 1

In the beginning was the Word, and the Word was with God, and the Word was God.
Gospel of John 1:1

But His command, when He intendeth a thing, is only that He saith unto it: "Be" and it is.
Quran 36:82

When we turn to the sacred scriptures of various religions, we discover that in every case the origin of the cosmos and of man is identified as a Reality which is conscious and in fact constitutes consciousness understood on the highest level as absolute Consciousness, which is transcendent and yet the source of all consciousness in the cosmic realm including our own. Whether we speak of Allah who commands things to be and they are, or the Tao, or the Word by which all things were made, or Brahman, we are speaking of consciousness. This truth is made especially explicit in Hinduism where the principial Reality that is the source of all things is described as at once Being, Consciousness, and Bliss. Nor is this unanimity of vision of the Origin of all things as identified with consciousness confined to sacred scriptures. Both Oriental and traditional Western philosophers speak of the same truth. The *tò Agathon* of Plato is not only the Supreme Good but also supreme awareness of the Good, and *nous* or intellect, so central to Greek philosophy, is of course inseparable from consciousness. Islamic philosophers consider being to be inseparable from knowledge and therefore awareness, and consider cosmic levels of existence also to be levels of knowledge and awareness. As for Hinduism, in its world view the existence of a thing, even a rock, is also a state of consciousness.

One can then assert safely that in the traditional world there was unanimity concerning the priority of consciousness in relation to what we call "matter" today. The Reality which is seen by all these traditional religions and philosophies to be the origin of things is also Supreme Consciousness and can only be reached when human beings are able to elevate their own level of consciousness. Even in Buddhism, which does not speak of an objective Supreme Reality and of cosmogenesis as understood in the Abrahamic and Iranian religions as well as Hinduism, *nirvāṇa* is the supreme state of consciousness and Buddhahood is also inseparable from consciousness. The only exception to this unanimous traditional view in the old days was to be found in certain anti-metaphysical philosophies of late Antiquity accompanying the death throes of Hellenistic and Roman civilizations and in certain marginal schools of ancient India which were thoroughly rejected by the mainstream orthodox schools of Hindu thought.

The privilege of denying the primacy of consciousness wholesale remained for the modern world, especially with the advent of the materialistic and scientistic philosophies which came to the fore after the Scientific Revolution in the seventeenth century. Furthermore, this transformation did not take place until the modern idea of matter, not to be confused with its understanding in Greek philosophy and science, was developed with Descartes and Galileo. By taking away from corporeal existence all its qualitative aspects and reducing it to pure quantity, these men, followed by many others, created a world view in which there was such a thing as pure inert matter divorced totally from life and consciousness but somehow mysteriously known by the knowing subject or the mind. Cartesian bifurcation created a dualism between mind and matter which has dominated Western thought since the seventeenth century, a dualism which has led many to choose the primacy of matter over mind and to establish the view that in the beginning was matter and not consciousness, even if some still hold to a deistic conception of a Creator God.

The prevalence of this supposedly scientific materialism, which, however, is not at all borne out by science as science—not as pseudo-theology or philosophy—gained momentum in the nineteenth century with the evolutionary theory of Darwin, which itself is an ideology in support of this so-called materialism and also based on it. The penetration of the view that all things begin with matter, which then evolves into life and later consciousness, into the world view of the general public in the West has been such that despite the total rejection of the classical view of matter in modern quantum mechanics, there still lingers in the public arena reliance upon a materialistic perspective which ultimately reduces all things to "matter." This reductionism has become part and parcel of the modern and even post-modern mindset. People believe that it is possible to understand a thing only through analysis and the breaking up of that thing to its "fundamental" parts, which are material. They are led to believe that the whole is nothing more than the sum of its parts, and physicists continue to search for the ultimate particles or building blocks of the universe, which the less sophisticated public envisages as minute billiard balls which are then accumulated together to create all the beings of the universe. In such a perspective based on materialistic reductionism, both life and consciousness are seen as epiphenomena of material factors, whether they be matter or energy. The whole rapport between consciousness and corporeal existence is thus reversed.

In traditional cosmologies Pure Consciousness, which is also Pure Being, descends through various levels of the cosmic hierarchy to reach the physical world, while remaining Itself transcendent vis-à-vis Its manifestations. In the modern reductionist view, things ascend from the primordial cosmic soup. Even if certain individual scientists believe that a conscious and intelligent Being brought about the Big Bang and originated the cosmos, consciousness plays no role in the so-called evolution of the cosmos from the early aggregate of molecules to the appearance of human beings on the planet. In the traditional world view, human beings have descended from a higher realm of being and consciousness, whereas according to the modernist perspective so prevalent in present-day society, they have ascended from below. These are two diametrically opposed points of view, one based on the primacy of consciousness and the other on the primacy of unconsciousness and blind material agents, forces, and processes.

* * *

How we view the nature of reality has a direct bearing upon how we live as human beings. For millennia human beings lived in a universe dominated by the idea of the primacy of consciousness over all that is corporeal and material. They fought wars and there was disease, but they lived in a world of meaning and beauty. They created traditional arts of surpassing beauty and lived, to a large extent, in harmony and peace with their natural environment. They knew who they were, where they came from, and where they were going. The denial of the supremacy and primacy of consciousness and the substitution of a materialistic reductionism in its place has given human beings greater domination over nature and certain earthly comforts while, needless to say, creating new discomforts. It has cured many diseases while opening the door to diseases unknown before. And it has been defended as being a way to peace while making possible wars with a degree of violence and lethal effects not imagined in days of old. But most of all it has destroyed the harmonious relation not only between man and God and the spiritual world, but also between man and nature, by permitting the creation of a science based not on wisdom but on power and by applying that science as a new technology which has the capability of destroying the very order of life on earth. On the individual level, it has taken away from human beings the ultimate meaning of life and destroyed the home which they considered the universe to be, making human beings aliens within a world view constructed by human minds.

* * *

Let us examine further the consequences of substituting for the primacy of consciousness, the primal reality of matter or matter/energy according to the modern scientistic perspective. Positing matter as the ground of all cosmic reality—and for many the only reality—has led to the development of a reductionism that reduces the spirit to the psyche, the psyche to biological processes, life to the activity of chemical agents, and chemical elements to the particles of physics. People continue to speak of finding the "fundamental" building blocks of the universe from which one could build up step by step to the greatest prophets, saints, sages, thinkers, and artists. The reality of higher levels of being is thereby seen as nothing more than phenomena resulting from purely material and quantitative entities and processes. Life is seen as an accident and consciousness as an epiphenomenon of life. The universe is depicted as "dead" and devoid of any life, meaning, soul, or consciousness. Consequently human beings are made to feel like an island amidst a vast, threatening ocean of blind and dead matter. They have no home in the cosmos as did their ancestors and feel alienated from all that is not human. Furthermore, this alienation has nothing to do with the alienation of the spiritual human being from the world as understood religiously. Nor is it in any way related to the saying of Christ, "My kingdom is not of this world." The new alienation from the world resulting from scientistic reductionism is of a very different order. Traditional men and women found their home ultimately in the Divine but they also saw in this world a domain dominated by God and full of souls and spirits which corresponded to different aspects of their nature. They never felt as if they were alone in a universe totally blind to their deepest hopes and aspirations. The modern forms of human alienation, whether psychological or social, issue from the cosmic isolation created by a world view which denies the primacy of consciousness.

Human beings are in need of meaning just as much as they are in need of air to breathe and food to eat. Modern materialistic reductionism has not only resulted in chemically infested food and polluted air, but also the loss of meaning in its ultimate sense. There can in fact be no ultimate meaning without the acceptance of the Ultimate in the metaphysical sense. It is indeed a great paradox that human consciousness in modern times has produced a view of the cosmos which has no room for consciousness. And when human beings do seek to find consciousness in the objective world, or experience what they consider to be encounters with conscious beings outside of the human realm, they are marginalized and condemned to the category of hallucinating men and women in need of psychiatric care. When our ancestors could encounter angels and even lesser beings in nature, and when such encounters were acceptable within the *Weltanschauung* in which they lived, they did not encounter "aliens" in the modern sense, nor did they feel the need to do so. Nor were they marginalized as abnormal in the societies in which they lived. And the conscious beings they did encounter were not alien to them.

The denial of the primacy of consciousness also resulted both directly and indirectly in the desacralization of nature and the reduction of nature to a pure "it," to a commodity to be used by human beings as they deemed necessary. The care for nature was turned into its rape as the prevalent view of nature became ever more impervious to its spiritual qualities, its mystery, its innate harmony and beauty. All those aspects of nature, celebrated over the centuries by sages, saints, poets, and artists, became subjectivized and made to appear as being objectively unreal. Turned into a commodity to be used by the ever growing avaricious appetite of modern humanity as consumer, the natural environment soon began to suffer, leading to the environmental crisis which now threatens the web of life on earth. Even today few want to accept the direct relation between the materialistic view of nature and the destruction of nature on the unprecedented scale that we observe everywhere on the globe today.

The materialistic world view and the denying of the primacy of consciousness have also had a direct bearing on the weakening of ethical norms and practices. In all civilizations morality was related to religion and a philosophical world view in which good and evil, right and wrong, had a cosmic as well as human dimension. We can see clear examples of this rapport not only in the Abrahamic religions, but also in Hinduism, Confucianism, and Buddhism. Ethics is always related in one way or another to metaphysics. In denying the primacy of consciousness in favor of the material, the modern paradigm has weakened the objective cadre for human ethics not only by marginalizing and weakening religion, but also by reducing the cosmos to a purely "material" reality in which good and evil have no meaning any more than does beauty. *À la* Galileo and Descartes, all such categories are relegated to the subjective realm and banished from objective reality. Ethics is thereby weakened wherever this world view has flourished, and secularized ethics based on such a truncated view of reality has never been able to gain widespread acceptance. Moreover, all this has occurred at a time when human beings are in the greatest need of an environmental ethics which would appeal to the vast majority of the human family, most of whom still closely identify ethics with God, with sacred laws and teachings of various religions. Nor is the need for ethics confined to the environment. It is also of the utmost importance to emphasize ethics in the dealing of human beings with each other when, thanks to modern technology, weapons of war and conflict have become lethal to a degree beyond imagination.

If in the beginning was only the soup of molecules, then our deepest yearnings and aspirations, our deepest feelings, our sense of love, beauty, justice, and goodness, are all ephemeral subjective states caused by blind evolutionary forces and truth has meaning only when operationally defined. What we call our humanity is only an illusion. What is real is what we experience of the outside world seen only as a domain of material entities and forces in various interactions and processes which are totally indifferent to our humanity. To deny the primacy of consciousness is in fact to confirm knowingly or unknowingly our own inhumanity and to admit that all that we consider to be the deepest elements of our thoughts, emotions, and even spiritual states are ultimately illusory and unreal, being reducible to material agents and forces. It is to surrender ourselves to the sub-human, which in fact we see manifesting itself, by no means accidentally, to an ever greater degree in the human order as it pulls humanity with ever greater speed downwards toward the abyss.

If consciousness in its highest sense is not the alpha of cosmic and human existence, it cannot, metaphysically speaking, be its omega either. By denying the primacy of consciousness, modern materialism has also cast doubt on the reality of the immortality of the human soul and the afterlife. Today in the West even many religious people do not take eschatological realities seriously. Besides the most tragic consequences for the human soul that denies such realities, the weakening of belief in eternal life also has a direct consequence on how we live in this world and more particularly upon the destruction of the natural environment. If life on this earth is the only life we have, then we should do everything possible to live a worldly life as fully as possible. For most people such a life means hedonism and consumerism to the extent possible. A few agnostics might be satisfied with "the life of the mind," but for most people loss of the fear of infernal states and the hope for paradise results in giving full vent to sensual passions and their gratification, which result in ever greater expectation of material "benefits" from their environment, with catastrophic consequences for the natural world as well as for the human agent within that world.

The consequences of the loss of the vision of the Sacred Origin of the cosmos and denial of the primacy of consciousness are so many and so multifarious that they cannot all be mentioned here. And yet, opposition to this view is so strong within the citadel of the modern scientistic paradigm that even scientific arguments for intelligent design of the universe, which implies of course the primacy of intelligence or consciousness, are brushed aside in dogmatic fashion by many high priests of the pseudo-religion of scientism. Despite this negative situation, the truth of the primacy of consciousness must be asserted whenever and wherever possible. And there are signs that more and more perspicacious people are awakening from their "dogmatic slumber" and realizing this truth.

If human beings were not to live below the human level, but realized the full possibility of being human, they would grasp intuitively the truth of the assertion of the primacy of consciousness. Their own consciousness would be raised to a level where they would know through direct intellection that the alpha and omega of cosmic reality cannot but be the Supreme Consciousness which is also Pure Being and that all beings in the universe possess a degree of consciousness in accord with their existential state. They would realize that as human beings we are given the intelligence to know the One Who is the Origin and End of all things, who is *Sat* (Being), *Chit* (Consciousness), and *Ānanda* (Bliss), and to realize that this knowledge itself is the ultimate goal of human life, the crown of human existence, and what ultimately makes us human beings who can discourse with the trees and the birds as well as with the angels and who are on the highest level the interlocutors of that Supreme Reality who has allowed us to say "I" but who is ultimately the I of all I's.

Sources*

1. *Religion and Religions: The Challenge of Living in a Multi-Religious World.* The Loy H. Witherspoon Lectures in Religions, The University of North Carolina at Charlotte, April 8, 1985. Charlotte: 1991.
2. *The Need for a Sacred Science.* Albany: State University of New York Press, 1993, Chapter 5.
3. *The Spiritual and Religious Dimensions of the Environmental Crisis.* London: Temenos Academy Papers No. 12, 1999.
4. *The Heart of Islam: Enduring Values for Humanity.* Harper SanFrancisco, 2002, Chapter 1.
5. Ibid.
6. "Who is Man? The Perennial Answer of Islam." *Studies in Comparative Religion* (Winter 1968), pp. 45-56.
7. *Sufism and the Integration of the Inner and Outer Life of Man.* London: Temenos Academy Papers No. 21, 2004.
8. "The Heart is the Throne of the All-Merciful." *Paths to the Heart: Sufism and the Christian East.* Edited by James S. Cutsinger. Bloomington: World Wisdom Books, 2002.
9. "The Meaning and Role of Philosophy." *Studia Islamica* 36 (1973), pp. 57-80.
10. "Theology, Philosophy, and Spirituality." *Islamic Spirituality: Manifestations*, ed. S.H. Nasr. New York: Crossroad, 1990, pp. 395-446.
11. Ibid.
12. "Existence (*wujūd*) and Quiddity (*māhiyyah*) in Islamic Philosophy." *International Philosophical Quarterly* 29 (1989), pp. 409-28.
13. *Knowledge and the Sacred.* New York: Crossroad, 1981. Chapter 4.
14. *Religion and the Order of Nature.* Oxford: Oxford University Press, 1996, Chapter 5.
15. *The Need for a Sacred Science*, Chapter 1.
16. Ibid., Chapter 3.
17. *Knowledge and the Sacred*, Chapter 5.
18. Ibid., Chapter 6.
19. Ibid., Chapter 8.
20. *Religion and the Order of Nature*, Chapter 7.
21. "In the Beginning was Consciousness." *Sophia* 9 (1), 2003: 5-12.

* All chapters except 21 have been abridged. For the full texts, along with the often detailed notes, see the originals.

Selected Bibliography of the Works of Seyyed Hossein Nasr in English

A bibliography of Dr. Nasr's writings through the year 2000 appeared in *The Philosophy of Seyyed Hossein Nasr* (pp. 831-964). Listed there are 60 books and 504 articles, typically with multiple editions and/or translations. Most were originally written in English, a good number in Persian, and a few in French and Arabic. Here we list chronologically the original editions of Nasr's major books in English, leaving out a few edited volumes and short monographs. Many of these books have been reprinted, often by publishers other than the one mentioned; those in print can easily be found on-line.

Three Muslim Sages. Preface by R. H. L. Slater. Cambridge: Harvard University Press, 1964.

An Introduction to Islamic Cosmological Doctrines. Preface by H. A. R. Gibb. Cambridge: Harvard University Press, 1964.

Ideals and Realities of Islam. London: Allen and Unwin, 1966.

Islamic Studies: Essays on Law and Society, the Sciences, Philosophy and Sufism. Beirut: Librarie du Liban, 1967.

Science and Civilization in Islam. Preface by G. de Santillana. Cambridge: Harvard University Press, 1968.

The Encounter of Man and Nature: The Spiritual Crisis of Modern Man. London: Allen and Unwin, 1968. New edition as *Man and Nature.* London: Unwin Paperbacks, 1987.

Sufi Essays. London: Allen and Unwin, 1972.

Shīʿite Islam, by ʿAllāmah Ṭabāṭabāʾī (translated from the Persian, with introduction and notes). Albany: State University of New York Press, 1975.

Islam and the Plight of Modern Man. London: Longmans, 1976.

Islamic Science: An Illustrated Study. London: World of Islam Festival Trust, 1976.

Ṣadr al-Dīn Shīrāzī and His Transcendent Theosophy. Tehran and London: Imperial Iranian Academy of Philosophy, 1978. Enlarged edition, Tehran: Institute for Humanities and Cultural Studies, 1997.

Islamic Life and Thought. London: Allen and Unwin, 1981.

Knowledge and the Sacred. New York: Crossroad, 1981.

Muhammad: Man of Allah. London: Muhammadi Trust, 1982. New edition as *Muhammad: Man of God*. Chicago: Kazi Publications, 1995.

The Essential Writings of Frithjof Schuon (edited and introduced). Warwick: Amity House, 1986. Re-issued as *The Essential Frithjof Schuon*. Bloomington: World Wisdom, 2005.

Islamic Art and Spirituality. London: Golgonooza Press, 1987.

Traditional Islam in the Modern World. London and New York: KPI, 1987.

Islamic Spirituality: Foundations and *Manifestations* (editor). Vols. 19-20 of World Spirituality: An Encyclopedic History of the Religious Quest. New York: Crossroad, 1987-1991.

A Young Muslim's Guide to the Modern World. Chicago: Kazi Publications, 1993.

The Need for a Sacred Science. Albany: State University of New York Press, 1993.

History of Islamic Philosophy (edited with O. Leaman). 2 vols., London: Routledge, 1996.

The Islamic Intellectual Tradition in Persia (Nasr's essays edited by M. Aminrazavi). London: Curzon Press, 1996.

Religion and the Order of Nature. New York and Oxford: Oxford University Press, 1996.

Poems of the Way. Oakton: Foundation for Traditional Studies, 1999.

An Anthology of Philosophy in Persia (edited with M. Aminrazavi). Vols. 1-2, New York: Oxford University Press, 1999-2000.

The Philosophy of Seyyed Hossein Nasr. Edited by L. E. Hahn, R. E. Auxier, and L. W. Stone, Jr. The Library of Living Philosophers, volume XXVIII. Chicago: Open Court, 2001.

The Heart of Islam: Enduring Values for Humanity. San Francisco: Harper San Francisco, 2002.

Islam: Religion, History, and Civilization. San Francisco: Harper San Francisco, 2002.

Islamic Philosophy from Its Origin to the Present: Philosophy in the Land of Prophecy. Albany: State University of New York Press, 2006.

Biographical Notes

SEYYED HOSSEIN NASR is University Professor of Islamic Studies at the George Washington University and President of the Foundation for Traditional Studies. The author of over fifty books and five hundred articles, he is one of the world's most respected writers and speakers on Islam, its arts and sciences, and its traditional mystical path, Sufism. His publications include *Sufi Essays*, *Knowledge and the Sacred* (the 1981 Gifford Lectures), *Religion and the Order of Nature* (the 1994 Cadbury Lectures), *A Young Muslim's Guide to the Modern World*, *The Heart of Islam: Enduring Values for Humanity*, and *Islam: Religion, History, and Civilization*. A volume in the prestigious *Library of Living Philosophers* series has been dedicated to his thought.

WILLIAM C. CHITTICK is a professor in the Department of Asian and Asian-American Studies at the State University of New York, Stony Brook. He is author and translator of twenty-five books and one hundred articles on Sufism, Shīʿism, and Islamic thought in general. Among his publications are *The Sufi Path of Love: The Spiritual Teachings of Rumi*, *The Sufi Path of Knowledge: Ibn al-ʿArabī's Metaphysics of Imagination*, *The Self-Disclosure of God: Principles of Ibn al-ʿArabī's Cosmology*, *Sufism: A Short Introduction*, *The Heart of Islamic Philosophy: The Quest for Self-Knowledge in the Teachings of Afdal al-Dīn Kāshānī*, *Me & Rumi: The Autobiography of Shams-i Tabrizi*, and *The Sufi Doctrine of Rūmī: Illustrated*. He is also co-author (with Sachiko Murata) of *The Vision of Islam*.

HUSTON SMITH is Thomas J. Watson Professor of Religion and Distinguished Adjunct Professor Emeritus, Syracuse University. He is widely regarded as the most accessible contemporary authority on the history of religions and is a leading figure in the field of comparative religion. His best-selling work *The World's Religions* (formerly *The Religions of Man*) has sold over two million copies. His many books include *Forgotten Truth: The Common Vision of the World's Religions*, *Beyond the Post-Modern Mind*, and *Why Religion Matters: The Fate of the Human Spirit in an Age of Disbelief*. His discovery of Tibetan multiphonic chanting was lauded as "an important landmark in the study of music," and his film documentaries on Hinduism, Tibetan Buddhism, and Sufism have won numerous international awards. In 1996 Bill Moyers hosted a five-part PBS television series entitled "The Wisdom of Faith with Huston Smith."

Index

For a glossary of all key foreign words used in books published by World Wisdom, including metaphysical terms in English, consult:
www.DictionaryofSpiritualTerms.org.
This on-line Dictionary of Spiritual Terms provides extensive definitions, examples and related terms in other languages.

Other books on Islam by World Wisdom

Islam, Fundamentalism, and the Betrayal of Tradition: Essays by Western Muslim Scholars,
edited by Joseph E. B. Lumbard, 2004

The Mystics of Islam,
by Reynold A. Nicholson, 2002

The Path of Muhammad: A Book on Islamic Morals and Ethics by Imam Birgivi,
interpreted by Shaykh Tosun Bayrak, 2005

Paths to the Heart: Sufism and the Christian East,
edited by James S. Cutsinger, 2003

Paths to Transcendence: According to Shankara, Ibn Arabi, and Meister Eckhart,
by Reza Shah-Kazemi, 2006

The Sufi Doctrine of Rumi: Illustrated Edition,
by William C. Chittick, 2005

Sufism: Love and Wisdom,
edited by Jean-Louis Michon and Roger Gaetani, 2006

Sufism: Veil and Quintessence, A New Translation with Selected Letters,
by Frithjof Schuon, 2007

Tierno Bokar: The Sufi Sage from Mali,
by Amadou Hampaté Ba, translated by Fatima Jane Casewit, 2008

Understanding Islam,
by Frithjof Schuon, 1994

The Universal Spirit of Islam: From the Koran and Hadith,
edited by Judith Fitzgerald and Michael Oren Fitzgerald, 2006

sential Titles from World Wisdom

e Essential Titus Burckhardt: Reflections on Sacred Art, Faiths, and Civilizations,
edited by William Stoddart, 2003

The Essential Ananda K. Coomaraswamy,
edited by Rama P. Coomaraswamy, 2004

The Essential Vedanta,
edited by Eliot Deutsch and Rohit Dalvi, 2004

The Essential Swami Ramdas,
compiled by Susunaga Weeraperuma, 2005

The Essential Frithjof Schuon,
edited by Seyyed Hossein Nasr, 2005

The Essential Sophia,
edited by Seyyed Hossein Nasr and Katherine O'Brien, 2006

The Essential Shinran: A Buddhist Path of True Entrusting,
edited by Alfred Bloom, 2007

The Essential Charles Eastman (Ohiyesa): Light on the Indian World,
edited by Michael Oren Fitzgerald, 2007

The Essential Sri Anandamayi Ma: Life and Teachings,
edited by Joseph A. Fitzgerald, 2007

The Essential Seyyed Hossein Nasr,
edited by William C. Chittick, 2007

The Essential Lord Northbourne,
edited by Lord Northbourne and Joseph A. Fitzgerald, 2008

The Essential René Guénon,
edited by John Herlihy, 2008

The Essential Martin Lings,
edited by Reza Shah-Kazemi and Emma Clark, 2008